THE WAR ON WOMEN IN ISRAEL

A STORY OF RELIGIOUS RADICALISM
AND THE WOMEN FIGHTING FOR FREEDOM

ELANA MARYLES SZTOKMAN

This publication is designed to provide accurate and authoritative information in regard to the subject matter covered. It is sold with the understanding that the publisher is not engaged in rendering legal, accounting, or other professional service. If legal advice or other expert assistance is required, the services of a competent professional person should be sought. —*From a Declaration of Principles Jointly Adopted by a Committee of the American Bar Association and a Committee of Publishers and Associations*

All brand names and product names used in this book are trademarks, registered trademarks, or trade names of their respective holders. Sourcebooks, Inc., is not associated with any product or vendor in this book.

Some names in this book were changed to help maintain anonymity.

Published by Sourcebooks, Inc.
P.O. Box 4410, Naperville, Illinois 60567-4410
(630) 961-3900
Fax: (630) 961-2168
www.sourcebooks.com

Library of Congress Cataloging-in-Publication data is on file with the publisher.

Printed and bound in the United States of America.
BG 10 9 8 7 6 5 4 3 2 1

Also by Elana Maryles Sztokman

*The Men's Section: Orthodox Jewish Men
in an Egalitarian World*

*Educating in the Divine Image: Gender Issues in
Orthodox Jewish Day Schools* (with Chaya Gorsetman)

This book is dedicated to all the feminist activists out there across different faiths who are writing, speaking, and protesting with their bodies and souls in order to create a better world—one that reflects the love and compassion that is so profoundly divine.
Keep up the beautiful fight.

CONTENTS

When a woman speaks her truth, it is as holy as prayer. At times the truth of another touches us so profoundly that it is a life-changing experience.

—*Rabbi Shoni Labowitz*

Listen to the women's voices. Listen to the silences, the unasked questions, the blanks. Listen to the small, soft voices, often courageously trying to speak up, voices of women taught early that tones of confidence, challenge, anger, or assertiveness are strident and unfeminine.

—*Adrienne Rich*

Preface
THE WAR ON WOMEN IN ISRAEL—AND EVERYWHERE

I t was a two-hour drive, mostly through endless desert and palm trees, to get to my daughter's army base. She had been inducted into the Israel Defense Forces (IDF) only a month earlier, as part of Israel's compulsory service, and had just finished basic training. We were on our way to her swearing-in ceremony, looking for a compound that was not listed on any map and had no road signs indicating its location. After taking a wrong turn to a different cluster of unmarked army bases, we were given the rather vague direction to "look for the row of palm trees on your left" to find our destination.[1]

Miraculously, we found those indistinct palm trees and the more obvious queue of cars filled with proud parents on the way to watch their children become soldiers. The whole process felt like an Israeli version of the typical American high school graduation. However, here, parental pride revolved less around their children's academic achievement and the start of their independent adult lives and more around their entry into a state-endorsed system of self-sacrifice in defense of their nation and the 3,500-year-old history of the Jewish people.

I parked the car in the desert heat and found my way to the

outdoor ceremony space, enclosed on each side by miles of sand dunes. One hundred twenty soldiers were being sworn in to the Military Intelligence Corps that day, two all-female units of forty and one coed unit. In intelligence, soldiers are not supposed to expose too much about what they are doing, so I had no idea why some groups were single sex and others mixed. To me, it was simply impressive that my daughter was standing alongside young men in this ceremony. It was a huge achievement, considering where women were only a generation or two ago, before the 1990s when they started fighting for equal rights in the IDF. When my daughter was young, there were few to no jobs available to women in the army, and those that existed mostly consisted of offering coffee and other personal services to the men in charge. Today, 93 percent of all IDF jobs can technically be held by women or men.

From a distance, the rows of soldiers emitted a certain sense of equality, not only between men and women, but among people of all different shapes, sizes, skin colors, and ethnicities. To my right was an extended Druze family; to my left, an Ethiopian family, all here with the same pride. In a sense we were all the same, embarking on this journey with the same skills and expertise, the same uniform, tools, and knowledge, the same expectations. This is actually considered one of the great legacies of the IDF. It is at times a wonderful social equalizer in which young people from all backgrounds train and serve side by side, wearing the same clothes, eating the same food, doing the same forty push-ups. In this institution, almost everyone has the same opportunity to prove themselves and get ahead in life and in Israeli society; even kids from troubled socioeconomic backgrounds can shine and emerge with the credentials to advance in life. As in the United States and elsewhere around the world, the Israeli army is known to help struggling adolescents find a strong path in life. Of course, there are certain ethnic and social groups that remain minorities in the IDF—ultra-Orthodox Jews, Muslims, Bedouin, Druze, and other non-Jews—even though members of these can form the backbone of some key units, such as trackers.

Seeing my daughter in her uniform, saluting and holding that gun, I was in awe of her presentation of strength. I suddenly felt the presence of Jewish women throughout the ages who dared to defy social expectations by being strong, outspoken, independent, and physical. I was filled with gratitude for all those brave women—and men—who gave their lives over the past 150 years so Jews would have the opportunity to simply stand safely and confidently in this space. Watching these young women, I could almost feel my grandmothers breathing over my shoulder, glowing in pride, sharing this incredible event, watching young Israeli women take charge and believe in their own power, ability, and mission to protect and defend their country alongside their male counterparts.

Still, I found myself looking for signs of proof of this claim to equality—for my daughter, for all the "others" who exist in society, and especially for women. Watching my daughter in an all-female unit next to a coed unit in a supposedly coed ceremony made me wonder if the IDF has a deeper ambivalence about female soldiers. On the one hand, they are equal to their male counterparts, but on the other hand, they are clearly still women. The young women in all units fulfilled the same roles and tasks throughout the ceremony as the men, saluting and holding their guns the same way. And even though it was a coed space, the women outnumbered the men. But as I sat there watching my daughter step into this new role alongside her male teammates, I knew that this rosy picture told anything but the full story. The status of women in the army is hardly perfect. I knew that, in practice, women actually serve in only 69 percent of army positions, and some of the most important jobs, such as sailors and special operative units, are still closed to them. In a country where army service is the main channel for cultivating political and economic leaders and serves as a stepping stone for most people's careers, that 31 percent of positions were not available to women could be incredibly significant in determining their future opportunities, for better or worse.

Despite all the problems, challenges, and uncertainties facing my daughter ahead, I felt proud. Here she was, being inducted into the Israel Defense Forces, a male-dominated, highly regimented, hierarchical, and gendered organization—an institution that is both beloved and flawed, like the state of Israel itself—off to a role in which she will be risking her life to protect a tiny but extraordinarily proud country that I have come to call my own. She is on a mission, as am I: to help ensure that the Israeli nation upholds the progressive moral and social vision for which it was established.

This, in a nutshell, is my constant struggle: love for the country where I've been living for more than twenty years and a commitment to the well-being of the people to whom I belong by birth and ancestry, along with a deep desire to see Israel continue to live up to its mission to be a compassionate refuge for all people, both male and female. These mixed reflections swirled around my head as I watched my daughter stand in an olive-drab row of erect, strong young people—she was so indistinct that, for much of the ceremony, I couldn't even figure out which one was her. At a certain point, I found myself feeling inspired. I was able to put these gender questions aside and see that this group of young women had arrived, fully at the center of this army experience. And anything was possible for them.

But the truth is, it's not. The cold, hard reality facing women in Israel today is that while Israel has made certain strides for women's rights, it has not yet achieved the mission for which it was created. It is not equal for all, regardless of gender. In fact, that vision of an egalitarian society is actually receding in alarming ways. Even more alarmingly, there is a growing faction of Israelis who are threatening not only equal rights for women, but also their fundamental freedoms and their presence in society.

In some ways, you might say that I've been gradually writing this book for many years. I've been living in Israel for more than two decades now, having arrived here as a young, idealistic, religious Jew along with my husband and then baby—now soldier—with the goal to help build this country and help it achieve its purpose. For much of that time, I have been a feminist activist, fighting for women's rights in different ways. Over the years, I have worked and/or volunteered for several different organizations, including Mavoi Satum (literally "the dead end," a description of women getting divorced in Israel), the Center for Women's Justice (CWJ), Kolech–the Religious Women's Forum, the International Coalition for Agunah Rights (ICAR), and others. I have also been writing and blogging about gender issues since my first feminist column was published in *The Jerusalem Report* in 1997 and at the *Jewish Daily Forward*'s *The Sisterhood* blog, as well as other publications, for many years. Then, in 2006, I completed my doctorate in the sociology of education at the Hebrew University of Jerusalem on the subject of gender identity among adolescent religious girls in schools. In 2012, I began work as executive director of the New York–based Jewish Orthodox Feminist Alliance, which leads the fight globally for religious freedom for Jewish women. In short, I've been fighting for Jewish and Israeli women's rights for a long time.

This book is in many ways a culmination of that work—though the work is hardly done—but more than that, it looks at the larger picture, the dire reality for Israeli women, and through them, for women all over the world. The purpose of this book is to tell the larger story, one that is not just about the individual issues of inequality that Jewish women face, but also about the disturbing trend happening in Israel in which religion increasingly is used as a stultifying force in women's lives to control and oppress them.

What makes this story particularly compelling is how religious women are leading the fight from within against these oppressive religious practices. This is also about women who have not dismissed religious life or relegated it to a corner designated for the fanatics, but rather who have continued to believe in the beauty of religion as a positive social-spiritual force and have dedicated their lives to protecting the world from fanatic, misogynistic ideas. It's a story well worth telling, one that the world needs to hear and get behind, because women all over the world struggle against this issue every day. The religious feminists in Israel are on the front lines of a really difficult battle: protecting the world from the spread of religious extremism. This book tells their story.

It's important for me to note how difficult this stance is. Like many religious feminists, I never planned a career trajectory as religious-feminist activist, yet here I am. Drawn by a pressing need to see Israel do better, my goal is one that rests on idealism and faith. Some may read it differently, as an attempt to destroy religion's place in Israeli society or paint Israel in a negative light. Nothing can be further from the truth. My goal in writing this book is very simple: I want to help create a more compassionate Israel for all and a more spiritually inspired Orthodox Judaism. I want the calls of women for equality, justice, and freedom to be heeded by Israelis and Jews around the world and, in turn, for that equality to be acknowledged and instituted for women everywhere. As we will see, when we work to ensure equality for women and men in every way, our entire society wins.

Introduction
ISRAEL: A LAND OF PROMISE AND PERIL

I srael, a country with some of the most complex social realities in the world, is drenched in both peril and promise.

When it was established in 1948, miraculous things happened. A tiny country with a population of less than one million people, 65 percent of whom were immigrants and 82 percent of whom were Jews, exploded in growth in ways that even the greatest optimists could not have envisioned.[1] In just sixty-six years, this tormented little nation has had tremendous technological and economic success, with a large list of vital inventions ranging from cell phones and computers to security, energy, and medical technologies, and has produced more start-up companies than large, peaceful, and stable nations like Japan, China, India, Korea, Canada, and the United Kingdom. Israel's $100 billion economy is larger than all of its immediate neighbors combined. It boasts the highest number of university degrees held by its population in the world, and 12 percent of Israelis hold advanced degrees. Israel also produces more scientific papers per capita than any other nation by a large margin—109 per ten thousand people—and has one of the highest per capita rates of patents filed. It has more museums per capita than any other country and has the world's second highest per capita rate of publishing new books. And it achieves all of this in spite of enormous internal and external tensions: in addition to fighting a war on its own borders every decade or so, Israel is also the largest immigrant-absorbing nation relative to its population on earth.[2] Not bad for a country smaller than New Jersey.

These statistics are certainly impressive. According to Dan Senor and Saul Singer, authors of *Start-Up Nation: The Story of Israel's Economic Miracle*, these successes reflect a culture that promotes ingenuity, independent thinking, and entrepreneurship. This may have emerged from a post-Holocaust mind-set that was determined to see the Jewish people succeed in their own autonomous country. As David Brooks gushed in the *New York Times* in 2010, "Israel's technological success is the fruition of the Zionist dream. The country was not founded so stray settlers could sit among thousands of angry Palestinians in Hebron. It was founded so Jews would have a safe place to come together and create things for the world."[3] According to its history, it certainly seems to be on the right track.

This impressive portrait, however, disguises certain troubling social realities. Gal Beckerman at *The Forward*, a New York–based Jewish newspaper, noted that the image of Israel as a "bastion of entrepreneurial spirit and technological achievement…skirts a discussion" of serious underlying issues of equality and discrimination that exist there, particularly for women.[4] In fact, Israel's success belongs predominantly to Ashkenazi Jewish men, especially those who served in certain elite units in the IDF that offer strong growth opportunities—units from which women are often systematically excluded.[5] Take, for example, the male-to-female ratio of business leaders for that impressive list of entrepreneurial achievements. Only about 8 percent of top executives in Israel's private sector are women, and the gender gap in executive pay for Israeli women versus men is currently at 25 percent and growing. An analysis of the total compensation packages for the five highest wage earners at the one hundred companies in the Tel Aviv 100 Index showed a gender wage gap of over 30 percent. "These numbers are amazing," Keren Kibovich, whose organization BDO Ziv Haft Consulting conducted the research on executive pay, told *The Marker*. "These are the largest companies in Israel, and these are the women who have reached the top. Nonetheless, the average wage gaps were even higher than the average for the entire population."[6] Israel currently ranks fifty-sixth from the top out of 135 countries in terms of its economic gender gaps, down from fifty-fourth in 2011, forty-fifth in 2009, and thirty-sixth in 2007, according to the World Economic Forum's Gender Index.[7] In other words, in terms of achieving gender equality in the workplace, Israel is way down the list and getting worse.[8]

But the gender issues extend beyond mere numbers of executives and their pay. The authors of the book *Start-Up Nation* mentioned previously make the case that one of the reasons why Israel promotes such an "entrepreneurial culture" is because of the training that people get in the army, especially in those aforementioned elite units. Perhaps the reason why only 8 percent of high-tech managers are women is related to the fact that they aren't allowed to be in most of these units, where they would gain those necessary skills and connections.

Women are also absent from high-level army positions. There is only one female major-general in the IDF—Orna Barbivai, appointed in 2011 and only the second woman ever to serve on the General Staff, the top tier of the Israeli military that is tightly connected to politics. No woman has ever been commander in chief of the Israeli army, a position that boasts a strong chance of becoming prime minister, like Ehud Barak and the late Yitzhak Rabin. Army types can also be found gaining high-level entry in the business world, like IDF generals Dan Halutz and the late Amnon Lipkin-Shahak. Needless to say, women have almost never been allowed to serve in these positions, and thus that avenue to business opportunities is essentially closed to them. In Israel, where the army culture is everywhere and often determines the careers and futures of most of the population, the absence of female leadership in the army, business, and politics is very telling of the lack of opportunities available to women.

To be fair, when Israel was in its infancy, it was in some ways way ahead of the rest of the world on gender issues. In the 1950s, while America was glorifying relegating women to the role of housewives and the nuclear family ideal of Ozzie and Harriet, Israeli women were already working outside the home and in fact were expected to be. According to Bar-Ilan University law Professor Ruth Halperin-Kaddari—who has been representing Israel at the United Nations Committee for the Elimination of Discrimination Against Women (CEDAW)—Israel implemented comprehensive maternity leave (today up to fourteen weeks paid parental leave for both gender parents as well as adoptive parents, funded for by the state) and instituted the 1954 Employment of Women Law aimed at protecting women, especially pregnant women, from workplace harm.[9] On kibbutzim (collective economic communities), in the army, and in the fledgling government offices, women were always present and working on some level. Moreover, women's workforce presence is etched into some national iconography: famous photographs of Zionist prestate pioneers show women working the land and donning army uniforms alongside men. And of course when Golda Meir became prime minister in 1969, it was an international celebration for women's rights. She was only the third woman in the world to hold such a position.

This progressive picture, however, was fraught with its own inequalities. For one thing, the portraits of early pioneering working women obscured more entrenched inequalities and sexism. Lesley Hazleton writes in *Israeli Women: Reality behind the Myths* that even as women toiled on the land, they were often not considered full-fledged members of their kibbutzim. As Hazleton notes, "The men at [kibbutz] Degania and the nearby Kinnereth were paid monthly wages by the Palestine office of the Zionist movement. The women were not. They were not even listed in the annual contracts drawn up between the pioneers and the Palestine office. When they insisted on being included, the women were told point-blank that they were working for the men and not for the Palestine office."[10]

Similar dynamics occurred in the army. As enlisted women demanded equality, Commander Yigal Allon mocked the "girls," restricting them to "domestic chore" positions such as wireless operators, nurses, and quartermasters—"exactly as women served in the British Army during World War II," Hazleton writes. "There were women who actually fought and died in battle, but it was solely on these exceptions that the rule of the myth [of Israeli women's equality] was to be based."[11] And Golda Meir, even as she broke a gender barrier, did not advance the rest of Israeli women. As Jewish feminist author Letty Cottin Pogrebin writes of Meir, "She was, in current parlance, a 'queen bee,' a woman who climbs to the top, then pulls the ladder up behind her. She did not wield the prerogatives of power to address women's special needs, to promote other women, or to advance women's status in the public sphere. The fact is that at the end of her tenure her Israeli sisters were no better off than they had been before she took office."[12] To date, there has not been another female prime minister in Israel since Meir.

Meanwhile, even some of the measures that Israel took to protect women in the early years ended up stifling them. Ruth Halperin-Kaddari explores the ways in which the 1954 Employment of Women Law, which established shorter "mother hours" for women, had the impact of preventing women from entering certain professions or increasing their income by working overtime. Similarly, by "protecting" women's rights as mothers, the socialist system established the cultural expectation that women would be primary caretakers—even while working full-time.[13] As Halperin-Kaddari notes, in essence this was a doubled-edged sword: women were included in the workplace, unlike many of their Western counterparts, but they also were expected to be full-time mothers and housewives too. So while Israeli women had certain advantages in the early years of the state, an entrenched culture of sexism infiltrated their work, their opportunities, and the general culture surrounding them, a sexism that still persists today. They were not much better off than their American or European counterparts.

Meanwhile, the women's rights movement that captured America and other parts of the world in the 1960s and 1970s took a while to pierce the public's mind-set in Israel. As Professor Hanna Herzog, academic director of the Civil Society forums at Van Leer Jerusalem Institute, writes, "Post-1967 Israel was pre-occupied with the question of borders and territories. In a society where the military, and more particularly a fighting army, is the centerpiece of social identification, civil society and civil demands are marginalized. Moreover, with the army as the fulcrum of the social ethos, the emphasis was naturally on men and on masculinity as the almost ultimate model of the 'civilian' who participates in and contributes to the life of the community." In fact, the wave of liberal feminism that washed over the Western world during the 1960s "left Israel largely, though not totally, untouched... In 1970, upon her return from the United States, Shulamit Aloni— founder of the Citizens' Rights Movement—was the first to ask, 'Does Israel need a women's rights movement?'"[14]

The answer was yes, most definitely, and the slew of feminist activists who have taken the stage in Israel over the past twenty years is proof of how badly Israel has needed this. In addition to numerous networks springing up of rape crisis centers, battered women's shelters, and legal aid associations, there are twenty-eight organizations fighting for Jewish divorce reform in Israel alone. Organizations of every type of feminism—Jewish, Muslim, interfaith, gay/lesbian, pacifist—have popped up, as well as lobby groups, economic empowerment groups, environmental feminists, groups promoting women in politics, and more. Feminism is starting to have its day in Israel, and on a certain level, this is invigorating.

But there is still a lot of work to be done. As Israeli society finally begins to seriously engage with these feminist ideals, new threats to women's rights have been emerging from different corners. The greatest is religion. As feminism has been on the rise, so has the growing power of religious forces in Israel, especially since the mid-1990s. These groups have brought with them increasingly fundamentalist calls to keep women out of power and out of the public eye at whatever cost.

Basic liberties that women had learned to take for granted—the freedom to ride the bus and sit wherever they want, to perform onstage, to have their pictures taken for public documents and media purposes, to sing, to wear jeans and a T-shirt, to marry and to divorce—are all under attack. This book sets out to chronicle each of these battles and the way they have escalated over the past decade, despite the cries of feminist activists.

Interestingly, the story of these rising tensions between religion and gender in Israel has more to do with money and power than with God. It's a story about the rabid growth of radical religious ideas—ideas that directly impact gender relationships and the lives of women—and the economic and political incentives that secular leaders have succumbed to, which have enabled their spread. It is also about a flawed if well-intentioned democracy and how its lack of separation between religion and state has given religious leaders new ways to intrude on and suppress women's basic freedoms.

In Israel, which was explicitly established to provide a safe haven for Jews persecuted by anti-Semitism for two millennia, religion is entrenched in the parliamentary political system, which rewards those protecting the narrowest of interests, even when those interests are expressly religious. As opposed to the American government where church and state are prohibited from mixing (at least in theory), in Israel, a party that is explicitly religious in nature and expressly forbids women from joining it has every right to run for government. In the United States, this would never be allowed. But in Israel, religion in any expression is considered as legitimate as values like freedom, democracy, and liberty and is upheld accordingly. In fact, for a large portion of Israelis, religion is considered a positive rationale for creating social and political policies. In other words, doing something in the name of religion—no matter how harmful it might be to others—is often acceptable.

A deeper look reveals that this entanglement of religion and politics is problematic not only for women, but also for Israeli society at large. For example, when the state was established in 1948 with laws about universal conscription, then-Prime Minister David Ben-Gurion made a deal with the ultra-Orthodox Knesset members to exempt ultra-Orthodox men studying full-time in yeshiva from army service and provide financial allowances for them. Considering how many yeshiva students perished in the Holocaust, the avowedly secular Ben-Gurion agreed to these demands out of either guilt or political expediency. At the time, there were four hundred students exempt, so it was likely the latter. But today, there are 37,000 exemptions.[15] These students, called *avreichim*, may receive up to 10,000 NIS (about $2,600 U.S. net, or 17,000 NIS/$4,300 U.S. gross) per month in stipends and other allowances from the government, an amount that is far above the average monthly salary for working Israelis.[16] They also create a huge economic burden on their non-*avreichim* counterparts to produce enough to support them, as we'll examine in more detail later on.

The situation with the *avreichim* raises the ire of many Israelis, both secular and working religious. So why does the Israeli government continue to allow this? Until the 2012 elections, religious parties had been willing to join coalitions in every single government, provided they met a very simple demand: continued funding for religious programs, especially the *avreichim*. For Israeli prime ministers, this was a relatively easy way to gain coalition support and push through their political agendas, even with its clear price tag. So government after government consistently paid this one faction.

Therein lies the problem: these governments have set a dire

precedent for giving seemingly boundless political and economic power to religious groups that do not believe in most of the basic principles of democracy, especially gender equality, and that do not really see themselves as bound by the laws of the land. For women in particular, the power that religious leaders have co-opted over the years to make rules for the rest of society has created a real threat to some basic liberties. The past decade in Israel has seen a frightening array of events in which religious parties seek to impose their own lifestyle on the rest of Israeli society—especially when it comes to controlling women. These include calls for gender segregation on buses and other public transportation, creating gender-segregated streets and shops, forbidding women from singing or speaking in public or on the radio, limiting women's roles in the army, and control over their right to marriage and divorce. And that's only part of it.

In ultra-Orthodox parties, women are not allowed to run for office, despite a 2012 petition to the High Court by women's groups to make such rules illegal, which was rejected. In fact, during the High Court hearings, the religious leaders emphasized their beliefs that the women's place is outside of the public eye, and with that, they won the case.[17] Moreover, state religious councils that provide municipal religious services are exclusively male and predominantly ultra-Orthodox. In fact, when the government ordered a woman to serve on the Jerusalem municipal council over a decade ago, the ultra-Orthodox men on the council protested by refusing to even hold a council meeting. This should help paint a picture of what life under Haredi (ultra-Orthodox) influence might look like for Israeli women.[18]

The ultra-Orthodox community has extended its antiwomen influence to government as well. For example, in the entire history of Israel, there has never been a female minister or deputy minister of religion, a position in the government routinely dominated by ultra-Orthodox men. There has also never been a female director of the rabbinic courts, state institutions meant to serve the entire public that are in fact fully controlled by ultra-Orthodox parties. And certainly any position that requires a "rabbi" title—such as rabbi of a city or rabbi of a school, both state-funded positions—by definition has never been held by a woman, since Orthodoxy is the only denomination recognized by the state, and Israeli Orthodoxy does not yet recognize women in rabbinical positions. In some cases, rabbis have also said that women shouldn't even vote.

But this culture of excluding women is not limited to ultra-Orthodox men and their beliefs. In some cases, Zionist rabbis share these views as well. Rabbi Dov Lior of Kiryat Arba, considered by some to be a leading authority of Halacha (Jewish religious laws) in Israel, wrote in 2010 that not only are women forbidden from running for public office in his jurisdiction, but they also are best off not even working outside the home. Women should be housewives, he said, "because it is important that everyone fulfill the role that the Holy One Blessed be He gave him [sic]."[19] Rabbi Elyakim Levanon of the Elon Moreh settlement also ruled in 2010 that women are banned from running for public office: "The first problem is giving women authority, and being on the council means having authority. The second problem is mixing men and women. Council meetings are held at night and sometimes end very late. It is not proper to be in mixed company in such situations... The husband presents the family's opinion... This is the proper way to prevent a situation in which the woman votes one way and her husband votes another."[20]

To get an idea of what kinds of expectations many of these

rabbis have of Jewish women overall, consider some of the restrictive rules that have emerged from different insulated communities in Israel and America: forbidding women from wearing high heels that make noise or wearing the color red; forcing women to wear coats on top of their clothes when they go to weddings, even in summer so as not to draw "excessive attention" to themselves; forbidding women from blogging or talking on cell phones in public; and more.[21] One Orthodox community in Israel established a "kashrut [kosher] department" for supervising clothing stores to check the length of the skirts and sleeves of the merchandise. This practice was justified by an Israeli group called the Committee for the Sanctity of the Camp to combat what they called "damaging our camp's modesty" due to women and girls "breaching" conventions.[22]

It's tempting for anyone, American, Israeli, or otherwise, to dismiss these practices as customs of a bizarre and exotic cultural group that is entitled to maintain its own rules within the larger Israeli society. But this would be a mistake. First, this is just another example of a culture created by men in which women do not get a say over their own lives. The culture in question is one that belongs exclusively to men—men who want to see women in a certain way and in certain places in society. It is about demanding that women comport themselves to the calls of certain men.

Second, the ultra-Orthodox acculturation of women into these gendered roles may have once affected only the women of the ultra-Orthodox community, but that is no longer the case. Today, all Israeli women are at risk. Religious groups increasingly call to extend these oppressive rules to all women, barring them from certain public places and enforcing gender segregation on the street, in shops, in municipal buildings, and more.

Even more alarming, ultra-Orthodox pressure to remove women from other areas of society, such as positions in the army, singing in the Knesset, dancing at public events, and receiving awards at public ceremonies, has been surprisingly successful. Recent reports show gender segregation on the rise in Israel's religious state schools, with a 40 percent rise in the number of gender-segregated students over the past thirteen years.[23] Images of women are also disappearing—from billboards, cereal boxes, magazines, schoolbooks, and television shows, anywhere that businesses or politicians want to attract Haredi customers or supporters and believe that eliminating women's images is the way to do that. According to a recent report in *Haaretz* of gender images among religious Zionist TV programming:

> *Public singing by women, even by 4-year-old girls, is no longer permissible, let alone on-screen. In fact, any mention of women has been removed from many of the schoolbooks used in religious schools... Many of the religious programs on the Internet are devoid of women, as are plays and DVDs... Singing by girls does not take place anymore in schools and kindergartens belonging to the religious Zionist stream...*[24]

All these issues are connected. In a system in which ultra-Orthodox groups are given free rein in politics and education, receive enormous public budgets for their institutions regardless of what is taught in them and exorbitant stipends for tens of thousands of *avreichim*, and are given positions throughout the Religious Ministry (where nepotism and back-door deals abound), the message is clear: ultra-Orthodox groups have disproportionate power over Israeli society. Those who desire women's total exclusion from the public sphere have no qualms about making such demands, and no doubt these demands will be met. And why shouldn't they? Over the past two decades, they have had political and business leaders alike cave in to their demands more and more without a second thought as to their implications for Israel as a whole. So long as there are no government regulations limiting the impact of religion on public life in Israel, these demands to control women in the name of religion will continue to be heeded to the detriment of all Israeli women—and men too.

This book is about Israel, yes, but not Israel alone. In fact, Israel is simply a case study of how religious radicalism—a disturbingly misogynistic religious radicalism—is spreading. This is a story that is happening all around the world, from Tel Aviv to Tehran, from Kabul to Kansas.[25] The story of Israel sheds important light on how religious extremism spreads and what can be done to stop it.

For example, as we have been witnessing over the past few years, Muslim countries are seeing tremendous threats to women's lives in the name of religion. We have seen the Taliban's violent persecution of women and schoolgirls in Afghanistan, Pakistan, and other places. Even Tunisia, once a bastion of secular Islam and a safe haven for Muslim women, has become a frightening place where members of the Salafist sect of Sunni Muslims beat up a school headmaster for refusing to allow a girl to wear a niqab at school, and rape and sexual violence in the name of religion are on the rise.[26] Even the once moderate Turkey is showing an increase in religious-based violence against women. According to a recent report, some 62 percent of Turkish men now say they believe that wife beating is justifiable.[27]

Similarly, violence against women in the name of Hinduism has also started to come to the forefront, following the public gang rape and murder of a woman in India in January 2013. According to the *New York Times*, "rape is just one facet of a broad range of violence and discrimination that leads to the deaths of almost two million women a year" in India, including an estimated 25,000 to 100,000 women who are killed each year over dowry disputes. Women who do not comply with expectations of femininity are at tremendous risk in India. "Many are burned alive in a particularly grisly form of retribution," the *Times* reports.[28]

It's tempting for some Americans to dismiss violence against women in Asia, Africa, and the Middle East as reflecting "foreign" cultures, i.e., non-American and therefore disconnected from their lives. But it's not just the developing world that has a problem with religious extremism and violence against women. Even in America, a country that prides itself on separation of church and state, there are increasingly vocalized opinions that violence against women in the name of religious beliefs is justifiable. During the 2012 American presidential election, Republican vice presidential candidate Paul Ryan's position on contraception was a horrifying example of the real threat that allowing religious rhetoric in politics presents to women's lives and well-being. Throughout the campaign, Ryan advanced the religious extremist theory of "personhood," according to which preventing a sperm from fertilizing an egg through birth control is equivalent to murder. This definition of what constitutes life is so extreme that it effectively criminalizes women who use certain types of birth control or seek to manage their own fertility. This idea also ignores the vast research showing that women's access to tools of family planning positively affects our educational and economic advancement. So even though America does have separation of religion and state, there is a remarkably antiwomen sentiment subtly infusing American politics. In other words, it's not just Israel.

As we've seen, the tension between religion and women's rights crosses national, ethnic, and religious boundaries—especially religious boundaries. Islam, Christianity, Hinduism, and Judaism all face real threats from fanatic religious ideologies built on the ability to control women's bodies and lives. Indeed, the situation in Israel is indicative of the trends of rising fundamentalism around the world. Women's freedom is often seen as a threat to men. Thus, wherever women are advancing, forces of backlash are intensifying. When women enter roles and positions of strength and leadership that were once the domain of men, it's often seen as a challenge to economic and political hierarchies and to men's privileged status within that society. This is especially true of places like Israel, where men are socialized into a belief system that their entire identity is a function of their political and economic power. In these societies, a challenge to those ideas, like women's equal rights, threatens their masculinity.

It should not come as such a surprise then that as women around the world challenge these gender constructs, some men assemble their resources and go on the attack in order to stop this advancement, using whatever tools they have at their disposal. In that sense, Israel is no different from any other society on the planet. Women seeking freedom and equality challenge the most basic assumptions of many men—religious and secular alike—and the result can be some difficult and painful social and political battles.

So why should you or I care about what's happening to women arguably half a world away from us? Because the whole world is threatened by religious extremism, and it will jeopardize our own freedoms too if we allow it to continue unchecked. We need to understand how it spreads and how it is to be stopped, and that is precisely what this book will explore. My argument is this: religious extremism spreads when it is *empowered, unregulated,* and *unopposed.* By *empowered,* I mean that political leaders, business leaders, or the media give religious extremists power. By *unregulated,* I mean that laws and practices enable radicalism. By *unopposed,* I mean that the *secular* public does not express any opposition to religious extremism with vocal protest, advocacy, or activism. It is the secular public that will ultimately pay the price for the spread of religious extremism. Yet so often, the secular public relies on misguided thinking around "cultural relativism"—as in, "Hey, it's their culture, leave them alone"—which ultimately gives religious extremism free rein. This confluence of factors is what leads to the spread of religious extremism, not just in Israel but around the world. In fact, it is clear that Israel, despite everything I describe in this book, is not the worst example of radical religious misogyny. But it's a story that is unfolding right now in dramatic ways, and so it is crucial for us to look at the Israel case to get ideas for what we as civil society can and should be doing to stop it.

Throughout the world, the groups working most intensely to halt the spread of religious radicalism are religious feminists across different faiths. I contend that secular, democratic citizens have a crucial role to play in helping to stop the spread of religious radicalism by working in concert with religious feminists.[29] As Allison Kaplan Sommer and Dahlia Lithwick wrote in the *New Republic,* "An unlikely alliance between Orthodox and progressive women will save Israel from fundamentalism."[30] Indeed, this call can be applied easily across religions.

This book tells the story of the rapidly spreading religious radicalism in Israel and the phenomenal ways that religious feminists are leading the fight for women's freedom against this increasing oppression. It looks at the different places where this struggle is taking place: on buses, on streets, at the holy site of the Western Wall, in courtrooms, in rabbinical courts, in the media, on the Internet, on billboards, and in the Knesset. It's a war that is still unfolding. Perhaps when you finish reading the book, you will discover that you have a place in this story as well, because as you will see, the war on women in Israel is a war on women—and men—everywhere.

Part I

NO WOMEN ALLOWED

*Erasing Women from
the Streets of Israel*

Chapter 1

SEPARATE AND UNEQUAL: GENDER SEGREGATION ON PUBLIC BUSES

One Saturday night in 1995, I was traveling home to Jerusalem, Israel, after spending a weekend at Bar-Ilan University with my husband and young daughter. When the bus pulled up at the university stop, my husband went to put our bags under the bus while I boarded with my then-toddler asleep on my shoulder. As I got on, a man in the front row looked at me, got up, and offered me his seat. He looked about twenty years old, and his black suit, white button-down shirt, and black fedora was the attire characteristic of men in the ultra-Orthodox community in Bnei Brak, the town where the bus had originated. I smiled at him in a gesture of thanks and he smiled back.

But as I was about to sit down, the gentleman next to him, an older man with a white beard and similar black hat and jacket, tapped him on the arm and shook his head in disapproval, whispering something as he waved his finger back and forth. The young man looked at his elder and then back at me, wiped the smile off his face (in what I think might have been his version of an apology to me or perhaps just embarrassment), and sat back down. The older man crossed his hands on his lap and looked straight ahead, apparently satisfied.

As I continued down the aisle in search of a seat, I noticed that all the front rows were filled with men in black hats. They either stared blankly at me or straight ahead as I walked past, none offering a seat. Toward the back, I finally saw women. One woman, dressed in jeans and a short-sleeved shirt, saw me coming with my sleeping child and quickly got up for me. I have never been so grateful for a seat on a bus in my entire life.

This incident took place years before the national bus company in Israel officially established gender-segregated bus lines, what have been called *mehadrin* bus lines, literally "glorified" or "extra kosher." When I took that bus ride, I had heard only faint rumors that such things existed. In fact, my only prior knowledge of gender segregation on buses was of the famed *mechitza* buses in New York, of all places, that went from the Jewish community of Monsey in Rockland County, New York, to Manhattan with a *mechitza*—literally a "partition"—down the middle. When I was growing up in Brooklyn, the *mechitza* bus was almost a joke. We mocked the vision of men and women bumping into each other in the aisles without actually seeing each other. It seemed so absurd it was laughable, a kind of exaggerated caricature of religious life taken to a ridiculous extreme.

But here I was, many years later, trying simply to get my family home to Jerusalem, and suddenly it wasn't so funny anymore. I felt as if I had unknowingly stepped into a cultural *Twilight Zone* where there were different rules and where my identity as *woman* now superseded all other circumstances and considerations. And I, as a mere woman, had no power to stop it.

A lot has changed in Israel since that incident, but not necessarily for the better. Over 150 segregated buses have been created by public companies in twenty-eight cities across Israel.[1] In fact, the social experiment I witnessed in gender segregation on buses that began in Bnei Brak in the 1990s has evolved into a state-supported system that has ignited people's passion around the world. Even more alarmingly, the phenomenon has spread beyond buses to public streets, health clinics, supermarkets, pharmacies, post offices, banks, amusement parks, municipal buildings, and more.[2] The issue has been examined and discussed by the Knesset, the Transport Ministry, and the High Court in Israel. It has led to violence, lawsuits, reports, regulations, and attempts at legislation. And the situation, which threatens to impose cultural norms of religious radicalism on everyone in Israel, reflects an intense, state-wide battle over some of the most basic rights of women.

The buses were the beginning. The first official segregation was established in 1997, when Israel's primary national bus company, Egged, under growing pressure from Haredi community leaders, began operating a gender-segregated line on a trial basis between Bnei Brak and Jerusalem. These were two of the biggest strongholds of Haredi ultra-Orthodox culture in Israel (and, not insignificantly, two of the poorest cities in Israel). On this bus, in acquiescence to demands of Haredi leaders (all male leaders, of course), women were to board only from the back door and sit in the back, not in the front, which was reserved seating for men.

In 2001, Egged announced to the Haredi community that the trial was a success and that bus line 402 between Bnei Brak and Jerusalem would become permanently segregated. In addition, a new segregated route would be added, bus number 350 between Ashdod, another ultra-Orthodox community, and Bnei Brak. In addition, Egged spokesman Ron Ratner added that the gender-segregated *mehadrin* buses would not play "inappropriate radio programs" on the loudspeakers of these buses. The bus routes were also redrawn so as not to go through perceived non-Haredi areas—which included the Jerusalem Central Bus Station—as demanded by Haredi leaders. Furthermore, even though these buses now would not be going through the Central Bus Station, Egged had apparently started pressuring shop owners in the station to change their displays to adapt to Haredi demands of so-called modesty. Already by the time of the announcement, an Internet café had changed its screen savers and a lingerie shop changed its window dressings. According to an Egged source, "we explained to the shop owners that if the Haredim boycott the bus station, it will mean less business for them."[3]

When the first gender-segregated line was created, Arik Feldman, the chairman of Egged, said at the time, "We hope that the new line will satisfy the chareidi [sic] sector, which is very important to us," and noted that Haredi Knesset members had been instrumental in making this happen. Itzik Kagan, spokesman for the other state-backed bus company, Dan, which was apparently part of the negotiations, added, "We regard all the service we provide very seriously, and especially our service to the Haredi sector."[4]

It might seem odd that the representatives of the bus companies were very enthusiastic about the establishment of these new segregated lines. After all, it goes against Israeli equal rights laws and discriminates against half their customers. But there were a number of incentives for them to appease the (male) Haredi market. The most obvious is that it represents an estimated 10 percent of Israel's 8.2 million-strong population. In addition, this is a population characterized by large families and a high rate of poverty. Many Haredim can't afford cars and thus are some of the most consistent consumers of public transportation. For this same reason, tickets on the 402 *mehadrin* lines became 20 percent cheaper than the regular 400 bus between Jerusalem and Bnei Brak (15 NIS instead of 18 NIS), indicating another cave to Haredi pressure.

The Haredi community met this new development with equal enthusiasm. During its first two weeks of operation in 2001, the new gender-segregated 402 line reportedly had an imposing 14,000 passengers.[5] The rest of Israel did not even know that this was happening, because it was never reported in the general press.

The Haredi community may have been proud of its victory in moving the entire Israeli political system to meet its demands, but the truth is this entire political deal to establish gender-segregated buses on public buses was struck behind closed doors. According to reports in the Haredi press, negotiations over this line had been taking place between Egged and the leaders of the Haredi community since 1997. A man named Rabbi Micha Rothschild representing a group called the Mehadrin Council (a self-described "modesty monitoring service for public transportation") was quoted as saying that his group was working with Egged to expand this model to other lines within Jerusalem and to "remove all the spiritual and educational pitfalls from the Central Bus Station in Jerusalem and from all the buses in the city."[6] But again, Egged never released a statement about these dealings to the general press. According to Shahar Ilan of *Haaretz*, "Egged wants the Haredim to know there is a deal and the secular community to think there isn't."[7]

Perhaps due to the backroom nature of these initial Haredi political steps to dominate the public bus system, secular politicians and leaders were rather slow to respond. Back in 2001, there were some reports that the antireligious Shinui Party was going to oppose all this, but Shinui eventually lost its seats and never got around to it. The Israel Religious Action Center (IRAC) announced that they were going to fight this with litigation, but it took almost six years for their first court petition on the subject. The rest of the country was mostly silent.

Meanwhile, the *mehadrin* bus phenomenon continued to expand, both numerically and culturally. As the number of segregated buses—both intercity and inner-city—began to grow with little opposition, Haredi leadership became more empowered by this consistent message from state organizations that their demands for gender-segregated spaces were legitimate and would be heeded, regardless of how harmful they might be toward women.

In retrospect, the seeming ease with which the general public in Israel acquiesced to the Haredi demands might have been a harbinger for events to come. Indeed, with this pattern of political responsiveness to Haredi demands, the culture of segregation became more strictly enforced and began to lead to bullying of women and eventually violence.

At first, violence against women on buses only consisted of verbal abuse and seemed to go largely unnoticed by the general population.

The incident that would eventually propel the issue into the public spotlight occurred in August 2004 with bestselling novelist and Jerusalem resident Naomi Ragen. Ragen writes that she got on an empty number 40 bus from the center of town to her home in Ramot—which she describes as "a neighborhood divided between secular, modern Orthodox, and Haredi inhabitants"— and sat on a seat near the front and began reading *Vanity Fair*. Suddenly she found herself "interrupted by an angry Haredi man who announced that I needed to move to the back of the bus. I looked up at him, astonished, feeling a flash of what Blacks must have felt in Alabama in 1950." She goes on to describe a series of tense verbal exchanges, during which the man "aggressively planted his two feet squarely in front of my seat and, in a loud and abusive tone and in no uncertain terms, demanded that I move to the back of the bus... He continued to rant and rave... The entire ride, I continued to be the target of intermittent abuse until he finally got off... All this time, the bus driver said nothing, even though it was clear to him what was happening."[8]

Ragen contacted Egged and was told that, "The number 40 bus is a public bus and passengers may sit anywhere they choose. However, on those lines (and number 40 is one) on which 95 percent of the passengers are Haredim, we allow the passengers to decide how they want to divide the seating. Egged doesn't interfere." In other words, gender segregation may not have been official policy, but Egged was allowing it to become the de facto practice. Haredi men were taking over the buses and moving women to the back—whenever and wherever they wanted.

According to one report from early 2006, two women who unknowingly sat in the front of a segregated Egged bus from Beit Shemesh to Jerusalem were verbally bullied by "two bearded men in suits and hats" who forced them to move to the back. "This is public transportation, I thought," one of the women told reporters. "I have a right to sit wherever I want to sit." The driver, she recalled, did not say or do anything to help the women. "I felt threatened," she said, and so she moved to the back. No other action was taken to protect her.[9] Verbal abuse then began to evolve into physical abuse. In December 2006, the first report of physical violence on the segregated line came to public attention. Miriam Shear, a fifty-year-old Canadian woman visiting Israel, was traveling on the inner-city number 2 bus in Jerusalem on her way to pray at the Western Wall when she was attacked by a group of ultra-Orthodox men for sitting too close to the front. On this particular morning, a man apparently demanded her seat, despite the fact that the bus was not yet full. She stated in a widely circulated email, which progressed into a later lawsuit about the incident, that she was "slapped, kicked, punched, and pushed by a group of men who demanded that she sit in the back of the bus with the other women."[10]

The events were confirmed by a witness, Yehoshua Meyer, the one person on the bus who came forward to talk to the police. "I saw everything," he said. "Someone got on the bus and demanded that she go to the back, but she didn't agree. She was badly beaten and her whole body sustained hits and kicks. She tried to fight back and no one would help her. I tried to help, but someone was stopping me from getting up. I yelled for the bus driver to stop. He stopped once, but he didn't do anything. When we finally got to the Kotel [Western Wall], she was beaten badly and I helped her go to the police."[11] It's astonishing that on the entire bus of people watching men beat up a woman for sitting in the "wrong" seat, only one person helped her at all.

But there was a deeper significance to this shockingly violent act: the number 2 bus wasn't even officially segregated. Much like the Bnei Brak bus that I unwittingly boarded back in 1995, the bus to the Western Wall was merely segregated de facto by the passengers acquiescing to established patterns of behavior.

The stories of Naomi Ragen and Miriam Shear began to wake up the public to the issue of encroaching religious radicalism on the buses. Religious feminist Israeli filmmaker Anat Tzruya wrote an exposé of the escalating violence in an article in *Eretz Acheret* magazine. She shared some other shocking incidents of gender-based violence on buses between 2007 and 2009. "When eighteen-year-old Oriyah Ferdheim boarded a bus in her neighborhood in the town of Beit Shemesh, her first time traveling this route on the way to the town of Yahud, she sat down in a chair astoundingly similar to the dozens of others surrounding it," writes Tzurya, and "had no conception of what was about to happen. She was sleepy and turned on her MP3 so that she wouldn't fall asleep and miss her bus. Oriyah was lost in her dreams with her music on when she was jolted by the first kick. The kick was a direct hit to her leg, and when she looked up to see the source of the pain, she saw her assailants facing her: four ultra-Orthodox men, and a woman…and they screamed 'shikseh' [a derogatory slur referring to a non-Jewish woman] at her and tried to tear her from her seat, all the while spitting on her, kicking her, and pelting her with all manner of objects."[12] But still, nothing was done beyond the press coverage to protect women.

It's hard to comprehend the driving forces behind this kind of violence against women—but it's possible that some Haredi men are getting instructions from their rabbis. The late Rabbi Yosef Shalom Elyashiv, for example, considered by the Haredi community to be the rabbinic leader of his generation, openly justified violence against women who refused to follow what he considered to be the rules of correct female dress and behavior, including sitting in the back of the bus. In March 2011, he gave an official ruling of Halacha in the Haredi paper *Kikar Hashabat*, instructing a young Haredi man on how to deal with a woman who sits in the front of a so-called *mehadrin* bus. According to the story, the man seeking Rabbi Elyashiv's counsel told the woman in front that this was a *mehadrin* bus and that she must move to the rear section reserved for women. When the woman refused to move, he screamed at her, insulted her, and verbally harassed her throughout the journey. But he had some doubts about the correctness of his behavior and wrote to Rabbi Elyashiv for a ruling on whether he should ask the woman for forgiveness. Rabbi Elyashiv told the man that since the woman should have moved to the rear of the bus, she was deserving of this treatment.[13] In other words, violence against women is justifiable in certain circumstances.

It's hard to know how many rabbis are issuing these kinds of rulings or how Haredi men internalize this message. Civil rights activists, however, reacted with horror. As veteran feminist activist and attorney Sharon Shenhav, representing the religious feminist perspective, responded in the *Jerusalem Post*:

> *According to Rabbi Elyashiv, we learn that a Jewish man can publicly humiliate a woman who violates Halacha.*
>
> *So now you know how to treat uppity women according to Halacha… While the case in question involved a woman sitting in the front of a bus, I have no doubt that Rabbi Elyashiv's [ruling] can be applied more broadly to women who do not conform to other Haredi standards.*
>
> *How about women sitting as civil court judges, especially the President of our Supreme Court? Then there are those women who serve as Members of Knesset and Cabinet ministers. Obviously, women who are CEOs of banks and corporations, as well as officers in the IDF are uppity. What about female academicians and scientists? Why, there's no end to uppity women today in Israel! They're everywhere, practicing medicine and law, appearing on television as entertainers and news broadcasters, writing articles in newspapers. The list is endless.*

...one can only imagine the results of this message! During the hot Israeli summer, the streets and public places are full of women whose mode of dress does not conform to Haredi standards of modesty. How are yeshiva boys going to find time to study Torah if they have to deal with all the uppity women?[14]

Haredi men are beating up women on buses because they are being taught that women who do not conform to social expectations of so-called modesty deserve it. "The lynching of Oriyah was carried out because she is a woman who refused to surrender to the ultra-Orthodox dictates of 'modesty,'" writes Anat Tzruya. "An ultra-Orthodox crowd did not hesitate to so severely punish the anonymous young woman who publicly violated the rules of modesty...[in an] event that left no impression on the Israeli public agenda."[15] Once violence against women was justified as being the women's fault, it was only a matter of time before the situation worsened.

While rabbis were issuing rulings and religious feminists were beginning to speak out, the number of segregated buses continued to rise—along with the accompanying bullying. It is difficult to put a precise figure on how many incidents of verbal abuse or threatening or hostile comments against women took place on these buses during those early years or how many women wanted to sit in the front but didn't do so, just as it is hard to know how women sitting in the back really felt about these new rules or how other passengers on the bus felt about these incidents. But what seems abundantly clear is that the culture of religious zealotry that justifies violence against women was spreading. As Anat Tzruya writes:

Nothing had prepared Oriyah for this attack. No detail in

what had begun as a routine trip on an Egged bus in the heart
of Israel foreshadowed the storm of rage and violence in which
she would be caught. There were just five zealots, but they
turned the routine trip of the passengers on Bus 497 from Beit
Shemesh into a scene taken from some kind of zany action film,
if one takes into account the ultra-Orthodox look of most of the
bus's passengers. In the unbelievable end of the episode, five
police cars and undercover police came to extricate the eighteen-
year-old Oriyah and the soldier who tried to rescue her from
the madding crowd, i.e. from the majority of the bus passengers
and from the residents of the Ramat Beit Shemesh suburb who
came to their succor.[16]

That said, it's not only the Haredi men who enable the violence, but also the bus drivers, who are usually not Haredi. When IRAC and Kolech began to respond to escalating segregation and bullying by collecting stories of violence on buses, they discovered a disturbing pattern of drivers enabling the bullies. For example, Ariela, a fourteen-year-old high school student who lives in the town of Beit Shemesh, writes in the IRAC report that emerged from this investigative work that she was returning from school with her friends and sat down in the front section of the bus. Two ultra-Orthodox men boarded the bus and stood next to the girls. "At that point, the driver turned to us and told us to move to the back of the bus, in order to make room for the two ultra-Orthodox men at the front of the bus," Ariela recalled. "I felt immediately that that was wrong. I knew that I could sit anywhere I wanted on the bus... Despite the fact that my friends and I felt humiliated and angry, we could not refuse to do what the driver asked and we moved to the back."[17] Segregation was on the rise, and women seemed to have nowhere to turn—not even to the mostly secular drivers employed by the public bus companies. Women's lives in public spaces in Israel were suddenly facing a new threat, and people did not seem to care.

The emergence of violence against women on the bus marks a critical moment in the evolution of religious radicalism in Israel. When a secular political system and a secular bus company enable the bullying of women to make them conform to their male customers' gender rules demanding silence, stillness, and total invisibility, we begin to see how easily political and economic forces can back the practice of violence against women. In this case, the opinions of radical rabbis and religious leaders on how women should behave and be treated are carried out by impressionable men and supported by the Egged bus company. Now it was time for women to start fighting back.

The first signs of feminist protest came in 2007, when IRAC, together with bullying victim Naomi Ragen and four other women who were harassed on *mehadrin* buses, submitted a petition to the High Court of Justice against the Ministry of Transportation, demanding the protection of women on its buses and other transport lines. "This issue clearly needs to be regulated so that what happened to Miriam Shear does not happen again," said IRAC attorney Orly Erez-Likhovski, who submitted the petition. "We are not asking that these lines be cancelled, but there needs to be order and the issue needs to be checked. Many of these buses serve people who are not ultra-Orthodox and there need to be alternatives."[18] The Ministry initially replied that it would not intervene in the practices of the bus companies because gender segregation is a "voluntary arrangement." However, the court then ordered the Ministry of Transportation to appoint a committee to examine the matter and report its findings.

In the nearly two years that it took for the Ministry's committee to present findings, issues on the street heated up. By the end of 2009, some fifty-five *mehadrin* lines were running throughout the country, and reports of violence and harassment continued to increase. Meanwhile, the committee received hundreds of letters from men, women, and organizations opposed to segregation—but it also received thousands of letters from Haredim supporting the policy.[19] Clearly there was a cultural fault line being created between those who believed in women's rights and those who did not—or between those who took instruction from a perceived word of God and those who followed their own sense of basic morality.

In October 2009, the committee concluded that gender segregation in public buses was illegal and coercive but added the bizarre recommendation to open both front and back doors of buses so that women can still board in the back of their own free will—implying that there are women who *choose* to sit in the back. This lack of a strong and clear verdict instantly created confusion and loopholes to get around the committee's conclusions. For instance, Transportation Minister Yisrael Katz, who was ordered by the High Court to issue instructions based on the committee's recommendations, formally wrote in February 2010 that although threats and violence were unsavory, segregation was ultimately "voluntary," and therefore buses could display signs that "suggest" gender-segregated seating without forcing it.[20] The Transportation Ministry was supposed to put up signs saying that segregation could not be coerced, but even this small step was not immediately taken. Moreover, these events had no impact on what was happening on the buses in which women continued being "asked" (or more often told) to move to the back. Tellingly, the Haredi community still considered this a victory.

Katz's utter failure to respond effectively and carry out the committee's orders brought louder protests from feminist activists and human rights activists—which in turn ushered in a new form of Haredi violence. In October 2010, several activists who were particularly vocal in their opposition to gender segregation claimed they were threatened and stalked by gender-segregation fanatics in Jerusalem. Avital Livny, the volunteer coordinator for the organization Yisrael Hofshit ("Be Free Israel"), whose contact details had been posted on flyers and Facebook pages in advance of protests against gender segregation on the streets of Meah She'arim, reported receiving dozens of threatening phone calls trying to stop the organization's activity. Similarly, Rona Orovano, then vice chair of the Bezalel Academy Student Union and founder of the Organizational Forum for a Free Jerusalem, said she received threatening phone calls, emails, and Facebook messages, such as "We are waiting for you with rocks" and "We know where you live"—and even a death threat.[21] Violence against women thus expanded into threats of violence against those working to *protect* women.

In some ways, this emboldened the activists who had begun to experience for themselves the intensity of the threat against women. Orovano's umbrella organization, for example, made up of more than twenty groups from across the religious and political spectrum in Israel, was conducting a series of protests along with other groups such as Be Free Israel against gender barriers on the public streets and on buses. "You had to see what was going on in

Meah She'arim during Sukkot," Orovano told me in an interview in 2010. "Haredi men were shouting in megaphones, screaming at people to separate. Men to this side, women to this side. You had couples walking down the street with a stroller, and these guys were screaming at them to separate. It's crazy."[22]

Similarly, Tali Feldman, a twenty-eight-year old activist with Elah, an international feminist student body fighting against sexual harassment at universities and for other feminist causes, was also shaken when she encountered the tension on the buses. "It's really frightening," she told me in an interview in 2010. "All these men screaming at me and staring at me—there have been times when I've been scared for my life. One time, there was so much scream-ing that the bus driver pulled over and refused to drive."[23] So as the violence seemed to be escalating over these years, the voices of activism finally were emboldened as well.

These events also began to forge a powerful alliance between secular feminists, human rights activists, and religious feminists—and perhaps even, in a quiet way, Haredi women. Although Haredi women faced some real risks in their insular communities if they were to join the protests—being branded as troublemakers would ostracize them in their communities and create difficulties in marrying off their children—there are indications that many Haredi women quietly supported the feminist activists.

"Haredi women were watching us from the windows during the protest," Laura Wharton, Jerusalem City councilwoman for the secular Meretz Party, who was instrumental in organizing the protests, told me in an interview. "We received…phone calls from Haredi women who said they were really grateful."[24] Kolech reported that they were being inundated with calls from ultra-Orthodox women, thanking them for speaking on their behalf.

"Haredi women can't speak out on their own without being subject to all kinds of threats," explained Dr. Hannah Kehat, the group's founder and CEO. "They are begging us to continue to protest, to bring back some normalcy to their lives."[25] Jerusalem councilwoman and Orthodox feminist activist Rachel Azaria said that some Haredi women actually joined the protests on the bus. "Many are not happy with the rabbis' orders which separate their families, but are afraid to speak out," she said.[26] "The truth is, there is probably only a small minority of people in the community who think that the extreme gender segregation is right," Wharton added. "But the rest are unwilling or unable to protest."[27]

The activists didn't stop there. One of the first major initiatives of the coalition was to collect information about what was really happening on the buses—in response to the Transport Ministry's claims that segregation was voluntary. Between August and October 2010, volunteers systematically boarded buses and collected data from 128 rides on the segregated buses. They found that there were complaints from passengers on thirty-one of these journeys (approximately one-fourth of the total sample), "including cases when women were prevented from boarding by the front door or from sitting in the front section of the bus. Many women experienced harassment and serious threats from other passengers, sometimes with the support of the driver. The complaints show that friction and violent confrontations continue to occur on the gender-separated lines due to the demand for segregation."[28]

Something was clearly starting to change on the streets, because the Transport Ministry began to pay attention. Following the release of this report on abuse on buses, it started collecting its own research. Out of 1,150 checks in which a female Ministry official purposely sat in the "wrong" part of the bus, in fifty-six instances, the official was asked to move, including fifteen instances in which the official felt personally threatened by other passengers to do so. Police Lieutenant Niso Shoham, Commander of the Jerusalem District, commented on the report, "Let's not delude ourselves into thinking that everything is good and quiet. The report does not reflect the enormity of this terrible phenomenon—and it is indeed terrible."[29]

This work had real impact. The first legal victory for women came on January 6, 2011—by which time there were 128 seg-regated buses operating around Israel—when the High Court of Israel ruled against the creation of additional segregated lines and ordered the Transport Ministry to be more assertive and proactive in protecting women. Egged was finally forced to put up signs saying that everyone has the right to sit wherever they want, and bus drivers were ordered to ensure women's freedom. This was seen as a great moment of justice for women and for democracy, sending a clear message both to the Haredi community and the Ministry of Transportation that male bullying of women on buses would no longer be tolerated.

According to the ruling authored by the panel head Justice Elyakim Rubinstein, "a public transportation company (like any other person) cannot tell, ask, or order women where to sit on a bus simply because they are women, nor what they should wear, and they are entitled to sit anywhere they wish. Of course, this also applies to the men, but for reasons that are obvious, the complaints [filed by the petitioners] have to do with the harmful behavior toward women. When I go back and read the lines just written, I wonder how is it that it is necessary in Israel of 2010 to write them. Have the days of Rosa Parks, the African American woman who collapsed the racist segregation on an Alabama bus in 1955, returned?"[30] This was the first time an Israeli leader took a definitive stance that gender segregation is against Israel's values of democracy and freedom. Egged buses were also ordered to publish ads about the cancellation of the *mehadrin* lines in Haredi newspapers. Interestingly, however, the newspapers refused to publish the ads, leaving Egged in contempt of court and demonstrating that not only was the war not over, but Egged also still had not decided whether it was on the side of the law or on the side of their radical religious consumers.[31]

Nevertheless, the High Court's ruling gave a strong boost to those resisting the Haredi takeover of public buses and helped bolster the collaboration between religious feminists and human rights activists. In a response submitted to the court, IRAC demanded real change on the ground. The rear door should be closed when passengers board in order to ensure that women will not be directed to board at the back and instead can freely choose their seats. "Theoretically, a person can sit wherever they want, even on a *mehadrin* line, but we're seeing that people are enforcing [the gender segregation] even on non-*mehadrin* lines and that's the part of the danger," Shear told reporters.[32] Others agreed. A large group of not-for-profit organizations and activists, including IRAC, Kolech, the National Council of Jewish Women (NCJW), Be Free Israel, Jerusalemites, and several more, stepped up protests against continued gender segregation on buses. The New Israel Fund and Shatil, two institutions that promote human rights and support what's known as the "Third Sector"—that is, the world of volunteer social activists in Israel—formed a roundtable composed of a coalition of religious feminist groups and human rights groups.

The group of ultimately more than thirty organizations met regularly to plan rallies, hotlines, petitions, video clips, online campaigns, and more, becoming a central force in coordinating protests and helping forge powerful working relationships between religious and secular activists to fight this increasing oppression of women.

As part of these protests, the NCJW, together with IRAC, began leading "Freedom Rides" in the spirit of the American Civil Rights movement. Hundreds of volunteers from both Israel and America—mostly women, to prove their point—began boarding buses to try to ensure that there was no coerced segregation. Here is how one volunteer, Diana Bletter, described her experience on a "Freedom Ride" in June 2012:

> *This was once a* mehadrin, *or sex-segregated, bus line—struck down as illegal by the Israeli Supreme Court on Jan. 5, 2011—but for these riders, sex-segregation is not a thing of the past. Men still ride in the front and women in the back...*
>
> *When I asked the driver where I should sit, he said, "In the back." But after telling him I wanted to sit in the front, he told me to do whatever I want, just to know that "people who ride this bus want it to be half-half: men in the front and women in the back. And I don't want to deal with any problems. I just want to focus on driving the bus."*
>
> *...I took my seat in front. The next woman who boarded the bus said to me, "This is a* mehadrin *bus. You should go to the back."*
>
> *"There's really no such thing as* mehadrin *buses anymore," I told her. "And did you know that in the United States, American blacks used to have to sit in the back of buses?"*

"That was for discrimination," she said. "This is for mod-esty. It gives men more respect."

...On my second bus loop around the city, the next bus driver told me that he's seen husbands and wives talk to each other on cell phones from separate sections of the same bus. He told me I could sit anywhere moments before a group of Haredi teenagers boarded. "Go to the back of the bus!" one of them said to me and then added, "Ichsa," which means disgusting.

"All passengers can sit wherever they want," the bus driver said loudly.

I said nothing but refused to move from my seat in the front. A short while later, an older woman with two shopping bags got on.

"Go to the back," the boys repeated.

"You can go sit in the back," the woman said, her voice shaky. "If it's your private car, you can tell me what to do, but this bus is for everyone." The woman plopped herself down next to me. "I keep kosher at home, I follow the laws," she said, telling me only her first name, Rivka, and her age, 64. "I should listen to them? They should tell me what to do?"[33]

The Freedom Rides were very effective at drawing public attention to the problem, which was a major goal of the initiative, but they weren't quite enough. As Shari Eshet, the director of the Israel branch of NCJW and one of the primary organizers of the Freedom Rides, told me in an interview, "I would like to see secular women on buses getting on those buses and sitting on the front, because this is not only an issue for religious women in Meah She'arim. It's about human rights and civil society."[34]

Another important shift came when IRAC and Kolech began

to sue for money. In December 2011, Egged was fined $1,070 for forcing a woman to sit in the back of a bus while traveling to Bnei Brak. "I explained to the driver that the line was not a segregated line, but the driver dismissed my argument and said that only the rabbis can decide whether a bus is segregated or not. It was humiliating and insulting," the complainant, who is Orthodox, said in court.[35] Around the same time, Tanya Rosenblit made international headlines as "the Israeli Rosa Parks" for refusing to move to the back of Egged bus 451 from Ashdod to Jerusalem, even after being verbally harassed and called names.[36] Then, in November 2012, the Beit Shemesh small claims court ordered the local bus company to pay 13,000 NIS (about $3,200 U.S.) to Ariella Marsden, a fifteen-year-old girl who was asked by the driver to sit in the back of the bus to let two men sit in the front.[37]

The police also started to support the women. In another instance, a female soldier who was physically attacked by Haredi men on the bus and called "prostitute" and "whore" received extensive media attention, and her attacker was arrested. "This isn't the first time this has happened; I just asked for help this time," the soldier, Doron Matalon, said, adding that she had been physically assaulted other times as well.[38] But it seems that the activism, protests, consciousness-raising, and lawsuits have also started to change the reality on the ground.

However, the story is not over yet. As the voices of protest began to rise, so did the violence. According to Shahar Ilan, the cofounder of the organization Hiddush for Religious Freedom and Equality, there was actually an increase in violence since the High Court ruling protecting women from being segregated on buses. "It's hard to document something that supposedly no longer exists," he said.[39]

To wit, in February 2013—long after segregated buses were ruled illegal, and even after the Transport Ministry ordered every bus to have a sign explicitly stating that people can sit wherever they want—two ultra-Orthodox men ordered twenty-two-year-old Noa Kanteman to move to the back of a public bus, shouting that she was "impure." One deliberately sat on the front steps of the bus near the driver to prove he was entitled to sit in front of her. The bus driver did not interfere, despite the High Court ruling. The woman's sister called the police, who sent squad cars to intercept the bus.[40] Ms. Kanteman got off the bus to talk to the police officers, and when she returned, there was a written note on her seat that read, "We are all kosher Jews. Please help us protect our kosher-ness and sit where women sit."[41] Essentially it implied that a woman's body in the presence of men makes the "entire Jewish people"—read, men—unclean. The conflating of women's bodies and the kosherness of meat leaves a chilling impression.

The Ministry of Transportation initiated disciplinary procedures against Egged for failing to protect Ms. Kanteman. Tellingly, she said that, "As a religious woman I know that where you sit on the bus is not something that is written in the Bible, but that people are just making this up. I don't know what it means to be a 'kosher' bus, but I do know that being religious is about respecting people, and that wasn't there." It seems, then, that one of the most powerful forms of resistance may be coming from within religion itself—most notably from religious Jewish women.

Along the same lines, in January 2013, twenty-two-year-old Miri Bleicher was verbally harassed by four Haredi man on a bus from Jerusalem to Arad for boarding the bus at the front. The men reportedly called her a "nuisance" and a "shiksa" and made vomiting noises. In a clear indication that the Haredi men were reacting not only to women, but also to the protest movements to support women's rights, one of the men shouted, "You're not respecting my rights."[42] Even as women began registering victories against encroaching radicalism, new fronts of the battle seemed to open up.

Thus the struggle continues. The activists' protests have raised awareness and forged a strong campaign to ensure and protect democracy and women's rights against the spread of religious radicalism. There are signs on buses, segregation is technically illegal, and the police at times intervene. But the religious radicalism seems to be impervious to surrounding pressures. And the segregation, which according to IRAC has been reduced from 150 bus lines to less than fifty, still persists.

So why do Egged and the government adhere to Haredi demands, even when these demands go against Israel's laws and basic principles of democracy? Sadly, or perhaps predictably, the answer may again be money.

To recap, the Haredi community makes up about 10 percent of Israel's population of 8.2 million people and is a disproportionately poor sector of it. Haredim generally live in insular communities and have an average of eight children per family.[43] Because they are so poor, Haredim are strong consumers of public transport. Haredim form a strong sector of the Egged clientele, and Egged actively woos Haredim with perks and cheap fares. Moreover, municipalities pay expensive tariffs to the Ministry for approval of stops and routes, so Egged has to work with local Haredi politicians on bus routes. Right here are two big financial pressure points for the nation's largest bus chain.

The greatest threat to this income for Egged, author Naomi Ragen claims, is when Haredim start to operate pirate transports—"*chapperim*" as they're known in Hebrew slang. These *chapperim*, which have cheaper fares and unofficial stops, lure riders away from Egged. It's no coincidence, argues Ragen, that the 2001 decision to institute the first *mehadrin* buses came only months after an unauthorized line began operating between Jerusalem and Bnei Brak. According to the Haredi press, the Vaad Mehadrin—the same group that loudly applauded Egged's institution of segregated buses—was behind the decision to start running these *chapperim* at half the Egged price (10 NIS [about $2.32 U.S.] per ride versus Egged and Dan's fare of 18.50 NIS [about $4.29 U.S.]).[44]

The battle over Haredi fares was particularly heated in the town of Beit Shemesh, where the *chapperim* worked hard to keep out the Egged 418 *mehadrin* line because it competed with *their* business. "When we first asked Egged to run a *mehadrin* line fourteen years ago, they refused, claiming it was not economically feasible," Shmuel Pappenheim, a spokesman for the Haredi organization HaEdah HaHaredit and a resident of Beit Shemesh, said in 2006 when the battle was most heated. "So we established our own transportation."[45]

Another Haredi businessman from Beit Shemesh, Shlomo Hirsch, established the Darka Acharina (the Other Way) transport company and was instrumental in fighting to keep Egged out of Beit Shemesh. According to the *Jerusalem Post*, "Egged eventually gained the support of Rabbi Natan Kupshitz, one of Beit Shemesh's leading rabbis, after running a *mehadrin* line from Beit Shemesh to Bnei Brak that was not in competition with Darka Acharina. With Kupshitz's agreement, Egged reinstated segregation on the 418." However, the 418 remained a source of violent struggle, and there were reports in 2006 of Darka Acharina supporters stoning buses that drove through secular neighborhoods.[46]

In effect, then, the Haredi bus clientele have the power to create mass boycotts of Egged if their demands are not met—demands that include not only conveniences and price breaks for Haredim, but also women-free spaces on the buses. Put differently, the religious radicalism that is finding expression on public buses has less to do with what Haredi men and women want than with the ways in which Haredi leaders wield economic pressure against businesses and political leaders in order to get what they want. Ultimately, this is about Israel's financial patronage to one group that operates on its own set of rules—and for whom obedience to gender scripts is a central value. For some people, it seems, the domination of women is a lucrative business.

The alarming phenomenon of gender segregation on public buses raises some troubling questions about Israeli society. One question that is raised is why does segregation of women persist in Israel and not in Jewish communities elsewhere?

This is not a hypothetical question: segregation has been tried and seems to have failed in New York, for example. In October 2011, the *New York World* posted a series of articles describing state-funded buses in Brooklyn, Kiryas Joel, and Orange County, New York, and reported a story of at least one woman who was asked by men on the bus to move to the back.[47] The rule consigning women to the back was posted in writing on the bus as well. This reflected what sociologist Samuel Heilman calls "a kind of cultural cross-pollination" between the ultra-Orthodox communities in Israel and in New York. "In Brooklyn they are getting their cue from Israel," he said.[48]

But it's not as easy to get away with this kind of thing in New York. According to Naomi Zeveloff, "the number B110 bus, which runs between Boro Park and Williamsburg, trolls a public bus route that the city awarded to the company as a franchise in a competitive bidding process. It must, therefore, play by the city's rules, which, in line with local and federal public accommodation laws, bar discrimination on the basis of gender or race."

Indeed, Mayor Michael Bloomberg was quick to respond. As soon as Bloomberg got wind of the story, he put a swift and abrupt stop to gender-segregated buses. "Private people: you can have a private bus. Go rent a bus, and do what you want on it." On city buses, he said, sex segregation was "obviously not permitted."[49] According to official reports, there is no more gender segregation on New York City buses. However, the *New York Times* reported in August 2013 that, unofficially, there is still segregation on the B110.[50]

I would like to say that in New York, the story of segregated buses fizzled because it lacks the kind of governmental and business support that the ultra-Orthodox leadership enjoys in Israel. But given the ambiguity of the facts on the ground, I'm not sure we can make that claim. Religious radicalism may be alive and well in New York—even when there are some attempts to quash it—simmering just below the surface.

Some would argue that religious radicalism feeds off of general perceptions of women's proper roles in society. It is arguably about religious groups feeling threatened by the spread of modern culture and the loss of masculinity. According to Kimmy Caplan, a professor of Jewish history at Bar-Ilan University who researches Haredi society, the trend toward gender separation in Israel is partly a response to the growing number of Haredi women entering the workforce. "[Haredi women] are meeting all kinds of people, and some Haredi leaders see this as dangerous," Caplan says. "It has the potential, as far as some leadership sees it, to be a danger because it can bring home questions, doubts, exposure to alternative ways of life. There are certain leaders who think there is a need to create a balance by having more segregation in the neighborhood to compensate for a drop of segregation by women going out to work every day."[51]

In other words, the more women advance in society, the more threatened and fearful male leadership becomes, and its religious extremists turn to the rhetoric of fear to impose restrictions on this progress. This in turn creates louder and stronger opposition and protest from those being oppressed and those who want to protect or help them. It's a vicious cycle in which religious ideology, in fear of the inevitable process of women's liberation, fuels its own movement toward the extreme, a move that we will explore further in the next chapter.

Chapter 2

NEITHER SEEN NOR HEARD: ERASING WOMEN'S PUBLIC PRESENCE

Professor Chani Ma'ayan is an impressive woman. A pediatrician and medical researcher, Ma'ayan has dedicated the past forty years to healing lung problems in children. As director of the Israel Center for Family Dysautonomia at Hadassah Hospital–Mount Scopus in Jerusalem—which she has been running since its inception in 1981—Ma'ayan has become a world-recognized expert in children's respiratory disorders and has written many books and articles on the subject and has worked with children all around Israel to help resolve their respiratory problems. For all these accomplishments, as well as for her commitment to Jewish religious practice, Ma'ayan was awarded a prestigious prize of the Health Ministry in 2011 in recognition of her research on the intersection of medicine and Jewish law.

Unfortunately, she was unable to accept it—or rather, she wasn't *allowed* to. This is because, despite all of her accomplishments, only one detail mattered to the Ministry of Health: she is a woman. And so, at the award ceremony in December 2011, a representative of the Ministry asked her and her cowinner nurse Naama Holtzer to refrain from appearing on the stage to accept the award in person and instead to send a man in their place. They were also asked to sit all the way in the back, far from where the men in the audience would be able to see them. In the end, some guy with no credentials was applauded and honored by a hall full of men at an event paid for by Israeli taxpayers, while the women who actually earned the award by putting in four decades of incredible work for children's health sat invisibly, anonymously, and quietly in the back row.[1]

Many Israelis were shocked by this, as the media reported. They wanted to know how it could happen. How could such blatant discrimination against women—in the name of religion!—take place at a state event, where it is not only immoral, but also illegal? How could a state institution like the Ministry of Health, in a secular democracy where everyone is supposed to be treated equally, become a conduit for religious radical ideology? Unfortunately, this incident raised more questions than it answered.

The situation remains murky. Who exactly is applying the pressure to eliminate the presence of women in public spaces? Who in the government is acquiescing to this pressure and why? The lack of answers is jaw-dropping for Israelis, with little recourse and power to effect change.

As we saw in the last chapter, the pressure to place women at the back of the bus, out of sight of men in the front, is just one form of the increasing demands from Haredi leadership to create, in essence, a woman-free world in Israel—a public space in which women physically are absent, their voices are not heard, and their faces are unseen. This is part of an alarming trend, a series of events all across Israel in which women are being removed literally and symbolically from public spaces. In this chapter, I explore women's exclusion from certain streets, shops, cemeteries, offices, and public events; the elimination of their pictures from billboards and newspapers; and the removal of their voices at public events, the Knesset, and radio.

I want to pause to note that even though I have been writing and blogging about these things since 2008, I was shocked at how far and wide this trend is. In fact, when I first began writing this book, I worried that perhaps there would not be enough material to fill a whole volume. I thought that the material for this chapter would be a few paragraphs. In fact, the amount of material I unearthed for this chapter is overwhelming, and it keeps coming. Almost every day, there is another story of women being excluded from an event, being asked to cover up, being told not to cross a bridge. The copious data here indicates that we are dealing with a trend that is far worse than anyone has even imagined, with no visible signs of abating.

What is perhaps most surprising about the rising oppression of women in Israel is the ease with which non-ultra-Orthodox people and groups capitulate to ultra-Orthodox demands to erase women from public. Professor Ma'ayan and Nurse Holtzer's situation is a perfect example of this alarming trend. The Health Ministry is an official government body and thus technically secular, so its actions and policies *should* be nondiscriminatory. In reality, however, they're not. The Ministry is one of many that have agreed to exclude women, for reasons difficult to understand. Even in my city of Modi'in (not to be confused with Modi'in Illit; though the two are in close physical proximity, Modi'in is an open, heterogeneous city, and Modi'in Illit is a closed and exclusive ultra-Orthodox town), we witnessed a municipal gender-segregated outdoor event following a major holiday, to the shock and dismay of many members of the municipal Women's Council.

In trying to understand why state or municipal institutions

would acquiesce to demands for segregation, the Women's Council meeting was an eye-opening case in point. Even here, in this avowed feminist space, women around the table had a hard time articulating their opposition to imposed gender segregation. "What's the big deal?" one woman asked. "It's a religious event, so let the rabbis have their say," another woman said. The assumption that any holiday-related event is automatically religious makes some people tie their own hands and give away power to the rabbis.

Interestingly, at this meeting, religious women were the most vocal in insisting that gender segregation is *not* the definition of religiousness and certainly should not dictate holiday events intended for the general public. As one of the religious women there, I oddly found myself explaining to my secular colleagues that the exclusion of women is an unwanted practice, like a rapidly spreading virus, and that we as a government body protecting democracy and equal rights have an obligation to stop this practice. It seems that secular Israelis are reluctant to step up their opposition to gender segregation out of a kind of misplaced, distanced reverence for religion. In fact, the secular members of the committee were more passive in their response to segregation than the religious members, precisely because of their well-intentioned desire to be tolerant of seemingly odd religious practices. The problem is, those good intentions can become women's worst nightmare.

Not only have government and municipal bodies shockingly agreed to create women-free spaces, but businesses and other groups in non-ultra-Orthodox areas have moved to exclude women as well. In the case of Modi'in, it seems that one of the three municipal rabbis simply told the planning committee that the event had to be segregated, and nobody questioned either the decision or the decision-making process. It was only the Women's Council that even raised it as an issue and decided to write a letter to the mayor about it. (Not that all this had any effect—at the event the following year, there was also a partition dividing women and men.) In many of these cases of segregation, there is an alarming obscurity about who is calling the shots.

As we've seen, the buses were only the beginning. Over the past five to ten years, Haredi demands for gender segregation in public spaces have spread to almost every conceivable public space in Israel. Here are some examples[2]:

- **HMO clinics.** In the mixed religious-secular city of Beit Shemesh, HMOs have separate hours for men and women or, in one case, wooden partitions in waiting rooms in order to, according to the signs, "enable men to avoid encountering women whom they consider immodestly dressed."
- **Post offices.** A post office in the Bukharian section of Jerusalem has separate lines for men and women, and a spokesperson for the Ministry of Communications said that more were on their way.
- **Banks.** The Poalei Agudat Israel Bank of the International Bank Group held a convention for its "customers" but only allowed men to attend and participate.
- **Libraries.** The public library in the Ramat Shlomo neighborhood of Jerusalem has separate hours for boys and girls.
- **City streets.** Signs on certain streets in Beit Shemesh tell women to cross to the other side.[3] Over the holiday of Tabernacles (Sukkot), women in certain areas of Jerusalem are asked—sometimes by the police, enforcing Haredi

demands—to move to the other side of the street. In 2009, the Jerusalem Day celebrations in the center of town were accompanied by gender segregation on the streets. Unofficial "guards" with yellow jackets stood in the crowd between the men and women and made sure the segregation was observed. When they saw men or women on the "wrong" side, they told them to move over.[4]

- **Hospitals.** In 2011, then-Deputy Health Minister Ya'akov Litzman announced his intention to establish separate psychiatric hospitals for men and women, starting with separate departments. This announcement was met with enormous opposition from professionals in the field who believe that gender integration is vital for patients' recovery in that it trains them in how to live in a normal society.

- **Trains and light-rail.** Some religious men regularly ask women to leave certain train cars because they want to pray and do not want to do so with women present, effectively creating an unofficial women-free train car. This is despite the fact that Orthodox women are considered obligated in prayer as well as men, by the way.[5]

- **Cemeteries and funerals.** Signs have been erected in funeral homes in several cities asking women to sit in a separate section. The Chevra Kadisha (Jewish burial society) in several cities takes it upon itself to impose rules on mourners, forbidding women from eulogizing or going to the grave. There are also signs in some cemeteries telling women to dress "modestly."

- **Universities.** Women were asked to leave the fitness center on campus at the Technion because two religious men walked in and demanded that they leave—the security guards helped remove the women from the treadmills at the request of the men.[6] At the Givat Ram campus of Hebrew University, it is already established practice: women are not allowed into the fitness center when men are swimming.[7]

- **Private businesses.** Some businesses catering to the Haredi community have imposed gender segregation, such as a "women only" side entrance to a candy shop, separate elevators at a banquet hall, separate hours for men and women at a supermarket, segregation at an amusement park, and more.

- **Magen David Adom (the "Red Cross" of Israel).** A "fun day" event for MDA volunteers was separated into two events, one for male volunteers and their sons and a separate one for female volunteers and their daughters.

- **Public conferences.** The annual conference of fertility and women's health run by the Puah Institute was gender-segregated, with no women speakers and women participants sitting at the back. At least one conference of the Ministry of Education asked women to sit in the back "so that men would not have to watch the presentation 'through the women.'" The annual Management Forum conference held at the International Convention Center in Jerusalem decided in its sixth year to no longer allow women to attend. Finance Minister Yuval Steinitz, Jerusalem Mayor Nir Barkat, and Bank Hapoalim CEO Zion Keinan addressed the audience during the conference, despite the ban on women, and security guards actively assisted in refusing entry to women.[8]

These practices cause tremendous distress to women and their families and friends. Women being told that they are not allowed into shops, post offices, or health clinics face the obvious problem of having to find other places to shop, send important correspondence, and receive medical care, plus the shame of knowing they are unwelcome. There are other consequences as well. We can imagine the experience of women being asked to leave the gym because a few religious men need the room—where will they go to work out? Women excluded from a banking conference lose out on the opportunity to learn important financial knowledge. This policy also perpetuates the idea that money is for men, which can have serious negative consequences for women, especially those trying to create careers for themselves.

There are also professional consequences. Women journalists who are excluded from entry to public events not only face the humiliation of being held at the door, but also face the professional problem of being unable to get the story. Professional women who are barred from presenting their expertise at conferences lose out on all the hard-earned and well-deserved opportunities that come with public recognition of their work.

Some of these demands place serious challenges on parents too. Segregated buses make it difficult for whole families traveling together; often a child of one gender will be forced to sit far from the family members on the other side of the bus. For example, an eight-year-old girl accustomed to taking the bus with her thirteen-year-old brother may suddenly find herself sitting alone in the back of a crowded bus, where she could get lost or harassed. A holiday amusement park event geared for the Haredi community is a nightmare for parents who have to drive their sons there in the morning and their daughters in the afternoon. The whole notion of people just being people—that a mixed-gender group or family can spend time together anywhere and that this is a positive experience—is at risk of being lost amid all these gender-segregated rules.

One of the most painful experiences of women's exclusion takes place at the cemetery, where women are increasingly being barred from their own mourning processes. Orly Erez-Likhovski went to the funeral of her friend's mother in October 2011 at the Shamgar Funeral Home in Jerusalem. "During the funeral, the men and women were segregated, with clear signs about where the women were to stand, and where the men were to stand," she recalled. "There was a curtain partition, with the eulogy stand, of course, on the men's side. My friend—one of six daughters of the deceased, who had no sons—requested to eulogize her mother, but the men of the Chevra Kadisha told her that that was not possible. The deceased's son-in-law and grandson gave the eulogy in her place."[9]

As if being denied the right to give a eulogy for one's mother wasn't devastating enough, the women were also pushed away at the graveside. "When the participants reached the cemetery, everyone gathered around the grave, and then men from the Chevra Kadisha ordered all the women to move away from the grave and stand far off, on the path leading to the gravesites. When I arrived, a short time after the start of the ceremony, only the men were standing around the grave and all the women, including the daughters of the deceased, were standing off to the side. Only my friend—who is an Orthodox woman, but was not prepared to accept her banishment from the site—insisted on standing next to the grave with all the men." Daring as the daughter was, even in her moment of grief, she had to withstand the bullying of the men of the Chevra Kadisha. "When she insisted that she would remain next to the grave, the men of the Chevra Kadisha informed her that if that was the case, the burial ceremony would not take place (!) but when she continued to insist, they relented. When I arrived I stood next to my friend and, slowly, other women came and joined."[10]

This story, one of many that have been reported over the past few years about this rising issue, illustrates some of the tremendous pain and distress that gender segregation can cause women. For perhaps obvious reasons, women who were prevented from saying eulogies or honoring their deceased loved ones at funerals faced significant emotional struggles. "As a religious woman, I felt outraged," said one woman who was sent to the side during a relative's funeral. "Why do I, at this moment, have to start worrying if I'm standing in the right place or not? Rather than dealing with mourning for my aunt, I'm wondering if I'm turning someone on. It's completely twisted." In another instance in the city of Petah Tikva near Israel's capital, Tel Aviv, a woman was prevented from standing next to her husband during his mother's funeral, and all women there were forbidden from speaking. "This was one of the most difficult moments of his life, and I wasn't even there with him," she said bitterly.[11] All over Israel, women are being denied the right to mourn their deceased loved ones and to grieve, the denial of which can inflict damaging emotional and spiritual consequences for years to come.

If women's exclusions from funerals are bad for women's well-being, imagine the impact of being excluded from the entire professional field of women's health. The Puah Institute—one of Israel's more prominent organizations dedicated (supposedly) to women's health, holds an annual conference on women's fertility in which women are systematically prohibited. They cannot speak, have a place on the podium, or sit in the main hall. There are only some spaces for them to sit behind a curtain in the back. This means that women's vital expertise is absent—particularly

given they are the subjects of the conference—and their questions, comments, and ideas go unheard. The image of this
men-only gynecology conference is particularly jarring because
it is precisely when the most intimate aspects of a woman's body
are up for public discussion and examination. But while their
anatomy and health are on show for all to dissect and analyze,
women themselves have no say.

Orthodox feminist organization Kolech has been fighting this
since 2010. "This conduct emphasizes not only the exclusion of
and discrimination against women, but also treats them as sexual
objects," the official Kolech position reads. "Many women have
complained to Kolech about Puah's conferences including both
participants in the audience and experts prevented from taking
part in the discussions… The rabbis have refused to recognize the
insult and injury felt by women arising from being prevented from
taking an equal part in the conference and from hearing female
experts in the field. We in Kolech assert that the exclusion of
women by the Puah Institute borders on a breach of the law, as
set out in recent rulings; exclusion and discrimination are criminal
offenses."[12] They're right, but unfortunately their call has gone
mostly unheeded, to the detriment of Israeli men *and* women.
Ignoring or forbidding women to voice their expertise about
their own bodies and matters of intimacy damages both sexes. It
leaves women's crucial knowledge of themselves out of public
conversations about these issues, prevents everyone from learning
about women's ideas and experiences and advancing female health
care and male/female relationships, and promotes the antiquated
and patently unhelpful idea that men know more about women's
bodies than women do.

But it's not just women's presences that are being excluded from public spaces: women's faces, voices, and bodies are made increasingly invisible in some of the most bizarre and grotesque ways.

Something strange happened to former Secretary of State Hillary Clinton on the streets of Israel on May 2, 2011: her face was erased. In an article covering the famous raid on Osama bin Laden, the ultra-Orthodox newspaper *Der Tzitung* ran a photo of the White House's Situation Room and literally photoshopped Clinton's face out of it. They bar the publication of women's photos, no matter who the women are, where they are from, the context of the story, or how crucial they are to it. Audrey Thomason, a counterterrorism analyst seen peeking out in the back of the original photo, was also erased.[13] The erasure of women's faces is not only disingenuous—after all, removing Hillary Clinton from the room is effectively rewriting history—but also promotes an unrealistic idea of a woman-free world—that the "right" world is one without women in it.

I wish I could say that the erasure of Hillary Clinton was an isolated example. But that's not the case. Member of the Knesset (MK) Tzipi Livni's face was erased from public posters all over the country during the country's 2009 elections for the same reason: so men wouldn't have to see women's faces. Following the elections, the two women appointed to the cabinet, Limor Livnat and Sofa Landver (a paltry representation in any cabinet), were also photoshopped out of pictures in several ultra-Orthodox publications. The daily Israeli publication *Yated Ne'eman* digitally changed the photo, replacing the women's images with pictures of two male ministers. The weekly *Shaa Tova* simply blacked the women out.[14]

It's not just political leaders whose pictures are erased or replaced with would-be ministerial men. Pictures of women and girls have been systematically omitted from newspapers, flyers, circulars, bus ads, and even cereal boxes all over Israel. One photo of actress Gila Almagor was removed from Isracard (MasterCard) ads in Jerusalem.[15] The National Transplant Center (Adi), an institute of the Ministry of Health, removed photos of women from their ads to encourage people to donate organs, showing rows of photos of men only as examples of people who have an Adi card. "We were receiving threats," the Adi spokesperson said as an explanation, "that the buses were going to be burned if they have photos of women on them."[16] This suggests that Haredi demands for women's erasure are at times accompanied by violence, or threats of it.

But it's not clear if businesses that capitulate are doing so out of fear of violence or fear of losing customers. For example, Bank Hapoalim, Israel's largest bank, replaced images of actress Alma Zack in its advertisements with an image of a dwarf and explained: "Bank Hapoalim respects all its customers, regardless of their religion, race, and gender and uses professional judgment only when it comes to advertising."[17] There is certainly some intense pressure on businesses and organizations to exclude women, including both economic threats and threats of violence. What is not clear is if these threats represent what the Haredi community wants or what only some radical leaders want.

The practice of excluding women's faces has become decidedly asinine in some instances. In a bizarre twist on the idea of preserving women's modesty, the Honigman clothing outlet "adjusted" (i.e., cropped) its nationwide campaign with model Sendi Bar, in which she appears wearing a modest wool knit outfit, so that in its ads in Jerusalem, all that one sees are her arm and purse, no face—literally a headless model.[18]

In the Shaare Zedek Medical Center in Jerusalem, women's pictures on the packages of orthopedic products sold in the hospital shop were covered with stickers. The store owner explained: "Eisler Orthopedic-Pharm respects different sectors of the population: secular, national, religious, and Haredi. As our branch also supplies its services to the Haredi public and as the issue is fundamental to them and does not hurt the professionalism of the services we provide, we agreed to the request of some of our customers to cover the pictures."[19] This practice has even migrated to ultra-Orthodox communities in America: an ultra-Orthodox group erased women's photos from a poster advertising an event at the Sheraton Hotel in Connecticut in 2009.[20]

How does this happen? Who is applying the pressure, and who is caving in and making the decisions? It's hard to know. In Jerusalem, where there is a strong ultra-Orthodox presence—some 146,000 of Jerusalem's 789,000 residents are Haredi, one of the largest Haredi clusters in the country[21]—the removal of women's faces from the public sphere was done gradually and secretly until the work was complete. By 2011, the advertising and bus companies quietly decided to officially stop putting images of women and girls on posters anywhere in the city. Did they collude about it? Were municipal authorities involved? Did the mayor of Jerusalem know? It all remains unclear.

The role of municipal government in the perpetuation of this practice also remains a question. For example, when the Ministry of Education put up posters all around Israel promoting the Oz Latmura educational reform system (a program that improves the wages and working conditions of high school teachers), the municipal government of the city of Bnei Brak called the ads "illegal" and sent inspectors around the city to cover them with stickers—because they include photos of female teachers. "We have nothing against the Secondary School Teachers Association," explained a municipality spokesman, Rabbi Avraham Tenenboim. "Our anger is directed at the company that posted the ads, which violate the agreement with the Municipality. The municipal law bans ads which include pictures of women in this city. It hurts the Haredi public's feelings, and therefore we had the women's photos covered. The signs that include pictures of male teachers only can be posted in the city without any problem."[22]

It is only because of the work of activists that some of these practices are starting to be challenged. When Jerusalem residents discovered that the removal or lack of women's images around town was due to the new official policies of these companies, they decided to do something about it. The group, formed in October 2011 and calling themselves "Jerusalemites," decided that the first battle in the fight to maintain Jerusalem as a "pluralistic" city— rather than let it become a stronghold of religious extremism—was the issue of women's images on billboards. First, they started putting up posters of women around the city to restore a public face to women. Rabbi Uri Ayalon, one of the founders, opened up a Facebook page called *Lo Metzunzarot* ("uncensored," in the female form), which invited women to submit photographs of themselves and the women or girls in their lives to display on Jerusalem streets.

"The idea is to return the city space to its natural state and turn the appearance of women into something boring, that no one notices," Rabbi Ayalon explained. One of the volunteers, Idit Karni, added, "I am not for cheap exploitation of a woman's body, but a minority can't take over the city and cause women and girls to disappear. I have four daughters, and I don't intend to leave them a city that has lost its sanity."[23] The group, which as of this writing has almost five thousand members, initially hung one hundred posters of women around Jerusalem's downtown area. Not surprisingly, this campaign did *not* go unnoticed by ultra-Orthodox extremists. Several incidents of violence were reported against people hanging up posters of women.

It's worth noting that this protest movement is also being led by members of the Orthodox community—especially Orthodox feminists. Rachel Azaria, an Orthodox feminist member of the Jerusalem municipal council, has been one of the most outspoken opponents of the erasure of women. In her 2013 election campaign, she purposely used her own face in posters under the heading "Women's faces will be seen again in Jerusalem." Similarly, Rabbi Jason Miller expressed this sentiment in a column at the *Jewish Week*, in which he argued that the altered image of Hillary Clinton "violates a central tenet of the Jewish legal principle of *g'neivat da'at* (deceit)," as well as explicit White House instructions not to alter the photo.[24] So as much as there is a slide toward more extreme views about women emerging from the Haredi community, there is also a growing movement of Orthodox Jews who actually want to see a gender-integrated public life.

But it doesn't stop there: protest movements working to restore women's faces to the public landscape are emerging from different areas of Israeli life. The Movement for Pluralistic Judaism petitioned the High Court of Justice to force bus companies and the Cnaan Media Company that monopolizes bus ads to include women's images on buses. They argued that their exclusion violates human rights and Israel's basic law protecting human dignity, equality, and freedom of expression. The petition demanded that the bus companies' licenses to operate public transportation only continue to be granted if they avoid gender bias or any other type of discrimination.[25]

Unlike in some other instances we've seen, this time the response was encouraging: the Court agreed with the petitioners and ruled that the bus and ad companies "are not authorized to refuse to publish an ad because it features a woman." In 2012, the Transport Ministry decided to include a condition in its licensing process: "A license holder will not discriminate in the services it provides, including in ads in and on buses on account of race, religion or religious group, nationality, origin, gender, sexual orientation, opinion, political affiliation, or personal status."[26] This agreement marked the first time that a government ministry in Israel took an official policy stand against the exclusion of women.

Rabbi Ayalon says that this victory was a watershed moment for women's rights in Israel: it was the moment secular Israelis finally decided to get involved. As a result, he says, women's images can now be seen throughout Jerusalem, and the vandalism and violence that marked the beginning of the campaign has all but disappeared. "The situation has changed radically since then, not because something has changed in the Haredi community, but because something dramatic has changed in the rest of society," the rabbi told me in March 2013. "The ethical stand of the pluralistic community changed—this includes orthodox, conservative, and reform—when we all agreed that gender equality is nonnegotiable, when we understood that raising our children, our girls and our boys, in an atmosphere of discrimination is not an option. And that realization, that there is no such thing as being sensitive to one group by erasing the other, is what has created real change."[27]

Ayalon adds that the perception that all Haredim support this radical approach to women is also a misreading of Haredi culture. "You can see it on the ground," he says. "The violence and vandalism against posters of women has mostly stopped. Most Haredim don't care." The fault, he asserts, is with secular organizations that are trying too hard to woo Haredim and, in the process, are making assumptions about what Haredim want. The other issue is they have no ethical qualms about hurting women in pursuit of their own objectives, and the public goes along with it. "We are censoring ourselves. The guilty ones are the bus companies, the HMOs, the municipalities, the non-Haredi decision makers who censor themselves in advance and abandon all morals. It's that simple."[28]

Interestingly, although the Jerusalem municipality has yet to come out with an official policy about the use of women's images in public, Jerusalem Mayor Nir Barkat has started to take ownership of the struggle. On his Facebook page in early 2013, he wrote, "Thanks to me, women's faces can now be seen in Jerusalem." This marks a real shift from two years earlier in 2011 when he had claimed there was no exclusion of women. The municipality also agreed to print images of women on the materials for the Jerusalem marathon, which it had refused to do in past years. "Mayor Barkat obviously realized that he didn't want to waste his time dealing with our complaints against women's exclusion and wanted to get back to dealing with the marathon itself," Rabbi Ayalon joked ruefully.

Today, the images of women have returned to the streets of Jerusalem. Studio C, for example, a women-only gym that had initially refused to put images of women on their ads even though they are the target audience, has recently agreed to restore women's images. Like Studio C, most companies, Rabbi Ayalon confirmed, are changing their stances. The only organization that dragged its feet was the Egged bus company. In 2012, the company declared it was avoiding all images of people, both men and women, on its buses.

Meanwhile, while Be Free Israel and Uncensored focused their attention—with important success—on restoring women's presence in ads and billboards, the erasure of women's faces continues elsewhere. In one instance in April 2013, the face of Rona Ramon—widow of Israeli astronaut Ilan Ramon—was blurred out on a poster for an event produced by the municipality of the city of Rehovot.[29] In another startling case in March 2013, a Haredi newspaper blurred out the faces of female Holocaust victims in an iconic Warsaw Ghetto uprising photo in which a crowd of men, women, and children are seen holding their hands up in surrender. "We show readers only what they need and want to see," the editor reportedly said as an excuse for this strange omission, as if the faces of the female Holocaust victims facing their own imminent murder should be considered more offensive to male readers than the atrocities they were about to face in that photo.[30] The erasure of women's faces from Holocaust artifacts marks a new low in the world of religious misogyny. It is quite a sad moment when the irrational obsession with removing all traces of the female body from the public sphere overtakes all other considerations—including honoring Holocaust victims.

Ironically, amid this increasing push to support women in public images, not all feminist activists see the fight for women's images on ads as the right battle. "We're fighting to allow ad companies to objectify women and sexualize women's bodies?" argues Orthodox feminist activist Robyn Shames. She has a point: there is a certain irony that supermodel Sendi Bar became at one point the poster child for women's rights, for example. After all, supermodels represent the commodification of women's sexuality—hardly a feminist cause. "I'm definitely against the exclusion of women, but I'm not sure that this is the right battle," Shames adds.[31]

For women like Robyn Shames, religious freedom for women is the primary cause. Writer Debra Nussbaum Cohen also describes this ambivalence about the exclusion of women's faces: "While I understand that it is a reaction to the immodesty that runs rampant in the world around us (have you seen those near-pornographic American Apparel ads?), it also shrieks of imbalance, pushing us into an archaic Catholic paradigm in which women are either virgins or whores. This one-dimensional view of women and girls leaves no space for wholeness."[32] Nevertheless, despite this ambivalence of using a supermodel as the poster child for women's equality, most feminist activists remain strong supporters of the struggle.

So the battle over women's public faces continues. But the story of how women's faces are being restored to the Jerusalem landscape raises some hopes that the tide has started to change. And the story provides a fascinating illustration of how religious feminists, in collaboration with activists for religious pluralism, have formed a powerful coalition that has become a force to be reckoned with. But it's not just women's faces that are threatened—their voices are under siege as well.

Ophir Ben-Shetreet is a talented young woman. The seventeen-year-old, a twelfth-grade student who lives on the religious cooperative village (moshav) Nir Galim near the Ashdod coast, has a gorgeous singing voice and a beautiful presence onstage. She garnered national attention as a contestant on Israel's 2012 reality show *The Voice*, where she eventually made it to second place. She also won the heart of the nation with her sweet openness, a voice that the judges called "clear, clean, pure, and angelic," and her choice of supersecular rock star Aviv Geffen as her mentor, rather than the traditional Sephardic Sarit Hadad or Shlomi Shabat. A clip of her gentle conversation with the mentors about building bridges and learning from one another went viral on Facebook and made at least one viewer cry (that would be me). "I have loved to sing since the time I was very young. I'm looking for a place to realize my talent," she said on the show. "I think the Torah wants us to be happy; it wants music to make people happy. I think you can integrate the two, and because of that, I made the decision to come on to the show."[33]

From this, it would seem like Ophir has a bright future ahead of her. But instead, she was punished and suspended from school. Why? For singing in front of men. "There is not a single rabbi who will permit a woman to sing in front of men, especially on television. It is simply not permissible by Jewish law," Zvi Arnon, the rabbi at Ophir's moshav, said in a television interview. He proceeded to describe a halachic prohibition against her singing and contended that the pressure to suspend Ophir came from other parents in the school.[34] That is to say, there were some parents in her religious girls' high school who were reportedly so upset that a girl would sing in public that they demanded she be removed from the school so her presence would not taint the educational experience of their children. Whether this is true or just the principal hiding behind what he believes to be parents' ideologies is hard to say. But what is clear is that whether or not the Orthodox or ultra-Orthodox public wants it to be this way, the female voice—like the female face and body—has become a symbolic object that religious men are increasingly seeking to control and own.

As an aside, it is worth pointing out that the issue of whether Jewish law prohibits women from singing is not so clear-cut. Ironically, any prohibition is actually aimed at men, not women. That is, men, according to some rabbinic authorities, are not allowed to listen to women singing because women's voices are viewed as a potential cause of sinful thoughts for men. But there is no actual prohibition against the women singing, so technically Ophir should be free to continue in her blossoming career.

"As an empirical statement, this is false," writes Orthodox feminist activist Shira Hecht-Koller of the claim that the Torah forbids women from singing. "Different individuals sometimes need different answers," she writes, meaning that if one rabbi at one point ruled in a community that women were not allowed to sing, this doesn't mean that this is the only true approach of the Torah. "When faced with a young woman with such talent and passion for song, the opinions that allow such singing (a popular view among some rabbinic sages) should be invoked."[35]

Rabbi David Bigman, a popular Orthodox rabbi in Israel and the head of the Ma'ale Gilboa yeshiva, ruled that women can sing "in innocence" in front of men. "There is no problem for the modest and pious of our girls to develop a singing career, even within popular culture, but without relinquishing the delicate foundations of the culture of the Torah and without cooperating with the vulgar commercial aspects of the culture surrounding us," he said.[36]

This is worth noting because it is important to realize that in all of these cases of religious war against women—women's removal from public places, the erasure of their faces, and the silencing of their voices—these are not singular, undeniable interpretations of

Jewish law. In fact, it is possible that they are not interpretations of Jewish law at all. And it is also not necessarily what religious people want. In Giv'at Shmuel, for example, when the Bnei Akiva youth movement (traditionally a modern, religious Zionist group) decided to hold their annual singing performances as a gender-segregated event, parents complained. Hundreds of Bnei Akiva movement members' parents sent the organization's Secretary-General, Benny Nechtailer, a letter in protest. "We could not believe our eyes," the parents wrote when they saw that the event would be segregated. "As former members of the movement, none of us remember Bnei Akiva as a movement segregating between boys and girls like an ultra-Orthodox movement."[37] All of this goes to show that the increasing emphasis on silencing women's voices is a recent and subjective invocation of Jewish law, one that does not necessarily represent a singular interpretation of Judaism or even a historic traditional practice. Thus, it's particularly sad that poor Ophir got suspended for supposedly violating Jewish law when it's not at all clear that she did.

The story of Ophir Ben-Shetreet is one of many attempts to silence women in the name of religion. In May 2013, Israeli megastar Yardena Arazi was excluded from a Jerusalem ceremony to honor citizen volunteers (*Yakir Yerushalayim*) because the organizers suddenly decided that they did not want to have female performers. In a high school volunteerism program in Tel Aviv run by the organization "Yehuda and Yisrael," in which youth were sent to alternative club venues around the cities in order to supposedly "instill the values of collaboration, unity, and contribution to society via theater arts," women and girls were also forbidden from performing.[38]

The exclusion of women's singing voices even reached the Knesset. New Knesset members are sworn in during a ceremony that traditionally includes the Knesset choir singing the anthem. At the swearing in of the Eighteenth Knesset in 2009, Israelis suddenly learned that there were only men in the Knesset choir, a policy apparently implemented by then-Knesset speaker Ruby Rivlin, in order to accommodate the "sensitivities" of his male Haredi colleagues. The all-male swearing in sparked a public outrage over the exclusion of women. Rivlin, rather than take a stand for women's rights to be heard and to sing in public—which might raise the ire of his religious political bedfellows—simply avoided the issue by not inviting the choir to sing for anything again. In fact, he took the policy of avoidance one step further at the 2012 swearing in of the new Knesset: for the first time in several decades, the new Knesset was sworn in without any choir accompaniment at all.

Ruby Rivlin's response of avoidance suggests that Haredi politicians hold more sway in Israeli public life than women do. This is despite the fact that Haredim represent only 10 percent of the population while women represent 51 percent. Rivlin, like so many other politicians, seems to fear the wrath of the Haredi sector more than he feels a commitment to uphold equality. "We have a problem, because if we invite an all-male choir, we are accused of excluding women," Rivlin told a Haredi newspaper as an explanation for this decision. "But on the other hand, if we invite women singers, we will hurt the souls of 18 [Haredi] Knesset members who serve the democratic state."[39] Much like Egged's decision to avoid images of both women and men on its buses, this response attempts to create a kind of "moral equivalence" between women's right to sing and men's right to silence women by avoiding having anyone sing at all. It represents an aversion on the part of politicians to stand up to Haredi pressures and a poor appreciation of the importance of protecting women's basic rights within the Israeli democratic system.

It is really important to note that there is no moral equivalence here: there is no such thing as a person's "right" to silence and exclude another. "People who are not okay with the values of Israeli democracy, which include equality for women, should not be in the Knesset," responded Rabbi Uri Regev of the Hiddush organization for pluralism in Israel.[40] The fact that some of Israel's leading political leaders are not fully committed to protecting women's rights—whether because they are scared of losing Haredi support or because they really don't understand that there is no moral right to squash other people's self-expression—is a major problem in Israeli life.

Interestingly, one of the places where women's silencing faced some of the strongest opposition was in the Israeli army, the IDF. In September 2011, ten Orthodox soldiers (not ultra-Orthodox, who do not yet serve in the army en masse, but rather the more moderate religious Zionists) walked out of an official army ceremony because a female soldier was singing. Dozens of soldiers tried to leave when the woman started singing, but Regiment Commander Uzi Klieger threatened to punish anyone who walked out. Many returned to their seats, but the ten who left despite the orders were summoned for punishment the next day. "It was spontaneous. We know it's forbidden, but we left quietly without coordinating it," one of them told *Yedioth Ahronoth*.[41]

For some reason, this story created much more of an uproar than the story about the Knesset choir. The blogosphere went wild about this event, and it was the top news item for days. The chief of staff was invited into a special session to review the issue, the Knesset

Committee for the Status of Women held a special committee session about it, and the Knesset Defense Committee discussed the role of rabbis in the army. Rabbis in Israel were issuing rulings on all sides. Meanwhile, the army quickly issued a statement saying that this would not be tolerated, which in turn invited backlash from some in the IDF rabbinical corps.[42] Israeli Air Force Chief Rabbi Moshe Ravad resigned from his post as head of a program that recruits Haredim after the IDF rabbinate released a statement saying that religious soldiers would not be excused from women's singing. Then Israeli Chief Rabbi Yona Metzger came out against the military's stance and publicly stated that the IDF should accommodate the demands of very religious soldiers. "It's certainly unjustified and inappropriate to deny them their status and rights for strictly obeying the Torah and its laws," he wrote in his official statement.[43] So while it is encouraging that the IDF responded more swiftly to protecting women's rights to sing, the battle is far from over. As one religious soldier said after Ravad resigned, "We'll find a way to get out of the IDF, because it has betrayed us."[44]

Both the soldiers walking out and the men spitting on buses point to a greater problem: the actions that young men like these are taking is based on messages they are receiving from religious leaders about acceptable ways to behave. Rabbis seem to be telling some religious young men that it is okay to both disobey one's commanding officer in the name of adhering to a particular religious belief or ruling and simultaneously disrespect women as equal human beings deserving of basic dignity. In addition, in the case of the soldiers, it's particularly difficult because they are receiving *conflicting* messages: serve the modern state, but be loyal to antiquated ideas that oppress women; aim to be equals with women in society, but do not respect them. The soldiers are torn between loyalties and codes, and because of the confines and codes of the religious doctrine with which they grew up, they have no skills or ability to stand up to their religious teachers, rabbis, or culture. If the rabbi says disobey and disrespect, that's what these young men are taught to do. When obedience to a rabbi or a religious belief system trumps obedience to a commanding officer and to basic moral rights, that's a problem.

Religious soldiers' unwavering obedience to rabbis is a threat not only to women's well-being, but also to the army more generally. The idea that a soldier will suddenly abandon the unit because of something his rabbi said can have grave political and strategic consequences. Although women won a tiny victory in this case when the soldiers were punished, one cannot help but wonder if the IDF was protecting women or simply trying to challenge rabbinic authority over their cadets. Major-General Orna Barbivai, who in 2011 became the IDF's first-ever female Major-General, told the Knesset Foreign Affairs and Defense Committee meeting on this subject that "a commander's authority trumps all others" and that "Halachic considerations must be congruent to commanders' considerations."[45] This is clearly not just about women's rights, but also about the army protecting its chain of command—which does not include rabbis.

Although this power struggle may not be entirely about women, it has a huge impact on them, since they are likely to suffer the most in a society driven by religious extremism. The IDF is just one more location in Israel where religious leaders are going to war and using women's bodies and lives as their ammunition.

The most extreme example of the silencing of women's voices has been taking place on the radio—and it's not even about women's *singing* but about women *speaking*, which creates a whole new level of silencing that has never been seen in Jewish life. Kol Berama, a publicly funded radio station established in 2009 and connected to the Sephardic religious party Shas, has a policy not only to exclude female singers, but also female DJs, news readers, voice-overs, announcers, and even callers into radio shows. During the 2010 and 2013 election campaigns, despite the fact that many women were running for office, Kol Berama—which literally means "a voice in the heights"—refused to allow the voices of any women to be heard on their radio station.

This is despite the fact that the late Rabbi Ovadia Yosef, spiritual founder of the Shas movement, ruled that there is nothing wrong with listening to women's voices. The station still eliminates women's participation from the most important places of radio life: women do not run programs, female Knesset members are not interviewed for their opinions, female artists do not have their songs played, female listeners cannot speak to broadcasters, and women cannot work anywhere close to a microphone. When a woman has a question for a talk show host, she can fax in her question to be read by a man or child at the station.[46]

When the Israeli public learned about the Kol Berama exclusion of women, there was an outcry. In October 2011, the Ministry of Communication ordered the station to allocate one hour a week in which women would be allowed to have their voices heard—not as singers, heaven forbid, but as callers and possibly announcers. The station refused, arguing that their listeners do not want to hear women. A month later, the station was ordered to allocate an hour each day to allowing women to be heard. The station refused again. Religious Zionist MK Uri Orbach, who is on a Knesset committee that regulates the communications industry, decided to get the Knesset Committee for the Advancement of the Status of Women involved, and in November 2011, religious MK Tzipi Hotovely, head of the Knesset Committee on the Status of Women, called a meeting to discuss Kol Berama's gender problem.

"The committee discussion reveals some vital insights into who is supporting religious radicalism. No one has the right to conduct such blatant discrimination," said the religious politician Orbach. "[It] is seeping into public life and is quickly becoming the norm. It's creeping into the buses, and official ceremonies; this is a new Judaism."[47] Hotovely also took issue with the idea that this is a reflection of religiousness. "We cannot permit developing a ghetto mentality," Hotovely said. "We do not want to become another Iran. We don't want to be our neighbors, and we are proud regarding our policies on women's rights in the Mideast, and I will not be part of any effort to take us back 100 years vis-à-vis women's rights."[48]

By contrast, the discrimination was defended by secular businessman Shai Ben-Maor, who said, "I am a devout secularist…a businessman seeking to earn a living so I will not be addressing Halacha here, but business, which is what my interest is." He argued that the Kol Berama clientele does not want to hear women. "This station is for a specific segment of the population, and this issue is different from that of the buses, because they serve the general public." Even ultra-Orthodox MK Yisrael Eichler agreed that this is not about Jewish law and said that there is in fact nothing halachically wrong with listening to a woman speak. But he also invoked the idea of "rights," as if Haredi men or secular businessmen have the "right" to silence women and that the state should protect this "right." "I completely reject the principle that the state can interfere with the freedom of the press in any way," he said, implying a false claim of moral equivalence, as if a woman's right to speak is the same as a man's right to silence her.[49]

So we have a situation in which the religious MKs were saying that gender discrimination on the radio has nothing to do with being religious, and the secular businessman argued that this is a business decision. What is clear is the overall agreement that the silencing of women has nothing to do with Jewish law but has everything to do with power and money. "There simply is no halachic prohibition here, just the station's own policy decision, something they made up," Orbach said.[50] It is also worth noting that in this entire debate, the radio management's assumption is that listeners are men. That is, only men would supposedly have issues listening to women's voices, and thus the entire notion of who the listening public is remains all male. That, in my view, is one of the most confounding aspects of this entire episode. It is a complete dismissal of women as clients, citizens, and members of society.

For religious feminist activists, this argument finally became a signal to action. The first approach was to get the radio to comply with the law. In April 2012, a coalition of thirty-eight organizations—some fighting for religious pluralism and some fighting for women's rights—filed a petition with Ilan Avishar, chair of the Second Authority for Television and Radio, a council that represents the public interest in the commercial broadcasting channels in Israel, demanding that they require Kol Berama to enable women's voices or lose their license. "This kind of behavior on the part of the Second Authority negates the principles of Israeli justice, including the principle of equality and respect for women," they wrote in their petition, "and it sends a damaging and humiliating message toward women."

Avishar responded that "we have been working very hard on this issue, and currently the radio station has committed not only to allow women's voices to be heard on separate programs, but also to allow women to speak on news programs aimed at the general public."[51]

Despite this agreement, the radio station did not entirely comply. The radio at times had one hour a week where women could call in but overall remained stoic in its resistance. The Second Authority decided to back down on its demand for six hours a week of women's voices and said that if Kol Berama would agree to four hours per week, the Authority would not press charges. But Kol Berama remained unmoved by the law, by morality, or by public pressure.

Realizing that the radio was acting out of perceived financial interests more than out of religious law, Kolech, along with IRAC, decided to take the battle one step further and went for the pocketbook. Kol Berama was trying to claim that 55 percent of the listeners would stop listening to the station if women were employed as broadcasters.[52] But Kolech decided to challenge the radio station on this premise. Kolech commissioned a survey of Kol Berama's two hundred thousand listeners—actual active listeners, people who had replied in detail about the content of the programs and knew the station schedule—conducted by the Sarid Institute, which showed that 40 percent of listeners said they were offended by the fact that women were not allowed to speak on the station's airwaves and that men spoke for them. In August 2012, a class action suit against Kol Berama demanded 104 million NIS (about $26 million U.S.)[53] in damages, the largest claim ever made for women's rights in Israel, and the first time in Israeli history that a class action suit was filed for gender discrimination against a radio station. "The exclusion of women from a publicly licensed radio station is against the law, offending the honor of women and their right to freedom of expression," said Orly Erez-Likhovski, the lawyer representing Kolech, in an article explaining the lawsuit.

The radio station replied, once again, with an argument that they have the right to discriminate against women. "We were thrilled to discover that Reform organizations and nonprofits submitted a petition to the High Court against the establishment of the station (before it even began to broadcast) because they wanted to block the rights of an entire sector of society from having its own media outlet that fits their way of life and system of beliefs," they wrote sardonically in an ultra-Orthodox web portal.[54]

"Kol Berama refuses to allow women on the air on any topic, whether it is regarding a news item, expressing an opinion on a particular issue or raising a question," Kolech claimed. "As religious women, we see no connection whatsoever in refusing to allow women on the air and Jewish law. The fact that in the name of Jewish law, women are excluded from the public realm, contradicts the value of human dignity and the perspective that women, like men, were created in the image of God."[55]

The story of Kol Berama is still unfolding, as court cases tend to take years. And the government is still hesitating about how much action to take. In March 2013, Kol Berama's license was renewed but "only" for a year.[56] In May 2013, the attorney general stated, for the first time, that this kind of exclusion of women is illegal. This will be an important test case in the battle over women's basic rights against encroaching demands of Haredi politicians and businessmen to silence women's voices. In January 2014, Kol Berama's license was renewed for another year, but only if the station actively increases female representation on the air and at the station, as well as placing no limitations on female callers, short of one hour of programming a day. IRAC and Kolech plan to listen closely to be sure the new requirements are followed.[57]

Women's voices, women's faces, women's presence—these are all different objects of attack from radical religious forces in Israel. But in this war over women's bodies, one of the biggest battlefields is where there are children and youth who have yet to be tainted by ideas of sexuality and identity.

Shiran Greenboim, a sporty and energetic ten-year-old girl from Ra'anana, Israel, loves to play basketball. Being the only girl on her team had never stopped her. That is, until one day in December 2012 when her team went to play against the team from Alfei Menashe, and the game was canceled. The other team, as it turned out, refused to play with a girl on the court because the boys—though all under the age of bar mitzvah and puberty—were nevertheless getting an early start on upholding the prohibition against adult men touching girls, called in halachic parlance *negiah*.[58] "The boys here are religious," the Alfei Menashe coach explained. "I can't let them play with a girl."

The Alfei Menashe coach asked the Ra'anana coach to bench the girl, but to his credit, he refused. "On our team, there is complete equality between everyone, regardless of sex, height or talent," the coach explained. "It's very insulting," a tearful Shiran said. She had never experienced this before, even when she played against other religious boys. "They are kids in the fifth grade, and there is no such thing as keeping the laws of *negiah* at this age," Shiran's mother added.[59]

The lives of youth form a major battleground in religious cultural wars across the globe. Take Tunisia, for example, where radical Islamists in Nabeul attempted to kill the headmaster of the Lycée Menzel Bouzelfa for refusing entry to a student wearing a niqab.[60] Or in the United States, where a kindergarten student in Georgia was forced to change her "short" skirt because it was a "distraction to other students" and forty high school girls were sent home from a winter dance in California after "degrading" clothing inspections "bordering on sexual harassment."[61] In Indonesia, Pakistan, France, and China, there is growing concern over religious extremism and the surprising ways its proponents are finding to assert it in schools. Religious extremists often seek control over youth, the thinking being that if you can control young minds, you can control the future.

In Israel too, schools have become a contested location of social and cultural control for religious extremists. One religious girl in the development town of Dimona who was working as a waitress in a restaurant to earn some money over the summer was expelled from school because boys also worked there. Efrat Daniel, at eighteen, spent three months at home because working in an environment alongside boys was considered against the school rules. "Why are they punishing her? Because she took a job?" her mother asked in frustration in a radio interview. "She is very hurt by all this. Her friends are out doing things, and she's sitting home crying." Rabbi Yaakov Hemed, the principal of the school, was mostly unmoved. "The school has a charter that we're all signed on, and we are committed to all the parents to keep to the charter. When one girl does things that go against the charter, we suspend her if necessary."[62] It is hard to understand why working would be a problem—but when it comes to religious extremists' ideas about women, logic can be elusive. These new religious extremist interpretations of what girls should or should not be doing are causing great suffering to young women.

As the tug of war continues, with religious radicals fighting for more control over young people's bodies, the ones to suffer are the young people themselves, especially young girls. For Shiran Greenboim, there was a lot of support surrounding her, but it did not necessarily help. Hanna Beit Halachmi, a feminist activist and Ra'anana resident, wrote in protest to Ra'anana Mayor Nahum Hofri, calling for an end to all municipal subsidies for organizations like the Elitzur basketball club that support the exclusion of women. Beit Halachmi also wrote a letter to Limor Livnat, minister of sport and chairperson of the Ministerial Committee on the Status of Women, calling on her to take action against the Alfei Menashe team and its coach. Ra'anana resident and feminist blogger Allison Kaplan Sommer wrote of her own outrage about the radical-religious sexualization of girls on her local community. "Many members of the secular majority ask—as Beit Halachmi has—whether they want their taxes subsidizing groups that would leave a little girl weeping on the bench as her teammates play basketball," she writes.[63]

As disturbing as the erasure of women's faces and the silencing of women's voices are, there is something about the cruelty to young girls that brings the war against women to a whole new dimension. The impact on girls is potentially stultifying—squashing their hopes and dreams and limiting their choices as they go through life. The good news is that the stories of girls like Shiran Greenboim have started to capture the attention of the Israeli public. Perhaps the picture of little girls suffering at the hand of religious extremists will have the potential to usher in real change.

But things will get worse before they get better. The next chapter explores places where religious radicalism turns violent.

Chapter 3
THE BATTLE OF THE "MODESTY SQUADS"

Last summer, during consistent one-hundred-degree heat in the Middle East, my then fifteen-year-old daughter casually told me that a Haredi man on the bus called her a "whore," presumably because she was wearing shorts. I reacted with horror, but she laughed it off. "It happens all the time," she said. It may happen "all the time" to her, maybe because she spends quite a bit of time on Jerusalem buses and does not abide by the ultra-Orthodox conventions of female attire. But I was still shocked—though sadly, I realized in retrospect, not really surprised.

The verbal abuse against women on buses is apparently so pervasive that only a fraction of the incidents are reported. These incidents are not only about the gender segregation that I described previously, but also about so-called modesty, a terribly misused term to describe what is really just a demand for female full body cover. The attempts to force women to cover their bodies in public have been creeping into the Israeli streets for decades. Indeed, I remember visiting Israel with my family in 1982, and my older sister, then fourteen, being given a scarf to wear around her shoulders and another one for her waist when we visited the Western Wall. She cried for a long time after that, but it was just "the way things were." A massive sign in the neighborhood of Meah She'arim imploring girls and women to dress modestly has been hanging for decades, and I remember as a student always remembering to wear a long skirt if I had plans to visit there. We took for granted that these kinds of demands were legitimate, even if by law we should have the right to dress how we want when walking along public streets. These days, as the example of my daughter showed, harassment for not following them has become almost expected.

In different Orthodox communities, public pronouncements about modesty by rabbinic leaders over the past few years have included forbidding women from wearing high heels that make noise or talking on cell phones in public, forcing women to wear coats on top of their clothes when they go to weddings (even in summer), forbidding women from wearing the color red, and more.[1] In certain ultra-Orthodox Jerusalem neighborhoods, even saying thank-you or owning an expensive baby carriage can be considered immodest.[2] One Orthodox community established a "kashrut department" for supervising clothing stores to check the length of the skirts and sleeves of the merchandise. This practice was justified by a group called the Committee for the Sanctity of the Camp, to combat what they called "damaging our camp's modesty" due to women and girls "breaching" conventions.[3]

Calls to cover women's bodies have become ubiquitous and at times absurd. Signs have been popping up on streets in cities all around Israel imploring women to "cover up" for the sake of the purity of the nation, respect for the inhabitants, or even respect for the dead. Yes, one cemetery in Israel features a sign asking women to cover their bodies because "an immodest woman is distressing to the dead." In some cemeteries, women are not allowed to be buried next to men. (Why, you ask? What might happen? Excellent question, with no real answer. Clearly this has reached obsessive and completely irrational points.)

What's more, the ubiquity of the calls for body cover seems to give license to violence. "Modesty patrols" have popped up in various cities to forcibly ensure that women are dressed according to ultra-Orthodox codes of appearance—long-necked, long-sleeved shirts, long skirts, tights, closed shoes, and head coverings for married women. The enforcement of this so-called modesty over the past decade or two has become one of the most dominating aspects of Orthodox Israeli culture, and it is increasingly enforced by violence. One example is the rise of the Sikrikim, or Sicarii, a Haredi group of men from the extreme anti-Zionist HaEdah HaHaredit sect charged with protecting women's so-called modesty using whatever tools they have at their disposal. Their tactics are mostly violence and bullying. There were reports in 2010 of Sicarii throwing bags of excrement, smashing store windows, and having locks glued in protest that stores were enabling women's immodesty by selling certain Internet or electronic equipment. Before that, in 2008, Sicarii activist Shmuel Veisfish was convicted for harassing and assaulting the owner of the Space electronics store in the Haredi neighborhood of Geula in Jerusalem. Supposedly, Veisfish objected to the sale of portable video players in the store, which he claimed corrupted Haredi youth with images of women. In numerous incidents, he and his gang would drive customers out of the building, block the entrance, and threaten to kill the employees and burn the store. According to the conviction, Veisfish and another Sicarii member, Ephraim Greenfield, once dragged store owner Binyamin Fredman out of the shop, where they beat him, leaving him with a broken nose, among other considerable injuries. Veisfish was finally sentenced to two years in prison for rioting, extortion, assault, and grievous bodily harm.[4]

This conviction hardly deterred other Sicarii gangs. In other instances, Sicarii allegedly sprayed "Promiscuity" in graffiti at the entrance of "a clothing shop selling dresses whose lengthy hemline and drab colors still were deemed too racy by the group," wrote a reporter for Reuters. "Other stores in the neighborhood, where men wear traditional black garb and women bare little but their face, have had their windows broken, locks glued, and foul-smelling liquid smeared on walls."[5] Although the Sicarii are arguably a fringe element of the ultra-Orthodox community, the views that they espouse about so-called modesty are not widely contested in their community. Because this message hasn't met with opposition there, it's been allowed to spread elsewhere too.

Indeed, while the bullying and violence has been escalating in more recent years, it has probably been going on for longer than we realize. Initially the work of a small group of extremists across Israeli cities, it has grown in part because of illegal financing. In January 2012, a money-laundering scheme to fund the extremist Sicarii group was uncovered in Jerusalem. According to a report in the *Jewish Daily Forward*, five men from the HaEdah HaHaredit were arrested on charges of money laundering, tax evasion, and embezzlement for allegedly using money earmarked for widows, orphans, and the poor to fund Sicarii gang violence. The money was allegedly spent on violent street demonstrations and attacks on buses, stores, and businesses that did not meet with HaEdah's approval of their activities, whatever the HaEdah decided those activities should be, as well as living expenses of Sicarii members. So it's not that the Sicarii are purely ideological; some are also in it for the money.

To make matters worse, Orthodox whistle-blower Shmarya

Rosenberg, who blogs at *Failed Messiah*, argues that the Sicarii violence has an effect on real estate by forcing non-HaEdah people to sell in frightened haste at lower prices and enabling HaEdah real estate owners to create an exclusive stronghold that must operate under its rules.[6] Another economic impact of the violence is on HaEdah businesses: for example, members of the Haredi community announced plans to create their own outdoor market in Jerusalem with separate women's and men's hours, a market that would compete with the iconic Mahane Yehuda Market, "the Shuk," where the Haredi community are a key consumer demographic.[7] Here, Haredi businessmen would obviously benefit. Modesty is perhaps nothing more than a tool of crowd control for the economic and political gain of certain leaders.

Like other areas where religious extremism thrives, in Israel too, economic and political forces conflate to empower these religious modesty thugs. The mayor of Beitar Illit is, as of this writing, under investigation for enabling the activities of "modesty terrorists" in his town. The two men accused of terrorizing female residents for "unchaste behavior" were employed by the city as youth counselors, and the mayor allegedly knew of their behavior, encouraged them, and tried to block police investigation into their activities.[8]

Meanwhile, although the Sicarii may have started as a fringe group, their impact is spreading. In fact, attacking women has become fully acceptable in certain circles. For instance, twenty-seven-year-old Natali Mashiah of Beit Shemesh was attacked in her car near her home in January 2012 by a crowd of ultra-Orthodox men. They smashed her car windows, punctured her tires, and spilled bleach on the inside of her car while calling her a whore and a shiksa and yelling at her to leave. She was hit on the head by a rock thrown from very close range as she ran from the scene. "Although a crowd was said to have gathered during the attack, no one reportedly came to Mashiah's assistance," *Haaretz* reported.[9] Though three men were arrested, no one stepped in to help her during the attack, which in effect silently condoned this violent behavior against her.

In another incident in July 2012, Vered Daniel, a mother of then seven-month-old twin babies, was pelted with rocks in Beit Shemesh for alleged immodesty as she was getting out of her car, holding her baby. "My heart was pounding, and all I wanted to do was get out of there," Daniel said of her ordeal. "I was terrified. I had my baby with me." Her windshield was smashed, though she was physically unharmed because two people helped her find cover during the rock storm. For what it's worth, she was modestly dressed, wearing a long dress at the time.[10] But according to the modesty mobs, that's not worth much.

Perhaps most tellingly, in June 2012, twenty-two-year-old Chananya Rabinowitz was arrested by the police for spitting on two women in Jerusalem, which he claimed he did "because they were not dressed modestly enough."[11] This may sound like a minor incident compared to the other two, but it's significant because his family claimed that Rabinowitz was not connected to Sicarii or modesty squads, an alarming indication that the Sicarii modesty wars are starting to be legitimized even outside their own circles. Beit Shemesh activist Nili Phillip echoed this sentiment, saying that while the "real violence is really just a few extremists, the spitting and cursing is much more widespread, as little kids are encouraged by their parents to yell out shiksa."[12] "Little" incidents like spitting cannot be ignored because they are merely the first expression of violence toward women. Rock throwing and acid pouring—acts with a much more sinister impact—are not far off after that.

Strangely, as the public has become more aware of this violence, the violence seems to spread. Voices of opposition have in essence become fodder to fuel the antiwomen rhetoric and modesty attacks. The uncle of one of the arrested bullies said, "It is regretful that this entire story is happening while the matter of the exclusion of women (from the public sphere) is making front pages and police are taking advantage (of the story)," as if to suggest that the family is really just the victim of protesters. "This is a pitiful neighborhood quarrel which, if it were any other case, the police would take no notice of."[13] The implication of the story is that increased public outcries about violence against women also give extremists more excuses for violence.

It seems, then, that while public awareness increases, the extremism is spreading as well. People like the uncle above have an "excuse" for the violence, because fundamentally, religious extremism abhors vocal or independent women. So protesters make for easy targets. In the Sanhedria community of Jerusalem in December 2011, Haredim called for a boycott of supermarkets that employ women as cashiers, arguing that the stores refused to accede to their demands to employ a "modesty supervisor"— that is, someone whose job it is to ensure that the store remains modest, whatever that means. Apparently all the other stores in the neighborhood had already acceded to these demands, and many had started to maintain separate lines for men and women in response to other demands in the name of modesty.[14] In Beit Shemesh, the number of HMO clinics and supermarkets bearing signs demanding that women dress modestly is also on the rise.

The pressure on women to cover up has also reached public

performances and municipal events. In a Jerusalem municipal event in 2008 to celebrate the inauguration of the new Bridge of Strings, also known as the Chords Bridge, a group of teenage dancers was forced to change their costumes and put on long dresses and head coverings that made their dance moves impossible to discern. Modesty squads were threatening violence and mass protests if they didn't. Then-Jerusalem Mayor Uri Lupolianski—himself an ultra-Orthodox Jew—was reportedly under pressure to cancel the dancers entirely, and thus the modesty requirement was considered something of a compromise.

Yaniv Hoffman, the company's manager, slammed the decision: "The parents and the girls were stunned and we're completely thrown. This company has been performing in every official city event for the past twenty years and this is the first time anything like this has happened. These are thirteen- to sixteen-year-old dancers. This is art; it's not like they're go-go dancers."[15]

This event was merely a harbinger of things to come. By March 2013, female performers were being excluded from municipal events. In a Jerusalem festival called Sounds of the Old City, a musical ensemble of seven musicians and a female singer called the Diwan Project was asked to cut their performance short, and the female singer, Liat Tzion, was asked not to return to the stage. "We started the show and already felt something strange," said Gil Ron Shama of the Diwan Project, adding that soon "a representative of the festival production walked over to the singer and asked her to get off the stage. I didn't know what it was all about but would not allow it and we went on with the performance. We later realized that Haredim were threatening that if the singer does not leave the stage, they will disrupt all other events in the festival."

In a similar vein, Marsh Dondurma, a group of fifteen musicians

(two of whom are women), was called a few days before the festival and asked not to let the women go onstage but instead replace
them with men. The group refused to comply. "I was told that
the issue was a problem since the event was taking place in the
Old City's Jewish Quarter," musician Dotan Yogev recounted.
"I was stunned. I said that the request was absurd and that I will
not back down. After two days of nonstop phone calls I was told
that the performance was to go on as scheduled." Once onstage,
Yogev's microphone was turned off as he tried to tell the audience about what had happened. Jerusalem Councilwoman Rachel
Azaria criticized the incidents, saying, "This is insufferable—that
in the old city of Jerusalem, to which the entire Jewish people
long [sic], this immoral, un-Jewish, and illegal act of excluding
women will occur. The mayor of Jerusalem must ensure that
no sign of exclusion appears in cultural events and fight Haredi
lobbyists who promote such exclusion."[16] Azaria's support was
admirable but did not change the outcome. Women's singing
voices remained unheard.

Unfortunately, the modesty squads are not just an Israeli phenomenon. As religious radicalism spreads around the world, there is a
particularly strong connection between what goes on in Israel and
what goes on in New York, a kind of cross-pollination between
the Haredi communities in both places, where each one watches
the other and listens for the most recent expression of extreme
behavior, especially when it comes to controlling women.

The Hasidic neighborhood of Williamsburg, Brooklyn, has
active modesty squads. Yiddish signs on trees that were later
removed by city workers instructed women, "Precious Jewish
daughter, please move to the side when a man approaches." In

New Square, New York, another Hasidic community, "similar signs remain posted," writes Naomi Zeveloff, "and residents walk streets strictly divided by gender, with women on one side and men on the other. Local women are also not allowed to drive, though this restriction stems from their deference to rabbinic decree and communal pressure rather than from injunctions promoted via public means."[17]

And Haredi men around the world are becoming more demanding. As of this writing, a case at York University in Canada is threatening the livelihood of a sociology professor who refused to accede to his student's demand to be excused from a group project because it would have forced him to work with female students. Professor J. Paul Grayson's administrators assert that he violated the university's "obligation to accommodate." The professor, in his defense, and in defense of women, said that the man's request "represents a great leap backward… When I was a student, you couldn't have gotten away with that—it wouldn't even have been considered."[18]

Moreover, just like in Israel, modesty and gender segregation are linked. In March 2013, the Barclays Center in New York hosted the Ringling Bros. and Barnum & Bailey Circus for a performance in which there were no female performers, to cater to the Orthodox Jewish community. In February, Barclays held a concert of violinist Itzhak Perlman with separate seating for men and women.[19] And the *New York Times* reported in January 2013 that modesty squads are bullying women and shop owners in New York as well for displaying women's clothing. "Modesty committees did not have addresses, stationery, or business cards, and…few people seem to know where their authority originated," the *Times* reported. "Hasidic leaders contend that the modesty committees are nothing more than self-appointed individuals who, indignant at some perceived infraction, take matters into their own hands… But many Hasidim say they have seen or heard how a shadowy group of men seeks to pressure parents to rein in children who wear dresses too short or stockings too thin, or who chat on cell phones with friends of the opposite sex. One family reported being harassed because the wife had stepped outdoors with a robe-like housecoat rather than a long dress."[20]

The significant difference between what's happening in the United States and Israel is that in New York, legal action is now being taken against some of these modesty bullies to protect women's rights. Seven businesses in Brooklyn are currently being sued by New York City's Commission on Human Rights for signs in their storefronts aimed at women, stating, "No shorts, no bare-foot, no sleeveless, no low-cut neckline allowed in this store."[21] Still, as we see in the case of the York University professor, even democracies can get flustered when confronted with the language of religious rights to erase women's presence.

Perhaps this is where Israel is currently faltering. In theory, the State of Israel should have similar legal tools at its disposal. Israel is a parliamentary democracy very similar to the British system, founded on principles of democracy though lacking an actual constitution. There are Basic Laws that guarantee a whole range of rights, and the Basic Laws are not meant to be abstract but practically applied in law and government. But the issue of separation of religion and state is one that Israel has never adequately dealt with. Religious political parties are given disproportionate power in coalition governments, municipal (tax payer–funded) rabbis are given inordinate sway in local decision-making, and employees of the Religious Ministry have enormous budgets and power with little accountability to anyone. These realities create a tangle of political and economic interests that continue to empower the violence rather than stamping it out. It is hardly surprising, then, that the Beit Shemesh municipality, frustrated by increasing violence, declared that they are "helpless" in fighting this rising oppression of women—as if to say that the Haredi bullying was more powerful than local government.[22]

And so, while there is a compelling sharing of cultures between Haredi communities in Israel and around the world, especially around modesty violence, the threat against women is particularly real in Israel. The victims of the violence in Israel are not just members of an insular community but all the women of Israel who cannot freely and safely walk down the streets knowing that they will not be attacked. In addition, while America has laws and mechanisms to limit the power of religious groups, as well as an elaborate system for keeping religion out of politics (despite the emergence of a powerful Tea Party that threatens to dissolve this separation at times), Israel has yet to seriously grapple with limiting the influence of the religious powers that be. This lack of attention to encroaching religious extremism poses a tremendous threat to the well-being of society, and Israeli women as a whole.

One of the major questions that comes to mind when discussing Haredi violence against women is: What do Haredi women feel about all this? There are two answers to this question, seemingly contradictory but both equally valid. One answer is that Haredi women are suffering the most, and the other is that Haredi women are complicit enablers of the misogynistic culture that oppresses them. Let's look at each of these realities.

The first victims of Haredi violence are undoubtedly religious women. For example, Dr. Hannah Kehat's seventy-eight-year-old mother, a lifelong resident of the ultra-Orthodox Jerusalem neighborhood Meah She'arim, did not ride her local bus for three years. As Dr. Kehat, founder of Kolech–Religious Women's Forum, told me in March 2012, her mother had lost her bus line because Haredi extremists would stone the bus every time it rode down her street. So Egged simply stopped the route, forcing her and many of her carless neighbors to walk long distances to find a different bus to get anywhere. "Women in her community are being completely neglected—they are at the mercy of the Sicarii," Kehat told me.[23] Not only are Haredi women often the first victims of this violent oppression; they are also often the ones to suffer most, even if they don't complain or call it suffering, and even if they say that they like it or choose this lifestyle over all other alternatives. As one Haredi woman told me, "I don't mind going to the back of the bus; it's not so bad."[24] She did not notice the irony or paradox in her own statement. The decision to embrace the culture as her own belies an admission or acceptance that these practices are "not so bad."

Choice, in this kind of environment, can be a dubious thing. Like Plato's famous image of the "happy slave," Haredi women who speak in glowing terms of their community's dictates about women's bodies may have made a choice to accept all the rules around them. But that doesn't mean that if tomorrow their rabbis declare freedom for women, the women wouldn't gladly embrace liberty instead.

Still, some Haredi women are also some of the strongest proponents of radicalism. This is not entirely unheard of. Women passengers in the back of the bus were among those who blamed Miriam

Shear for her own beating, for example, accusing her for failing to comply with the "rules." In fact, women internalizing religious-based sexism and becoming the staunchest advocates for their own oppression can be found in many religions. Genital mutilation in Islam is often carried out by women, child marriages in India are often carried out by women, and some American women lead the antiabortion movement in the name of Christian faith. Women embracing misogyny in the name of religion, what Dr. Tova Hartman calls "jailer-mothers," are frequently a product of religious radicalism itself. In other words, women who live in a culture that calls for complete control over women's bodies will at times become powerfully complicit in the transmission of that culture.[25]

Indeed, there is a good motive for women to condemn fellow females for stepping outside the box: these complicit women who side with their own oppression frequently gain a strong measure of approval in the communities or societies in which they live. If we accept the idea that there is nothing that human beings want more desperately than to be loved and accepted by others, then conforming to social expectations of the only community you know will inevitably deliver that. Certainly, full body cover is an act of total conformity to a set of radical religious beliefs. It's not about protecting women but about keeping women under control. Even when women do it to themselves, it's internalized control. But with that control comes some social rewards. Women who are deemed "most" religious, "most" pious, "most" good are often revered by their communities. Human beings will often go to great lengths to achieve that kind of status and respect. Moreover, many religious women genuinely want to be "good." If women who have a sincere desire to be good and God-fearing are told that the only path toward that end is extreme body cover and body control, it should not be too surprising that many women will choose that path on their way to achieve their life purpose of being the best in the eyes of God.

Still, it can be surprising to see just how far some women will go to internalize and accommodate the sexist demands that religious extremism puts on them. The most radical expression of this internalized sexism comes from the rise of the Haredi burka sect, so-called "Taliban mothers," which started in Beit Shemesh. Followers dress in layers upon layers of clothing, revealing not a speck of skin anywhere, not even hands or eyes. Hannah Katsman, who writes extensively about this group, explained to me that the women wear a special fabric over the eyes that is perforated in a way that they can see out but people cannot see in. They are called Taliban mothers because such total body cover—*shalim* in Hebrew—has been unheard of in Judaism until now; the only frame of reference that observers have is to compare them to Muslim women wearing burkas.[26] Although this phenomenon began years ago, observers note that it has now reached the tipping point where it is an established phenomenon not likely to go away any time soon. *Haaretz* reporter Allison Kaplan Sommer writes that "twenty of the families in Beit Shemesh sent a letter to their town, saying that the ultra-Orthodox school their children attend is inappropriate because the teachers' wives do not veil, and the group expressed a desire to start an exclusively 'pro-veiling' school. This would institutionalize the phenomenon and give them a base for growth."[27]

So it should not be surprising that body cover is sometimes spearheaded by women and led to the extreme. After all, the messages of so-called modesty that have been pushed throughout the Haredi world—that women's body cover is the most important thing, that nothing signifies being religious as much as full modesty to the extreme, that there is nothing more noble for women to do in this life than cover their bodies—have been fully internalized by these women. They are not "different" or strange or insane. They have simply acquiesced to the messages that they have been infused with and have chosen to adopt these ideas completely. And why wouldn't they? If a woman genuinely desires to do the right thing, to be "good" and noble and virtuous—not bad goals in and of themselves—she will likely do what she is told is the way to achieve them. And if the only way she has been taught to be good is to cover one's body, then by covering completely, she is being as good as she possibly can. What's wrong with that, right?

Let's take a look at some of the results. A leader of the sect, Bruria Keren, a face-covering mother of twelve, was convicted of child abuse and sent to jail for four years. In keeping with her extreme views about religious women's behavior, she habitually punished her children by pouring water on them, locking them outside, and restraining them in the storage shed for perceived violations of modesty. Her children were so confounded by her fanaticism that her son and daughter actually had incestuous sex in that locked punishment shed.[28] So much for protection from deviant sexuality. In the end, extremism breeds extremism.

Nevertheless, more women seem to be joining the sect despite Keren's conviction. The group apparently went from fifty members in 2008, right after Keren's conviction, to several hundred by 2011, and the petition for pro-burka Jewish schooling was signed by husbands as well. But it is interesting to note that some Haredi men are not entirely happy with this. Allison Kaplan Sommer reports that a group of husbands of veiled women have been pleading with their rabbinical leaders to call for a ban against full veiling (the women veil at home as well, all day).[29] It is interesting that they are using the main tool at their disposal to help them see their wives that others in their culture use to oppress them.

It is also fascinating to see how some members of the Orthodox community try to disassociate themselves from this radical approach to women's modesty while still enforcing the practice in other ways. Shmuel Pappenheim has said that the women of the cult are "crazy," as if his own "regular" Haredi culture that creates Sicarii and modesty squads bears no resemblance to the women's behavior. "Even the strictest rabbis who require women to wear black head coverings and black stockings understand that a woman must allow herself to be a woman," he added.[30] In other words, he is promoting an ideology by which "normal" body cover dictated by men makes women "womanly," but an amount of cover dictated by a woman transforms from "womanly" to "insane." It seems that women—bombarded with radical messages of body cover supposedly in the name of God—are somehow expected to know the difference and follow it. In truth, given the predominance of this rhetoric in the Orthodox community, it was only a matter of time before women internalized the modesty messages to the extreme. Of course, that has become the women's fault, not the men's. Women have merely taken it "too far."[31]

The "burka women" raise a crucial question about whether Haredi women are victims or complicit in the spread of radical violence against women. The answer, as mentioned, is that they are both. In some ways, they are empowered; after all, they have taken ownership of the life that they were given. They have taken the messages that they received and made them fully their own. If male leaders say that their bodies cause societal sin and impurity, then they comply completely, owning their bodies completely. And more cover means more boundaries. The fact that the burka women's husbands can no longer see them or touch them also gives them a certain power—they can say no to unwanted advances. With that, the women who choose extreme body cover are still living within male-created rules intended to keep women's bodies out of a public landscape. No matter how much women own these practices, acclaim women's modesty, or say "it's not so bad," they are still accommodating and enabling practices based on institutionalized misogyny, practices that confine them the most. As Lisa Fishbayne Joffe writes in her book *Gender, Religion, and Family Law*, there is a complex and ongoing feminist negotiation between advocating for religious women's rights and respecting women's agency.[32]

It's not just Jewish women who suffer from rhetoric and rules of body cover, but American Christian women as well. In fact, America is now experiencing the growth of a Christian movement called Modest Is Hottest in which women are encouraged to cover up to the max.[33] This is promoted by groups such as "Secret Keeper Girl," which promotes mothers covering their daughters as early as eight through intense sleepovers and "bod squads." This body cover is touted as "protection" for girls.

However, it's really girls' body cover as "protection" for boys. The "slut-shaming" practices to cover girls are reaching new heights. According to recent reports, two girls in Ohio were turned away from their prom for being "improperly dressed," because they were only allowed to wear dresses that had "no curvature of their breasts showing."[34] This Modest Is Hottest movement about observing and nit-picking girls' bodies teaches girls to cover themselves to the greatest extent possible. This is not Beit Shemesh, Israel, but Ohio, United States of America.

Like religious feminists in Israel, there is a groundswell of activism in America that is challenging these disturbing trends from within the culture itself. Some American activists are starting to question whether this movement is the hottest idea after all. *The Friendly Atheist* blogger, writing about "the ugly side of modesty," argues that "teaching of modesty to teen and preteen girls reinforces the idea that men are slavering goons, hapless at the sight of a tantalizing shoulder or waist. It is the woman's responsibility to mitigate men's desires by covering up all of their 'problem bits.'"[35] One man wrote the essay "Is Modest Really Hottest?" and describes how "I watched my female classmates forced to line up in the hallway, one straight line of girls kneeling. As they waited, a teacher would walk by and measure the distance between the floor and the hem of their skirts, then the distance between the lowest point on their blouse and their clavicles. If the distances were too great, they were sent home or forced to wear the school's official 'ugly sweater,' my school's version of the scarlet letter A."[36]

Perhaps the greatest irony of the Modest Is Hottest movement is that it's telling girls to be modest *and* hot. Yes, cover up so men won't sin, but still strive to be sexually attractive anyway. Women and girls are trapped in a set of double expectations—be pure but be beautiful; be prudish but also hot. Not unlike the Taliban mothers in Israel, American girls are becoming trapped in a culture that sexualizes them, then puts all the blame for men's sexual urges on them too.

Marinda Valenti at *Ms.* magazine summarizes the problem of Modest Is Hottest well:

> *The concern for overly exposed young bodies may be well-intentioned. With society fetishizing girls at younger and younger ages, girls are instructed to self-objectify and see*

themselves as sexual objects, something to be looked at. A laundry list of problems can come from obsessing over one's appearance: eating disorders, depression, low self-worth... But these dress codes fall short of being legitimately helpful. What we fail to consider when enforcing restrictions on skirt length and the tightness of pants is the girls themselves—not just their clothes, but their thoughts, emotions, budding sexuality, and self-image. Instead, these restrictions are executed with distracted boys in mind, casting girls as inherent sexual threats needing to be tamed. Dress restrictions in schools contribute to the very problem they aim to solve: the objectification of young girls. When you tell a girl what to wear (or force her to cover up with an oversized T-shirt), you control her body. When you control a girl's body—even if it is ostensibly for her "own good"—you take away her agency. You tell her that her body is not her own... You recontextualize her body; she now exists through the male gaze.[37]

From America to the Arab world to Tel Aviv, the spread of religious radicalism across the world is incredibly uniform in its attempts to control the female body. The rhetoric of modesty cuts across religions and cultures and threatens girls' and women's well-being. It also adds to an already punishing culture in which women are expected to dress for the way their bodies look to men. As we've seen throughout this chapter, the situation in Israel is just one example of how this radicalism spreads: from small extremist pockets into the dominant culture, where sexist views of women still persist. It is stopped only when all people speak up and speak out against it—religious and secular women, men, and governments alike.

Chapter 4
THE PLIGHT OF THE WOMEN OF THE WALL

The Old City of Jerusalem is the center of the world, or at least that's the legend in several religions. But that's not the initial sense you get when you enter it. As you leave the bustling modern part of Jerusalem and go into the Old City, the walls feel heavy, worn, and, well, drab. This monotonous first impression is misleading though. A closer inspection reveals hues in the walls, little cracks and fissures, and wrinkles of character and memory, like the face of a wise old woman or the trunk of an ancient tree.

As I walked along the slippery cobblestone streets enclosed by these ancient walls of heavy cut rock on a recent February morning, I couldn't help but think that the Old City is not so much the center of the world as a world unto itself. Walking through the Dung Gate—a decidedly ironic (or perhaps appropriate) name for the entrance to this site that has been violently fought over for centuries because everyone thinks that God lives there—I was mostly struck by the contrasts. To enter the world of the Old City is to leave behind certain comforts of cosmopolitan life. The standard buses and light-rail cannot cope with the narrow pathways and curves, leaving residents to manage most of life on foot (or, in some quarters, by donkey). In this city on a hill, every trip, no matter how long or short, requires a tricky navigation of slopes, stairs, and slippery alleys. During the rainy season, even maintaining your balance can be a challenge. Water drips down the sewage clefts in the middle of the streets, and your feet struggle to grip the ground to avoid sliding down the steep stone paths. The temperatures always feel extreme too—either you're burning with heat in the exposed Middle Eastern sun or you're chilled to the bone from the walls of cold rocks.

Perhaps the city mimics its inhabitants. This is not a place with bike paths, expansive parks, or soccer fields. The central squares are filled with merchants peddling religious objects, tourist souvenirs, and sunflower seeds in close succession, where the sounds of the muezzin mix with the call of shopkeepers who compete with tour guides for the attention of passersby. Groups of American tourists are instantly recognizable by their sneakers and baseball caps, cameras in hand and water bottles around their necks. But they're not to be confused with the packs of foreign Orthodox students who are more likely to be characterized by long skirts and prayer books for girls and, well, almost any attire for boys. Both young men and young women, on a break from formal schooling and family life, often seek out the Old City, a seemingly exotic space where they may find independence, historical narratives, and perhaps some bizarre and strangely attractive religious ideas and practices.

Every square meter of the Old City is infused with layers of narrative, some of it thousands of years old, some still in the making. Ruins of a medieval synagogue bearing a sign describing its cycle of destruction and rebuilding stand alongside a Temple-era ritual bath where priestly artifacts were recently unearthed. Visitors there are greeted by an old lady sitting on its stoop calling out "*zedaka*"—"charity"—as she shakes a can of change. Next door to her are a falafel stand, a yeshiva, and an advertisement for a 3-D film about the history of Jerusalem.

People walk down the alleyways of the Old City with purpose and intensity. On this February morning, as I sat in a coffee shop waiting for prayers to begin, a man walked past me wearing ritual fringes and phylacteries (small sacred pouches containing a piece of parchment inscribed with verses from the Torah for morning prayers). Only here in the Jewish Quarter of the Old City, I thought, can a man safely walk down the street dressed this way and fully expect—and be validated in his expectation—that nobody would think him unusual.

I have some fond memories of the Old City. It was here in 1988, as one of those wide-eyed, purposefully pious, post–high school girls, that I dated my now-husband. He was a student at Yeshivat HaKotel, a famous institution that overlooks the Western Wall, and it was here in the Old City where he often found me, the sincere if perhaps misguided yeshiva girl I was back then, searching for truth and meaning, and maybe some freedom, in the aisles of a local bookstore. I spent a lot of time at the Western Wall that year, having bought into the belief system that prayer and closeness to God—or at least to the outer walls of what was once the Temple—are ingredients to divining a good life. I still hang on to aspects of that belief system, though I've long since searched for meaning beyond the Western Wall and now am more likely to find it in the solitude of my garden, in yoga, or texting with my kids.

These days, the Western Wall brings out very mixed feelings in me. People often talk about how important the Western Wall— the Kotel—is to Jews. The last remaining bit of the famed Temple in Jerusalem, built by David's son Solomon, the Wall has been the center of Jewish ritual life for a millennium. It is considered the most sacred site for Jews who hold by the tradition that the *shechina*, or God's spirit, rests there. It is the endpoint of pilgrimages from people of many faiths and the spot where people bring their dreams, desires, and hopes, written onto little scraps of paper, and place them in the crevices of the rock for safekeeping and, ideally, fulfillment. The Kotel has been the location of conflicts, pillages, destruction, reconstruction, and endless prayers. I smile at the thought. Kind of like my own spirit and identity.

But it's a tough place to be a woman now, for sure, especially if you want to pray. Here's why: to be a woman at the prayer service at the Kotel, it's all about the fingers. You stick your fingers through the holes of the partition separating the men's and women's sections of the plaza, reaching for a peek at the action, which is exclusively on the men's side. It's a combination of spectator sport and prison: a six-foot-high partition separates the men's side, where the prayer occurs, from the women's, where women are forced to sit in silence, separated from the ceremony and rituals they came here to participate in. The partition and ambient noises obscure any direct contact or view of the prayer services and destroy one's ability to feel like a real participant. It is really hard for me to watch women—mothers, grandmothers, aunts, sisters, cousins—scurry for a spot on the plastic chairs so they can get a real view over the partition, women scampering around looking for a spare chair they can squeeze in between a few other women, ignoring the oddness, discomfort, and sheer humiliation of comporting oneself this way while dressed up for the occasion in high heels, stockings, and fancy suits.

Standing on one of those chairs, an experience I have often vowed never to repeat, involves the adjustment from a position

of reverence to a role void of all dignity. For me, it was an acquiescence that my purpose in life is to be a silent observer, while a
child—a mere thirteen-year-old who still relies on his mother to
make his lunch and remind him to comb his hair—can experience and have a presence in a sacred part of this world that I shall
never have. I remember well the awkward experience of my own
son's bar mitzvah (which was not at the Kotel). Though I was far
older, wiser, and more experienced, I was nothing more than an
uncounted woman, and he, though still a child, was considered
a man, ready to be a full equal among men. In this world of
Orthodox Judaism, no matter what I do, I will never achieve what
he has achieved simply by being born as a different gender. I will
never be more than the fingers through the crack, the tippy-toes
on the chair, the eyes peering over the top of the partition.

It took me a little while to realize just how much I hated this.
It took me forever, it seems, to learn how to talk back to my
own culture, to find the courage and the wisdom to acknowledge
my own experiences, to even give myself permission to be an
observer and driver of my own thoughts and feelings. In the
Jewish community I grew up in, I was so used to being told what
women want and need that I had to find both the courage and the
understanding to question the veracity of all that.

Eventually, I figured out what bothered me so much. Being a
woman at the Kotel feels like being robbed of your own story,
your heritage, your nationality. You think that this belongs to
you, that this is a central part of your identity—isn't that what
everyone has told you since the time you were five years old? You
think that this sacred place has a central location in your Jewish
personhood. And then one day, it dawns on you. You think you
are a Jew, but really, in the eyes of Jewish culture and society, you

are just a female. You're barely a person. You're not really there. The desperation with which you stick your fingers into the holes, hoping to hold on to some bit of that story, belies the futility of the exercise. You will never be fully present there, and it will never be yours.

And that realization makes it all worse. You're angry and longing and confused, and nobody seems to notice. Everyone around you keeps battling for that space on the plastic chair, as if they have it all figured out. And you, you're just perplexed. Your heart aches, you don't know where to turn, whether there is someone in your world who may understand you, and the voices in your head of your teachers and your family that once gave you comfort morph into a noisy cacophony of empty words. Your search for meaning has brought you into this maze. And ironically, that urgency of desire, that search for meaning and truth that began in earnest when you were eighteen, has not ceased within you. This is where it has led you.

In 1998, somewhere around the time when I was starting to honestly face my own true feelings about my gendered religious upbringing, I discovered a group called Women of the Wall. I had first heard about them in 1990, because I once went to a lecture about them at college, when they had just started. But at the time, the whole notion of women's prayers and women's empowerment within religion was such a foreign concept to me, something so alien, that at the end of the lecture, all I could do was angrily spew back some of the rhetoric about arrogant women changing tradition, rhetoric I was brought up on and didn't yet know how to unpack and analyze. I ran out of that lecture and didn't look back.

But in 1998, at age twenty-eight, with three children under the age of five, I was in a different place. I was ready to start being honest with myself about how I felt living the life of the Correct Orthodox Jewish Woman. And it was during that period of honest searching that Women of the Wall showed up in my life.

It was the holiday of Purim in Jerusalem, a holiday that has become a central event for Orthodox feminism as women are granted permission in Halacha to publicly chant the Scroll of Esther, *Megillat Esther*. My dear friend Rabbi Dr. Haviva Ner-David, one of the first women to receive Orthodox rabbinic ordination and one of the leaders of Women of the Wall at the time, asked me if I would read chapter five for her women's prayer group. Women of the Wall (WOW) gathered at the Kotel on the first of every Jewish month, Rosh Hodesh, to pray and chant Torah, as well as on certain holidays like Purim. I had never chanted megillah, the Scroll of Esther, before—or Torah, actually, something I wouldn't do for another few years—but when Haviva asked me, I felt something somewhere inside me wake up. I *wanted* to do this. I had no skills, no experience, and no viable plan for learning the ancient chants effectively enough for a public reading. But I had listened to the megillah reading a zillion times, I love the biblical texts, I love music, and I have always connected to the cantillations. I *really* wanted to do this. So I agreed.

The fact that it was going to be at the Kotel was an added bonus, like a kind of "proof" in my young mystical mind that this was a really significant and spiritual event. The fact that I was participating in a women's prayer group and leading some of the chanting was a positively thrilling prospect for me. I felt invigorated for the first time in a while.

I got hold of a recording to help me study chapter five. I would practice while my kids—ages five, three, and eight months—were playing, while I was nursing, while I was preparing dinner. My husband, for whom all this feminist stuff was new as well, was helpful and supportive in every way possible. But there were still some logistical challenges in taking on this task to read megillah. I needed to be hands-free in order to read, and it's hard to do that and chase around three little kids at the Kotel. My husband decided to take the two big kids elsewhere that morning, and my parents, who happened to be visiting Israel then, came with me and the baby and were charged with looking after her from the back of the women's section. Predictably, as my turn to read approached, my beautiful child only wanted to be held and screamed while wrestling with my parents. Somewhere around the middle of chapter four, my mother came and brought me my baby to hold.

I was nervous enough without her, trying to remember my cantillations, the stops and starts on a scroll that lacks all punctuation and markings. But though terrified, I dutifully took her in my arms and continued. And as one might imagine, as chapter five came along and I started to read with my beautiful daughter perched on my hip, I choked. I made so many mistakes that the chapter was mostly unrecognizable. It was awful, just a big mess. But the worst part for me was not embarrassing myself in front of this incredible group of women that had given me an opportunity to read for them—nor ruining their megillah experience as well. What was really the worst was that my father was watching and listening from behind. A seasoned Torah reader in an Orthodox family with four daughters and no sons, he had raised us on the belief that chanting Torah was a man's job. I was raised believing that Torah reading was in the category of things—like, say, practicing medicine, balancing a checkbook, driving a car, or venturing outside after dark—that were meant to be done by men. Here I was, the first woman in my family to ever have the opportunity to prove all that wrong, and I failed. Totally failed. I was living proof of why men were leaders and women should stay home and look after their babies. I left the Kotel mortified, completely ashamed, and dejected. Perhaps even for a moment, I was lost.

Or perhaps I was found. Despite how it turned out, something inside of me shifted that day. The singing and dancing of the women at the Kotel—a historic event for the group struggling for its own legitimacy at the Wall, a mission I had not appreciated at the time because I was drowning in my own issues—were enthralling. I loved being among women who were doing religiousness in a whole different way. I did not have the language at the time to describe this new feeling, but the word I was probably looking for was *empowered*. Or perhaps just *liberated*. I really did love chanting megillah and being in the presence of women taking ownership.

I also knew that something really important was happening with the Women of the Wall, that this energized and alive group of women was changing the rules about gender and religious practice. This group was giving me a language and a visceral experience with which to challenge so many of the assumptions about religious life that I had been brought up with. That experience with Women of the Wall awakened in me something that had lain dormant for years, possibly my whole life. It was a totally new way of being at the Kotel and a new way of being in prayer. It was about no longer being a spectator but about making the women's section alive, with women's power and women's voices and bodies. The experience of enabling women to be active players in the spiritual journey of singing out to God—even if they couldn't participate alongside men—and to be fully alive and emboldened human beings brought me back to life. It would be years before I got over my shame and took on megillah reading again, and with our move away from Israel and Jerusalem for a few years, I would only go back to the Women of the Wall sporadically during that time. But in the meantime, my new journey had finally begun.

My story here, however, is only a tiny piece of the story of Women of the Wall, and it is one of the most peaceful. After all, since 2011, women have started to be arrested at the Wall for praying with this group, a development that is shocking even to the most jaded observers. But before I get into the details of how the police force of the Jewish state has come to arrest women at Israel's holiest site for the crime of *praying*, it's important to look at the broader context first. This is not only about the Wall, but also about women and religion in Israel. It's a story of politicians heeding the calls of religious bureaucrats whose primary demand seems to be about controlling women. It's about a confluence of interested parties—religious, political, economic—who are all willing to sacrifice the well-being of women for their own symbolic needs, for their own perceptions of power, God, and masculinity. It's about encroaching religious fanaticism in Israel up against the work of some dedicated activists to protect democracy and freedom.

The Women of the Wall have had a really tough run. This multidenominational Jewish women's group, formed twenty-five years ago in order to conduct an all-female prayer service at the Western Wall, has experienced constant physical and verbal abuse, prolonged legal battles, and ostracism from the very culture that they so desperately want to cling to—religious Judaism.

But it didn't start that way. The group that made the decision on December 1, 1988, to conduct this prayer group was eager and almost naïve in their intent to create a beautiful spiritual experience for Orthodox women. "We brought a small folding table with us, upon which to rest the Sefer Torah (Torah scroll)," cofounders Phyllis Chesler and the late Rivka Haut recalled. "We stood together and prayed aloud together; a number of us wore *tallitot* (prayer shawls)."[1] The purpose was very simple: to enable Jewish women to pray together as a group.

The concept of a women's prayer group was born in the late 1960s, not in Israel, but in Lincoln Square Synagogue on the Upper West Side of Manhattan, of all places. It began on the holiday of Simchas Torah, which celebrates the reading of the Torah and dancing with Torah scrolls, practices from which, until then, women had been excluded in the Orthodox world. In this brand-new service, women read the Torah portion aloud and gave *aliyot* [call-ups] to women.

The first Women's Tefillah Group was a major coup in a culture in which women literally don't count. Group prayer in Judaism requires a minyan, a quorum of ten, but in Orthodoxy, only men count in that quorum. The spread of the practice of women's tefillah groups throughout the 1970s—in which women would typically gather around Rosh Hodesh to pray and read the Torah—was a way of women counting themselves, even if they were not officially a quorum. It was the closest thing to experiencing a minyan. All this was well and good until the infamous Yeshiva University responsum (answer to a religious query) of 1985, in which five high-profile Orthodox rabbis came out with a public ruling against the groups, arguing that the women's prayer groups were halachically invalid, formed "merely" for feminist purposes.

The impact of the ensuing maelstrom was actually quite empowering for women: many rabbis came out defending women's tefillah groups and distancing themselves from the responsum. Rabbi Avi Weiss published the first book supporting women's prayer groups, and a number of the groups came together and formed the Women's Tefillah Network as a source of support and resources for women. By the late 1980s, women's tefillah groups spread throughout New York and to more isolated communities of Jewish women. By 1988, there were an estimated twenty groups in the United States with more about to form in Canada, Israel, England, and Australia. According to the Jewish Women's Archives (JWA), these groups represented nearly four thousand Orthodox women.[2]

Within this context of growing women's tefillah groups, Women of the Wall, made up of Israeli and American women, became arguably the most visible and public women's tefillah group. The only group that met outdoors and the only one that prayed on a national site in Israel, WOW took the tefillah groups to a whole new level. No longer "underground" and fearful, the women of this group were out there, literally, claiming sacred ground for women, unafraid to let their bodies be seen and their voices heard.

"Our service was peaceful," wrote Phyllis Chesler and Rivka Haut about the first meeting of some seventy women in 1988, "until we opened the Torah scroll on-site. Then a woman began yelling. She insisted that women are not permitted to read from a Torah scroll. This alerted some Haredi men, who stood on chairs in order to look over the *mechitza* (partition). The men began to loudly curse us. Despite the jeers, curses, and threats of many onlookers, we managed to complete our Torah reading. We were not stopped by the late Rabbi Yehuda Getz, who was then the Kotel administrator. In fact, a woman who happened to be standing near Rabbi Getz heard him tell the female complainer: 'Let them continue. They are not violating Halacha.'"[3]

In the twenty-five years since then, WOW have continued to pray at the Kotel every month—and have continued to be yelled at, abused, cursed, and worse. Their struggle has become a symbol of women's struggle for equality in Israel in the face of religious fanaticism. There are certain aspects of the WOW story that are especially alarming, in particular the practice of arresting some of the participants, which began in 2009. These incidents have become a symbol of the rapidly deteriorating status of women in Israel where religious politics are involved and the frighteningly increasing use of police forces to control women.

From its inception, WOW faced the often violent opposition of Haredim, both men *and* women. "The men began to infiltrate the women's section, encircling us in the midst of our prayers," recalled WOW cofounder Dr. Bonna Devora Haberman about that first experience:

> *They began to jeer at us, then tug at our clothes and prayer shawls. Some women were thrown to the ground. "The Torah belongs to men," shouted some ultra-Orthodox women as they sought to wrest the holy scroll from our custody. The female assailants laid their hands directly upon our bodies, a gesture usually reserved for blessing, and instead intoned curses that we should never bear children and that we should die young, in traffic accidents. There were catcalls of "whores," "Nazis," "dogs," "witches."*
>
> *Jolted from the vulnerable moment of prayerful intention into a defensive deployment, we closed in around each other in tight concentric circular formation, arms supporting each other, delineating and protecting. We gripped one another in one mass. I was in the center, arms wrapped around the Torah,*

which I had grasped in time before the table on which it had
rested was overturned by the disrupters. Prayer books spilled
onto the ground; pages printed with God's holy Name scattered
in the commotion. I stood, frozen, gripping the Torah. Acts of
desecration shattered and dispersed the sacred letters; women's
bodies and prayers were routed from holy space.[4]

The women were both shocked and emboldened. The violence
they experienced was traumatizing for sure, but it also reinforced
their commitment to persevere in their efforts to create safe spaces
for women at the Kotel. The group vowed to convene for prayers
every Friday and every Rosh Hodesh.

The Friday meetings, which Dr. Haberman described as "an
oasis of spiritual sustenance," a practice that continued for three
and a half years, stood in stark contrast to the Rosh Hodesh
meetings, which regularly drew violent reactions. On Fridays,
she wrote, "we came to be respected among many of those who
frequent the site; we were even recognized and anticipated. We
said our prayers and wordless meditative melodies with confidence
and even abandon."[5] Perhaps because the group was relatively
small and there was no Torah reading involved on Fridays, these
prayer services were, for the most part, peaceful—except for one.

"The only truly nasty incident on a Friday involved a woman in
a green dress." Dr. Haberman continued:

One Friday morning, in the midst of our prayers, and with no
advance warning, the woman in the green dress rushed at us,
grabbed us, cursed us, and flailed. She took hold of Barbara,
a slight, middle-aged, gray-haired woman, and bit her arm.
Millie, one of our regulars, always carried a camera in her bag.

She pulled it out to photograph the woman, who became even more infuriated. She lunged at Millie, who was flanked by her terrified children, struggling to wrest the camera from Millie's hands. I gripped the arm of the woman in green as her whole body writhed with malicious intent. No official came forth to intervene. Finally exhausted, the woman ceased her attack as suddenly as she had begun it, and fled.[6]

The women filed police reports, but nothing came of it. They eventually received a notice that the case was closed due to "lack of public interest."

Although this kind of violence was unusual for the Friday prayers, it was fairly typical of what the women experienced on Rosh Hodesh, when WOW had a larger group, the prayers involved the disputed Torah reading, and the Kotel itself was crowded with yeshiva students, tourists, and throngs of worshippers, any of whom could take offense at what they were doing without warning. Chairs were regularly thrown at the women (a bizarre and frightening experience that has been captured on film and can be seen all over YouTube). Meanwhile, there was no police intervention to protect the worshipping women. They were on their own.

After repeated pleading for assistance, the first official response from Israeli authorities came in 1989 when then Religious Minister Zevulun Hammer and Rabbi Getz met with WOW and officially declared that their prayers were off-limits. Rabbi Getz, in a gesture of conciliation, offered the women the use of his own private synagogue "deep in the recesses of the enclosed northern segment of the wall."[7] During the group's initial tour of the enclosed site through underground passageways and tunnels, his assistant, Rabbi Zvi Hersh, turned to the group to offer his advice. "He emphasized to us that our opponents were violent and formidable. As soon as the ultra-Orthodox community learned of our intention to pray within the holy tunnels, he said 'they would bus in thousands of people bearing knives.' Keys to the passageways were easily procured. We would be trapped inside the tunnels and massacred, he warned. We would be much safer outside."

They were confused by this seeming attempt to deter them, but despite this frightening and menacing proposition, the group considered the use of the space. However, as they were about to respond with readiness to accept the compromise, they received notice that the offer was rescinded, without explanation.[8] The women returned to their space outside and continued to endure the unimpeded chair throwing and curses with no support or protection from the police or the Israeli government.

For the holiday of Purim 1989, WOW was offered another proposal by Hammer: he would agree to deploy police to protect the women on the condition that the women arrive without prayer shawls or a Torah scroll, two essential components. (One can only imagine the outcry if a government anywhere around the world told Orthodox men that they were allowed to pray but only without a *tallit* or a Torah). The women agonized over their decision.

Nevertheless, the women eventually agreed to the terms—but things once again did not turn out as they expected. On that fateful morning, some 150 women arrived at the Kotel, supported by another hundred men, as the police tried to clear a path for them. Rows of Haredi men surrounded them, cursing and spitting at them. As the women began their prayers, men began hurling chairs and even tables at them. A woman was hit in the head and taken to the hospital. This time, however, the women were expecting to be helped by the police and called out for assistance. The police, however, stationed at the back of the plaza, remained unmoved, refusing to even get out of their vans. They watched the women being attacked—the women they were supposedly deployed to protect—and did nothing. Finally, after some twenty to thirty minutes of observing the attacks, the police decided to take action: they threw tear gas at the crowded wall. "I recall my first inhalation of the scorching gas, the burning in my throat, nose and eyes," Dr. Haberman recalled painfully. "Clutching my shirt and hat to my face, I regretted not having my *tallit* to enshroud me. Coughing and gagging, we retreated, horrified. We had been utterly betrayed."[9]

It is important to note that all this happened in 1989, before the Supreme Court issued any rulings about the Women of the Wall, before any women had been arrested, before the famous Anat Hoffman got involved with the group. It happened while the first George Bush was president, before any of us heard of the Internet, before there were cell phones and digital cameras. It happened before there were segregated buses in Israel and before Islamic terrorism was a blip on anyone's radar. My point is that intense antagonism against women's singing voices, women's prayer accoutrements, and women's ritual empowerment has been present in Israel for decades. Since its inception, the women have been pressured to avoid singing, to refrain from using a Torah scroll, and to leave their prayer shawls at home. The lack of opposition to this oppression of women is in essence an endorsement of it. It is a practice in which the most extremist and misogynistic interpretations of Jewish law are adapted by the powers that be. It's as if to say these are aspects of religious life that, when women engage in them, violate some kind of state law. And rather than showing signs of responsiveness to public outrage, the phenomenon is getting worse.

A nagging question is why, from a legal standpoint, this is allowed to happen, and the answer remains disturbingly unclear. The Western Wall is governed by an Israeli statute related to the administration of the holy places, explains Boston University law Professor Pnina Lahav. The Ministry of Religion has the authority to regulate holy places, under which the Ministry created a position called the Rabbi of the Wall. The rabbi does not create laws but can issue regulations. In the 1980s, the Rabbi of the Wall issued a vague regulation prohibiting any prayer that is not "in keeping" with Jewish custom (*minhag hamakom*). Since then, the men who have held the position of Kotel Rabbi have interpreted *minhag hamakom* according to the customs of the most extreme ultra-Orthodox groups. This means that prayers are segregated, that women have to dress modestly, and that women must refrain from ritual activity. "Put differently, the abused women, not the men and women who abuse them, are accused of breach of the peace," Lahav explains. "Thus in the clash between the worshippers' right not to be offended as they exercise their religion, and the right of WOW to free exercise of its form of religious worship, the worshippers (mostly men, backed by male rabbis) have the upper hand."[10]

Since its inception, WOW was a group that worked in tight partnership with American women, both those living in Israel and those living in the United States. Early on, WOW formed an American entity called the International Committee for the Women of the Wall (ICWOW), which included many active feminist and veteran civil rights activists, including Phyllis Chesler,

Rivka Haut, and others. "The ICWOW were ardent supporters of the State of Israel, and looked upon Israel as a progressive polity which shared American values and sensibilities," wrote Lahav. But the Committee did not fully appreciate the complexity of Israel's form of democracy, "where constitutionalism was only beginning to assert itself, and where orthodoxy was rather fundamentalist, patriarchal and in possession of political power."[11] Moreover, explains Lahav, "religious pluralism, while taken for granted in the United States, has been (and to a large degree still is) a marginal phenomenon in Israel, at least in the Jewish sector... Theories of feminism and gender equality have been slow to penetrate the Israeli consciousness. By 1988, when the violence against WOW began to escalate, the Israeli public was still hostile to feminism and most women felt an inner desire to keep their distance from it for their own safety."[12] For American women, accustomed to the language and practices of civil rights, these events woke up a need for justice and action against gender discrimination at this holy site.[13]

The abuse of women at the Kotel was initially based on "regulations" but not in any real law. Because of this, WOW decided to try to challenge the legality of these positions by petitioning the Israeli Supreme Court, a process that ultimately took the better part of fifteen years. The first round in the Supreme Court came shortly after the tear-gas event. In 1991, WOW petitioned the court to protect women's right to pray, as well as to provide the women with one of the many Torah scrolls that have a home at the Kotel and to create a protected space at the plaza for the women to pray in peace. Not a single member of the government supported the women's petition; rather, many very publicly sided with the Ministry of Religion. In addition, perhaps emboldened by the support, the Ministry hired female security guards to remove women from the Kotel if they "sing."

Over the years, while WOW members were doing their best to comply with orders not to sing—and at times being dragged away by guards—the legal system was joining arms with rabbinical leaders without any law experience recruited as "legal experts" in the validity of women's prayers. Not surprisingly, the supportive briefs submitted to the Supreme Court about why WOW should be banned came primarily from Orthodox rabbis: "This is an offense to all the righteous women of all the generations," wrote then-Sephardic Chief Rabbi Mordechai Eliyahu in his brief to the Court. "This is definitely the work of Satan," wrote then-Ashkenazi Chief Rabbi Avraham Shapira. "Never have we heard, never have we seen anything as strange as this since the time of Moses our Rabbi until today. The women...neglect their husbands and their children rather than helping their husbands, which is why they were created," wrote Rabbi Menashe Klein. "Women who are stubborn and who wish to fight and make changes are considered heretics who do not have a share in the world to come," wrote Rabbi Moshe Feinstein.[14]

"Although women are halachically permitted to touch, hold, and even read from a Torah, any gathering of women...is based on the desire to equate the status of women to that of men in the world of Jewish men...with an intention to make it seem that women are as important as men," wrote Professor Eliahu Schochetman, adding that such women are "heretic" and "desecrating holy places." Rabbi Herschel Schachter, who, like Rabbi Feinstein, lived in America and had no connection to the Israeli legal system, also submitted a brief in which he claimed that "the women's main motivation is to create something new for its own sake, to get newspaper publicity, glory, to be known as leaders, and sometimes just to rebel against tradition… It is our obligation to fix their souls, as the rabbis taught, 'Teach yourselves to be normal.'"[15] The irony inherent in the idea that it is "normal" and even praiseworthy in men to want to pray in a group, to sing to God, to read Torah, and to lead, but it's "abnormal" for women to want to do the same was completely lost on the brief authors as well as on the chief justices.

What is most astounding is that not a single one of these rabbinic opinions actually spoke to the law or even to Halacha. Rather, their responses were all based on societal views about the status of women in Israel. In fact, some, like Schochetman's, were even couched in admissions that the women's actions were completely in line with Jewish law. This utter lack of a legal basis for their claims and their conspicuous hostility toward women's religious empowerment proved that their opposition had nothing to do with religious law and everything to do with maintaining the comfortable status quo for men. Even the regulations invoked, "the custom of the place," are a euphemism for male authority over social practice, which has become the core rationale for oppressing women.

WOW, supported by their sister organization ICWOW, lost their petition. In 1994, the Supreme Court ruled against WOW, with only one of the three (male) justices supporting the women's rights to pray at the Kotel (Justice Shlomo Levin). Interestingly, Justice Menachem Elon, whose decision was against WOW, actually wrote a lengthy opinion in which he demonstrated that WOW had Halacha on their side. Nevertheless, the court did not uphold the idea of WOW's halachic legitimacy and threw the job back to the government rather than the courts: they recommended setting up a commission to resolve the issue.

Following that first court decision, WOW had legislative battles to defend while it requested to review the decision. The appointed commission, the Mancal Commission, was an all-male panel—not a Haredi panel but a modern, mostly secular panel—that was charged with coming up with a viable solution for WOW. The commission missed their first deadline, and then their extended deadline, and then their third deadline, while WOW and its sister organization ICWOW looked for ways to force the commission to make its recommendation. The Mancal Commission finally issued its report in April 1996, which looked at four possible locations, and proposed WOW be moved to the southeastern corner of Jerusalem, outside the Old City of Jerusalem in Arab East Jerusalem. WOW immediately appealed for a new commission, which took its time, while there were new elections in Israel that increased the number of ultra-Orthodox Knesset members. In March 1997, a day after the Supreme Court ordered the state to "show just cause about why Women of the Wall's lawsuit against the government should not succeed," members of the religious Shas party passed a Knesset bill in a preliminary vote that would turn the Kotel from a national site into an ultra-Orthodox syna- gogue. According to no. 1924, an amendment to the Holy Sites Law of 1967, a woman who read Torah or wore *tallit* or *tefillin* at the Kotel would be imprisoned for up to seven years.[16] Although the bill did not pass, it revealed the underlying intentions of the ultra-Orthodox powers that be and became a disturbing harbinger of things to come.

Finally, in May 2000, more than a decade after WOW first filed its suit, its hard work paid off. The Supreme Court issued a unanimous opinion in favor of WOW, arguing that the government has a responsibility to protect the women as they exercise their right to freedom of worship. However, in a bow to the Knesset politics (or perhaps out of loyalty to Shas legislators and cabinet members, in an act characteristic of the men's club that is so often Israeli politics), the Court did not actually provide a solution or demand immediate government action of any sort. Rather, it gave the government six months to make appropriate arrangements to implement the ruling. Just a month later, the attorney general petitioned the Court for a "further hearing." His petition was granted.

Despite the fact that the 2000 court decision was unanimous, the court appointed a nine-person panel to review the decision. And then, after nearly fifteen years in the courts, in 2003, a panel of nine judges ultimately ruled against Women of the Wall, five to four, on the grounds that WOW represented "a threat to public safety and order." The Court required the government to provide an alternate site, Robinson's Arch. The Ministerial Commission issued its report shortly thereafter, recommending that WOW be considered illegal, a report that was adopted by the state in its response to the Supreme Court. WOW was defeated, in both the judicial system and the legislative system, and the ultra-Orthodox politicians driven by radical views of women's role in public life, religion, and society at large won. They won not only the official battles, but also the surprising support of secular political leaders. WOW was up against a wall—literally and metaphorically—and had nowhere left to turn.

Frances Raday, the attorney representing WOW in the Supreme Court, said, "Robinson's Arch is not a site for communal prayer of the Jewish people. The decision that the Women of the Wall should pray at Robinson's Arch is therefore…a form of exclusion and banishment and so is certainly separate but in no way equal."[17] Bonna Devora Haberman added: "Robinson's Arch is a beautiful site; it is not the core of our collective gathering… Until women's voices, lives, bodies, work, and prayers are fully part, we will not be whole. Humanity will not be whole."[18]

This was not only disappointing, but also indicative of the corruption in the process. As Raday told me in an interview in May 2013, "There were four judges who had already ruled in WOW's favor, so we thought we were in a good position, but the secular Justice Cheshin was there, and he joined with Justice Barak and the two religious judges and one more, and that was the absolutely last judgment."[19] In other words, the real loss sadly for the women came not from the ultra-Orthodox men throwing chairs but from the secular Supreme Court male justices who supported the position of religious men. Once again, it's clear that the real threat to women's religious freedom in Israel is not from Haredi men but from powerful, secular men who give Haredim undeserved authority.

When WOW lost their legal battle, ultra-Orthodox leaders with radical antiwomen views were effectively empowered by both the legislative and judicial branches of government. The concept that women's voices of prayer are "offensive" morphed into the principle that they are now officially "illegal." In a disturbing irony, Israel became the first country in the history of the modern world to penalize Jewish women for praying together. One can only imagine how such laws would have played out in other modern Western democracies, if it became illegal for a certain group of Jews to hold prayers at a spot designated for prayer. There would certainly be outrage, mass protest, and indignant cries of anti-Semitic discrimination and biased, hate-based regulations.

Yet here in the modern Jewish state in the twenty-first century, there is now a Supreme Court ruling that declares that women may not violate the *minhag hamakom* and that it is up to the ultra-Orthodox, unelected, unregulated Religious Ministry appointee—that is, the Kotel administrator—to determine what constitutes such custom. In other words, this one man has the power to single-handedly decide how Jewish women in Israel are allowed to pray in public. He also has the power to dictate to the Israeli police force what counts as legal and illegal at Judaism's holiest site and to order them to enforce that. An unbridled religious radicalism won out over forces of democracy and basic fairness to women.

Nevertheless, following the court ruling, WOW continued to hold its monthly meetings and tried to comply with the regulations. When Robinson's Arch was opened in 2004, they began meeting there. They would start the service at the Western Wall, wearing their prayer shawls as scarves so as not to cause any offense, singing quietly through the service, and then moving to Robinson's Arch when it was time to begin the Torah reading part of the service. The violence against them quieted down, and they continued to hold their monthly meetings with their new guidelines. It was not ideal for WOW, but they were doing everything they could to comply while retaining the integrity of their own prayer services.

In November 2009, the détente between WOW and the Kotel rabbi began to show signs of cracking. For no apparent reason, the police suddenly began arresting women. Nofrat Frenkel, a fifth-year medical student, was arrested while praying with the Women of the Wall. Her crime? Wearing a *tallit*. It is not clear, explained

Lahav, "whether the police were given the green light to tighten the rope around WoW and, if so, by whom."[20] There had never been arrests before, but someone had clearly given the police free rein to raise the stakes in the battle to stop Women of the Wall.

The abuse continued—as did the arrests—even as the women continued to try to comply with the court's rulings. "We were forbidden to continue praying with ritual objects, forbidden to read from the Torah in the women's section," Nofrat Frenkel later described. The women would wear their *tallitot* under their coats so as not to offend anyone. The Torah scroll was hidden until the group was ready to move to Robinson's Arch. "We were allocated another space, away from the main Kotel plaza, a place for second-class citizens, in which we could pray without, God forbid, forcing the offended public to be exposed to the brutal sight of women performing the mitzvahs of tzitzit and reading the Torah."[21]

Then, on the morning of Rosh Hodesh Kislev, something suddenly changed. As Nofrat Frenkel, the medical student who was arrested at the Wall, wrote:

> *As we were exiting [the main square to go to Robinson's Arch] with me carrying the Torah, a policeman met us and began forcefully pushing me toward the nearby police station. Our pleas and explanations that we were on our way to the alternative site were of no use. I was transferred for questioning to the station at David's Citadel. All I had on me was my* tallit, *my siddur, and a Sefer Torah. In my interrogation, I was asked why I was praying with a* tallit *when I knew that this was against the Law of the Holy Places. I am an Israel Defense Forces officer, a law-abiding citizen, a volunteer for the Civil Guard—I have never incurred even a parking fine—and the*

idea of having broken the law was most trying... I was banned
from visiting the Kotel for two weeks, and a criminal file has
been opened against me.[22]

Frenkel's arrest was just the beginning. In January 2010, WOW's leader, Anat Hoffman, was detained by the police. "It is unthinkable that a citizen of the State of Israel is arrested for donning a prayer shawl and holding a scroll," Hoffman declared. "There were hundreds of people on the other side of the screen who did the same and nothing happened to them."[23] Despite the outcry—most of which interestingly came from American Jews rather than from Israelis—Anat Hoffman was arrested in July for bringing a Torah scroll to the site of the Wall. The police treated Hoffman with particularly strong force, pulling the Torah out of her arms as the group was exiting the Kotel to go to Robinson's Arch.

"We were not reading from the Torah," Hoffman told me that day shortly after her arrest. "We were merely holding it on our way to Robinson's Arch to complete the service." I then spoke to the spokesman for the Israeli police, Micky Rosenfeld, who said, "Anat Hoffman was arrested by police because she violated the agreement of the high court by praying with a Sefer Torah." The event was captured on video and shows clearly that Anat Hoffman and 150 worshippers were carrying the Torah on their way to Robinson's Arch when she was arrested. The ensuing arrest is not a pretty sight. But for anyone who believes in the holiness of the Torah, it is actually very painful to watch. According to Michelle Handelman, a Georgia State University graduate and immigrant to Israel, the gathering was "relatively calm" until Anat Hoffman took the Torah out. Then a dozen officers started to pull the

Torah out of Hoffman's hands in a wild scuffle caught on video that is chilling to anyone who values human dignity or the sanctity of the Torah. "The Torah looked like it was about to tear apart," Handelman said. "It was shocking."[24]

Rabbi Steven Wernick, executive vice president and CEO of the United Synagogue of Conservative Judaism, who was at the prayer service, said, "It was just heart-wrenching to watch a Jewish woman arrested, on Rosh Hodesh, for holding a Torah in her prayer service. And it's unfathomable that the police in the Jewish state will arrest a Jewish woman for that."[25] After a five-hour interrogation, Hoffman was fined $1,300 and banned from the Kotel for thirty days.

The arrests continued every month after that for more than two years, and women were arraigned for "disturbing the peace," fined thousands of shekels, and banned from the Kotel for different periods of time. "Frankly, I don't know why they started to arrest us," WOW board member Peggy Cidor told me. "We do not know for sure, but we believe that it was [Kotel administrator Rabbi Shmuel] Rabinowitz's initiative, who apparently couldn't allow the relative calm at the Kotel during our tefillah and felt the urge to remind us all he has the power."[26]

Rabbi Rabinowitz, who had been leading a campaign to make the entire plaza gender-segregated, said that the women were being "provocative, trying to turn the Kotel into a place of controversy." He later told the *New York Times* that the Kotel "is not a site for any kind of protest" and "not a place for the individual, where everyone can do what they want."[27] In addition, Anat Hoffman "violated the ruling by praying with a Torah," police spokesman Rosenfeld told me, adding, "Read the court protocol."[28]

I did. The forty-nine-page 2003 Supreme Court decision is

vague on this point, mostly pointing toward *minhag hamakom*. Hoffman maintains that while reading from the Torah is banned for women at the main Kotel plaza, merely holding the Torah is not. "The police took it upon themselves to reinterpret the ruling—and that is a very dangerous development," she said. "It's a slippery slope. Today they say women cannot hold the Torah. Tomorrow it will be women cannot look at the Torah. Then it will be women cannot be at the Kotel at all. Before you know it, all of Jerusalem will be segregated. That is where we are headed."[29]

Since the first arrest, there has been a growing public outcry in favor of WOW, yet the police have only intensified their actions against the women. As is often the case for women in extremely religious societies around the world, the more progress the women of WOW made, the more backlash they experienced from religious radicals.

As the arrests kept occurring—and started to get worse—American Jews and Israeli Jews began to take a growing interest in what was happening. This was part of the growing awareness in Israel that WOW is fighting for basic human rights that should concern each and every citizen of Israel and the world. Police began confiscating the ritual shawls and phylacteries of women as they entered the Kotel plaza.

This spreading awareness was just in time. In October 2012, the arrest *again* of Anat Hoffman—in what was to become one of more than thirty events in which WOW members were arrested—took on particularly ominous tones. As Daphna Berman described in her profile of Anat Hoffman in *Moment* magazine in February 2013, "She gathered to pray at the Wall with 250 Hadassah women from the United States as part of [Hadassah's] centennial birthday." This gathering also included three IDF veterans who had wrested the Wall from the Jordanians in 1967, a huge form of symbolic support in the Israeli consciousness. "[The group was] reciting the Shema prayer when a police officer separated Hoffman from the group...and arrested her. Although never charged with a crime, over the next twenty-four hours, she says, she was handcuffed, strip-searched, shackled, dragged on the floor, and forced to spend a night in a tiny cell in Jerusalem's Russian Compound prison, alongside a car thief, a prostitute, and a woman who was charged with hiding evidence of child abuse in an ultra-Orthodox polygamous sect. A police spokesman called the allegations 'not accurate and not right.'"[30]

When the American groups and Israeli veterans began joining WOW, public opinion in America and in Israel began to shift as well. A few months later, three female Knesset Members—Stav Shaffir, Michal Rozin, and Tamar Zandberg—also began joining the group, and because of their parliamentary immunity, they could not be arrested for wearing a *tallit*. The group thought that perhaps this signaled real change. Dahlia Lithwick of *Slate*, who joined the group in February 2013 after twenty-two consecutive months of arrests, wrote, "It looked as though arrests wouldn't happen this month." But such was not to be the case. Ten women were arrested.[31]

In February 2013, the arrested women included Rabbi Susan Silverman, sister of comedienne Sarah Silverman, and her seventeen-year-old daughter Hallel. They were held and inter- rogated and barred from returning to the site for fifteen days. "So proud of my amazing sister and niece for their balls-out civil disobedience," Sarah Silverman tweeted.

Like in so many other aspects of increasing violence against women, here, too, Haredi justification of violence against women tries to blame the women. Rabbi Shmuel Rabinowitz continuously blames the women for disrupting the unity of Israel and causing conflict—as if women's prayer was the offensive, disruptive act, rather than other worshippers' throwing chairs or spitting at them. Rabbi Avi Shafran of the ultra-Orthodox Agudath Israel of America called WOW "guerillas" and "political agitators." He then made the argument that Haredi men are "allergic" to WOW and non-Haredi practices, like a school child who is allergic to peanut butter and around whom fellow students must refrain from eating or using peanut butter. "A Halacha-abiding man may not be literally allergic to women's chanting. But in a way he is."[32] Once again, we hear a twisted rhetoric justifying the exclusion of women, as if it is legitimate for a man to be "allergic" to the sound of a woman's voice, as if women's voices are "poison" to the rest of society. If one were to replace the word "woman" with the word "Jew," I wonder whether Shafran would be so quick to consider that a legitimate line of thinking.

The claim that the status quo must be maintained is also flawed at its core. "There is no status quo at the Wall," Anat Hoffman wrote in 2010. "Things change all the time. Men and women used to enter the Western Wall plaza together through the Jewish Quarter's Dung Gate; in 1994, separate, gender-segregated entrances were created. Within the past decade, women soldiers were still allowed to sing the national anthem during ceremonies at the Wall—now they are instructed to be content with mouthing the words." She added that even the police attitude toward women continually changes. "If you want a quick lesson on the growing gender segregation and discrimination in Israel, I suggest taking a look at the policies in place at the Western Wall, which are being constantly revised to deny women equal access at this sacred space. Things have changed tremendously in my 21 years of going to pray with Women of the Wall every Rosh Hodesh."[33]

In addition, there is now more forced separation between men and women. The main entrance gates to the Kotel have been rebuilt and now have large signs for "men" and "women" and another sign on the side that reads "the segregation continues beyond the security checkpoint." Also, it's not clear why, but women are strongly discouraged from going to the northern side of the Kotel plaza during festival times—the area that also happens to have the restrooms, including women's restrooms. Segregation is extended during the holidays beyond the entrance and exit to the buses, and there are "modesty guards" on the buses, a direct violation of the law.

The situation continued to worsen. In April 2013, the police announced new measures: women would be arrested if any of them said the Kaddish mourning prayer, one of the prayers that requires a quorum and which WOW officially does not do. The outcry that followed was significant in that it came from an Israeli public, for whom reciting mourners' Kaddish is a sacred act. Even in Orthodox synagogues where women do not count for a minyan, women are often allowed to recite Kaddish as men answer. Even secular Israelis who had not taken an interest in WOW until then started to speak out. *Ynet* columnist Arianna Melamed wrote following the Kaddish announcement that "it's time for Women of the Wall to start breaking the law."[34] Following the outcry, Rabinowitz announced that "no women will be arrested for saying Kaddish."[35] The arrests promptly stopped. This was an enormous moment for WOW, who had never seen any kind of backtracking from Rabinowitz. This statement made two things clear: Rabinowitz truly was pulling the strings of the police, and the public anger was starting to have its impact.

For twenty-five years, while WOW were being harassed and then arrested, the prime ministers remained silent. But in December 2013, that chapter came to a close as Prime Minister Benjamin Netanyahu announced that he was appointing the high-profile, universally adored former prisoner of conscience Natan Sharansky to find a solution to the problem. Significantly, Netanyahu made this announcement in English in the *New York Times*—in other words, Americans found out about it before Israelis did. This indicates that he was responding less to Israeli pressure and more to American pressure. That's good news for Americans who may wonder if they have any impact on civil rights in Israel, although it is perhaps less good news for WOW supporters in Israel who may feel powerless to impact their own leader without international voices.

Perhaps Netanyahu realized that notions of religious freedom are more deeply entrenched into American life than Israeli life. As American Rabbi Elyse Frishman, one of the four women arrested in December 2012 for wearing a *tallit*, said, "This is really an issue of religious freedom, and this understanding that within Judaism that there's more than one path to God... And this sense of rigidity and of gender distinction and of discrimination is something that's absolutely intolerable."[36] Alternatively, this had more to do with Netanyahu's relationship with American Jewry than with women's rights. Or as Jodi Rudoren wrote in the *New York Times*, "This has deepened a divide between the Jewish state and the Jewish diaspora, in which some leaders have become increasingly vocal in criticizing Israel's policies on settlements in the Palestinian territories; laws and proposals that are seen as antidemocratic or discriminatory against Arab citizens; the treatment of women; and the ultra-Orthodox control over conversion and marriage."[37]

Sharansky's work coincided with increased activism in America as well. A prayer group in solidarity with WOW met in New York in March 2013 and had several hundred worshippers. Similar solidarity meetings have been held all around North America with significant media coverage. All major American news outlets ran stories in 2013 about WOW, and the international outrage seemed to contribute to the urgency of Sharansky's task.

Sharansky came out with a proposal in April 2013 that was intended to create a pluralistic space at the Kotel. His proposal was to expand the Kotel so that Robinson's Arch is part of the main plaza and then convert the archaeological site into an extended plaza that will be used by non-Orthodox groups in prayer. The plan was initially greeted with excitement by many groups that felt that there would now be real religious pluralism in Israel at the Kotel. Rabbi Rick Jacobs of United Reform Judaism threw his support behind the proposal, calling it a "unique opportunity" for the Jewish people.[38] Netanyahu also expressed support for it, as did many WOW supporters initially it. Even Rabinowitz initially supported it.

The support quickly gave way, however, to other concerns. In addition to being expensive, unfeasible, and destructive of antiquities, it also maintained the idea that non-Orthodox practice is outside of the norm of Judaism. With this proposal, Women of the Wall were uniformly cast as non-Orthodox, despite the fact that many of its members and founders are Orthodox women seeking a space for an all-women's prayer group—a practice that has been part of Orthodox life for over thirty years. The proposal also did not address the needs of the women praying in the current women's section. Women praying at the Kotel with a *tallit* or Torah were still subject to harassment by the Haredi public and arrest by the Israeli police. "For me, it's not a solution," Orthodox WOW board member Leora Bechor told the press. "As Orthodox women, all we are asking for is to give us our space where we can feel comfortable eleven hours of the years—eleven and not twelve because we don't hold our service on Rosh Hashanah."[39] In other words, according to his plan, a women's tefillah group would be lumped together with mixed egalitarian groups, and an all-women's group in the women's section at the Kotel would still be an arrestable offense.[40]

At one point, Anat Hoffman offered a much simpler solution. At a lecture at a conference of the Hadassah Brandeis Institute in April 2013, she suggested making a removable partition, so that parts of the day are segregated and parts of the day are mixed. But so far nobody in any position of influence on the Kotel seems to have heard.

Somehow amid all the useless commissions and Supreme Court petitions fluttering around WOW, one woman in Jerusalem changed everything. For the first time since women started being arrested at the Wall, the charges were thrown out. On April 10, 2013, around the same time that Sharansky was releasing his proposal, five women who were arrested for disturbing the peace at the Kotel came before Judge Sharon Lary-Bavly, who had the prescience to say that arresting these women "is likened to blaming a rape victim for the clothing that she wears."[41] After twenty-five years of suffering misogynistic abuse at the hands of religious radicals, abuse supported by a secular court system and legislature, one judge had the power and the courage to say that it is not the women who are at fault for disturbing the peace but rather those who abuse them. The appellate court upheld the ruling, effectively reversing everything that WOW had been experiencing for twenty-five years.

The women of WOW were ecstatic. In May 2013, they finally prayed as they wanted, with song, with prayer shawls, and with a Torah. It was going to be a victory celebration. For the first time, police could be seen actually protecting the women rather than protecting the Haredi men. Several Haredi men who had thrown chairs were arrested. It was a complete reversal of everything that WOW had experienced. As Yair Ettinger blasted in *Haaretz*, "On 1st of Sivan, 5773, Women of the Wall became a legitimate stream of Judaism."[42]

But the battle is not yet over, the drama still unfolding as I write these words. Because as we've seen happen with religious extremism, the greater the threat, the more extreme the response. The Haredi community decided to bus in six thousand young women, eighteen-year-old seminary students, to protest that day. And so, while police were protecting WOW, seminary students were standing around in protest. But the real violence came from rock-throwing Haredi men.[43] Haviva Ner-David, who introduced me to WOW in 1998, was at the Kotel that day with some friends and some of her children, and her twelve-year-old daughter was hit in the head with a rock. "It was really scary," she told me later. "I've been to scary protests before but not like this." Her daughter is okay, physically at least, but the battle is far from over.

And then came a dramatic turn of events that altered the history of the organization: Anat Hoffman announced that Women of the Wall would accept Sharansky's proposal. And the Orthodox women on the WOW board revolted. A group of WOW women formed a new splinter group, Original Women of the Wall (OWOW), which announced its commitment to remaining at the current Kotel plaza rather than Robinson's Arch.[44] "We, the Original Women of the Wall (OWOW), will continue to pray in the Ezrat Nashim because our hearts and our heads tell us this is right for us, the State of Israel, and the People of Israel," Susan Aranoff wrote in *Times of Israel*. "The courts of Israel have recognized the validity of OWOW's aspirations three times and strengthened our resolve. The Court of Three Strands Will Not Be Quickly Broken."[45] And so the saga continues.

The story of Women of the Wall illustrates some key issues underlying the increasing empowerment of religious radicalism in Israel, an otherwise democratic society. Take, for example, the fact that throughout this twenty-five-year saga, as abuse against women of prayer turned into violence, there were no arrests against the perpetrators of this violence. In addition, it is telling that the entire discussion of *minhag hamakom* never questioned whether verbal or physical abuse of these women constitutes an offense to someone's prayer or violates the sanctity of the place. In fact, this failure to address that could be seen as condoning the abuse itself. These questions demonstrate how certain ideas held by a small but vocal extremist group can become accepted when they are given support (or at least aren't denounced) by a secular, liberal political system. In this same way, when women have no political power, their customs, traditions, ideas, and spiritual needs are invisible.

The truly disturbing question, however, is not why ultra-Orthodoxy demands extreme measures like the treatment of the WOW women to uphold its beliefs but rather why the Israeli police and the government have then taken these demands more or less as the law. The idea that an extreme version of Judaism practiced by a small minority can come to be considered important enough to support with the entire law force of a seemingly democratic state—even to the detriment of the majority of citizens—is nothing less than frightening.

Chapter 5

WAR WITHIN THE RANKS: RELIGION AND GENDER ISSUES IN THE ISRAEL DEFENSE FORCES

When twenty-five-year-old Shani Boianjiu served as an infantry instructor in the Israel Defense Forces, her job occasionally involved having to touch other soldiers—teaching her students how to hold a gun correctly, how to lie on the ground in position, or how to protect themselves from enemy attack. Although this was an acceptable part of the job and made her an excellent instructor, it also caused problems for certain soldiers, specifically religious ones.[1]

In an essay in the *New York Times* in September 2012, Boianjiu described the first time this happened. She was teaching a soldier to sit correctly in the field. "I came up behind him and put both hands on his shoulders, gently shaking him. I wanted to explain, 'Look how easy it is for me to shake you out of position,' but I couldn't, because the soldier was yelling at me like he was on fire. I couldn't make out what he was saying, but he was still in training and I was shocked by his disobedience. I thought maybe he was confused, so I bent down in the sand and grabbed his foot, moving it so that his toes pointed forward. If anything, he screamed louder. It was only when the drill ended that I caught what he was saying: 'I observe touch.' What this meant was that he couldn't touch or be touched by girls or women. I was his superior and trainer, but I was also a girl."[2]

Female soldiers have made tremendous strides in the IDF over the past two decades. According to the IDF spokesperson's office, women make up 33 percent of the IDF, female officers with the rank of colonel doubled from 2 percent in 1999 to 4 percent today, and the percentage of female officers with the rank of lieutenant colonel has grown by 70 percent in the last decade, from 7.3 percent in 1999 to 12.5 percent today. Moreover, over half of all soldiers in officer courses are women. During the last three years, an average of 55 percent of all staff officers in the Officers' Training Course were women, an average of 53 percent of those OTC graduates went on to become officers in combat support positions, and an average of 3 percent of all combat officers were women. Perhaps most significantly, in March 2011, the IDF appointed Brigadier General Orna Barbivai as the first-ever female major general.[3]

From the statistics, it's clear that women are still a small minority of officers, though their numbers are rising. But as a country with mandatory conscription since its founding in 1948—the only country in the world in which women are also subject to this conscription—these advances for women are significant. Gone are the days when women in the army are relegated to jobs of making coffee and typing men's memos. Also, even though, according to the IDF, women only serve in 69 percent of the 93 percent of all roles that are open to them, they are present in far more areas of the Israeli military than ever before.[4]

But as Shani Boianjiu's example shows, women's advances are also potentially problematic for religious men. And this could signal the beginning of a troubling trend for women in the army.

Women's advancement would be on a positive trajectory except for the fact that there is increasing pressure in Israel to recruit

Haredi men to the army. The call was especially pronounced during the January 2013 elections by Yair Lapid's new Yesh Atid Party, which won a surprising nineteen seats (16 percent) under the banner of "sharing the burden"—a reference to making Haredi men serve in the army and work. Haredi men have benefitted until recently from the IDF exemption called the Tal Law that enabled men to be full-time students of Torah rather than become soldiers. The Tal Law expired in August 2012, and the government is currently scrambling to figure out what to do with these men now.

Haredi conscription is a hot-potato issue in Israeli political life and discourse. Coalition talks initially stalled in large part because of disagreement over Haredi army service. In fact, Lapid's insistence that "sharing the burden" is nonnegotiable eventually kept Haredi parties out of the government for the first time in thirty years.

The tension surrounding Haredi men's conscription is not without good reason. The issues dividing Haredi men from the rest of the country are economic and cultural. The economic burden of the Haredi men's exemption, which comes with a whole series of government stipends as described in the introduction, is a cause of major resentment among secular Israelis. That economic resentment is compounded by a more visceral resentment based on the fact that some people are forced to risk their lives while others are not. Average Israelis give two to three years of their lives to the army, at key ages—eighteen to twenty-one. So while American kids are off to college and starting careers and building their lives, Israelis are wearing uniforms and guarding borders—or worse, sacrificing themselves in war—while they put their own lives on hold. Then there is reserve duty. All soldiers are supposed to do reserve duty until their early forties, although in practice, the burden falls on some 23 percent who serve more than twenty-seven days a year.[5] Imagine picking up for one month a year every year, leaving your job and your family to sleep in a tent and guard an outpost in the desert. So it's no wonder that Israelis feel a little resentful that a whole group gets an exemption in which they do not have to work or fight but can sit and read Talmud all day.

At a symposium of the Open University on gender and religion in the IDF, Brigadier General Hadass Ben-Eliyahu of the Center for the Advancement of Women in the Public Sphere at the Van Leer Institute explained that many groups are pressing to recruit Orthodox men without considering the impact on women.[6] Beyond the Tal Law, there are strong economic, political, religious, military, social, and cultural pressures relating to the recruitment of ultra-Orthodox men into the IDF.

There is mounting pressure to recruit religious men into their own specially designed units within a special program called Shahar in which the Haredi soldiers will have all their cultural and religious needs met. And right now, the army and the government are trying to figure out just how complicated those needs might be. In March 2013, the army produced the first issue of its signature magazine, *Bamachane*, aimed at Haredi men. The editors of the magazine, which included articles by rabbis permitting army service and interviews with wives of soldiers, did what they thought would appeal to Haredi recruits: they removed all photos of women.[7]

One of the driving points behind Haredi opposition to serving in the army has always had to do with women. Army life has commonly been perceived in the religious world as a place of sexual danger and secular temptation. Haredi men who serve in the army are often derided in their communities as *hardakim*, both an acronym for Haredim *kalei da'at* ("frivolous ultra-Orthodox") and a play on the Hebrew word for insects, *harakim*. Flyers demonstrating opposition to Haredi recruitment claim that these men "replaced their identity with the army and national service."[8] Behind this rhetoric, the real accusation is that their willingness to engage in activities where women are present is a negation of their entire identity. If one point becomes clear from this entire book, it is how much separation from women is increasingly a key element of identity for religious Jewish men. It seems like religious men are increasingly unable to reconcile the idea of working alongside women and maintaining their identity as religious—and that has serious implications for both sexes.

What's interesting is that the exemption of Haredi men is actually a reversal of the original system. In the early days of the State of Israel, this threat of "mingling" between the sexes was thought to endanger women more than men. In fact, although women have been drafted to the army since the beginning of the state, women were the first ones to receive exemptions on religious grounds, and since 1948, religious women have received an easy exemption— religious Zionist women have an option of serving one or two years in National Service duty in places like hospitals, schools, and welfare organizations, while ultra-Orthodox women can receive a complete exemption. The rationale for this has always been a form of "protection" of women from sexual "dangers."

Still, just because they were drafted does not mean that rabbis approve. In 1951, both chief rabbis of Israel ruled that "the drafting of women, even single, into the military system, in any sort of manner, is absolutely prohibited."[9] In 2011, the Chief Rabbinate republished the official position of women in national service that had been circulating for several decades—written originally in the 1980s by then Chief Rabbi Avraham Shapira—a position that women's army service is against Halacha: "We should not make peace with a situation in which one third of all female graduates of state religious schools are recruited into the army, and we must therefore 'attack' the issue at its core... The girls of Israel should be educated to withstand temptation, to retain a pure mouth, and avoid sins of being alone in the presence of men, and forbidden sexual relations."[10] Women who are drafted are assumed to be at risk of committing those sins of "impurity" based on uncontrolled sexuality. In fact, in January 2014, the Chief Rabbinate reissued the ruling prohibiting young women from enlisting in the IDF.[11] This time, they added something new: they categorized the prohibition as "*yehareg v'al ya'avor*" (better to be killed than to perform the transgression).[12] That is, even if someone holds a gun to a young woman's head and says, "either enlist or you will die," the rabbis are telling the woman that it is better to die than to enlist. Up until now, over the past two thousand years of Jewish legal history, there have been only three transgressions in this category of "*yehareg v'al ya'avor*": murder, idolatry, and incest. Now, women's enlistment has suddenly been included in that category of the most heinous of transgressions. The rabbinic assumption is that the very act of enlisting brings about a sexual transgression akin to incest.

In the state religious school system, there is tremendous pressure on girls to do national service instead of army service. Arguments that army service is against Halacha for women are cited in discussions in girls' religious high schools, in synagogue talks, in discussion by other rabbis, in religious chat groups, in blogs, and more. The perception in many Orthodox settings is that women's army service signals that a girl is "less religious." There's discouragement in some places and outright disapproval in others: Of the 120 registered high schools for girls, only forty even allow army representatives on campus, and some of the schools that do ask applicants to sign a commitment that they will not wear pants or join the army.[13] Only half of the religious girls "drafted" actually serve.

Indeed, the rabbinic pressure to keep religious girls from serving in the army remains fierce. In January 2014, the chief rabbi of Safed, Rabbi Shmuel Eliyahu, stated his opinion in a widely circulated letter: "Military service exposes the girls to situations that are not appropriate, that harm the girls religiously, emotionally, and unfortunately also sometimes physically. [It] is not appropriate for a Jewish female... We wish to emphasize the total prohibition against girls going into the army... We recommend that educational institutions not open their doors to organizations encouraging military service and call upon everyone to reinforce the girls' desire and need to serve the people and the land through sanctity... In addition, we are establishing an entity that will come to the schools and explain to the girls about the dangers lurking for them in military service."[14]

The IDF was particularly unimpressed by the position of Eliyahu and others, claiming that a line had been crossed. "As long as the army has a dispute with the rabbis over the drafting of girls, so be it, but the moment that an official entity of the State of Israel, on official stationery, tells a state educational institution you shouldn't let the army or any other civilian entity provide an explanation regarding the service options, that goes beyond the legitimate dispute," a senior army spokesperson told *Haaretz*.[15] Finance Minister Yair Lapid also called on the chief rabbis to step down because of these statements. Yet, the ire of IDF officials and the finance minister seem to have little impact. Even Lapid's number two in his party, Education Minister Rabbi Shai Piron, supported the chief rabbis and announced that women should not serve in the IDF.[16]

In addition, this figure that only forty religious girls' schools allow IDF representatives to speak was worrying to the IDF, which does not like people trying to get out of service—even women. In fact, the army has always wanted women and encouraged them in their service, especially religious women. Since 2008, the army has been initiating programs to attract religious girls, such as fast-track engineering programs for religious girls that include receiving a degree (an attractive proposition when one has an eye on early marriage and may also want to serve wearing a skirt). There is an entire organization, Aluma, dedicated to attracting religious young women. The IDF said back in 2008, long before any discussion about the Tal Law expiration and integrating Haredi men into the army, that they were willing to accommodate the needs of religious girls in the army in order to help gain more recruits.[17] For now, the work to recruit more religious women is being done quietly, without much fuss and possibly with some success.[18]

Still, it is unclear how much these initiatives have impacted the discussions at high schools. The pressure on religious girls to avoid the army and do national service remains fierce. Rabbinic opposition remains strong too. "There is no rabbi that would give outright approval for this," said "Anna," a religious woman serving in the Intelligence Corps, skirt and all, in 2012. "Religious girls serving in the army are not exactly a common thing. From my entire school class, I am the only one."[19]

Indeed, while in 2008, the IDF was citing a 55 percent draft rate for religious girls, by 2012, it was 45 percent. This drop is likely an indicator of increasing fundamentalism throughout the religious world, perhaps a response to all the language of modesty and pressure on girls to be more devout—which includes marrying young and avoiding army service. But "Anna" is proud and happy in her service. "Religious army service is the call of the hour, in my opinion. In addition to the challenge and struggle, the girls who get drafted will live with secular Jews in the future. It's inevitable that you'll meet people with different lifestyles—religious, secular, girls, boys—so it's a great way to learn to see everyone as equal."[20]

While religious young women grapple with pressure within their own communities to avoid the "sin" of army service, the issue of the "sin" of army for religious men has taken much larger proportions in Israel. First, the rhetoric for men to avoid army service is also many decibels louder than the rhetoric for women. For instance, Rabbi Aharon Leib Shteinman, the spiritual mentor of the United Torah Judaism ultra-Orthodox political party, and the late Rabbi Ovadia Yosef of the ultra-Orthodox party Shas vehemently opposed universal draft legislation. In January 2012, Yosef declared that ultra-Orthodox yeshiva students may have to leave Israel rather than serve in the army. "We are surrounded by haters…by enemies…by evildoers who despise the Torah," he told his followers.[21]

In a similar manner, "there is no room for compromise," said Rabbi Israeli Zikerman at a rally protesting the draft of Haredi men, "just like you cannot compromise by having one eye plucked out instead of two. No child of ours will go to the army. We would rather go to prison." Another speaker said that the rally should have taken place inside an army base, as "soldiers know that we are the ones protecting them with our studies and prayer."[22]

For religious soldiers who are serving—even those who do not identify as Haredi but as religious Zionist—there is still a perception that the army is a sinful place. Like Boianjiu's recruits, many religious men are taught that they must avoid certain behaviors, such as being touched by a woman, hearing a woman sing, looking at women, and more. Boianjiu recalls her shock upon discovering her students walked out of her lecture on the topic of grenade launchers when she brought an actual grenade launcher to class to demonstrate how to use it. "The moment I touched the weapon, one of the soldiers got up from his chair and left," she recalled. It seems that the vision of women handling weapons such as grenades is considered by some rabbis to have sexual connotations. For some men, sitting in this class was akin to watching pornography. "Soon, the room was filled with the sound of scraping chairs. I proceeded with my lesson plan until I was left alone with one bespectacled soldier, who had been furiously taking notes. It was only when I stopped talking that he looked up, horrified to find that the two of us were alone."[23]

Boianjiu is not alone. As the changes in the Tal Law have placed pressure on the army to absorb religious men and adapt to their needs, the real threat toward women in the IDF has started too as this pressure mounts. According to retired General Avi Zamir, some religious recruits have been imposing a whole series of requests—or perhaps demands—on the army. Before his 2011 retirement as head of personnel in the IDF, Zamir presented the chief of staff with a document outlining some of the requests that were heard: removing women from visible posts because of modesty, preventing women from performing formal functions at ceremonies (and not just singing), prohibiting women from being infantry instructors, forcing women to attend private classes so as not to "distract" male soldiers from study, and more.

The document, which was exposed in *Haaretz* in 2011, is rife with troubling examples of religious male soldiers demanding that the IDF move women around for the men's religious needs. One female officer who graduated with honors was refused entry into the elite unit that she was meant to attend because the commanding officer did not want women as officers in his unit. Women were removed as instructors following complaints from religious soldiers. In some instances, soldiers refused to take orders from their female infantry instructors (like Boianjiu). Discussions were being held about limiting the roles of women in armory. In the Intelligence Corps, women were asked to teach only while standing behind a desk in order to keep a kind of "partition" between them. Religious soldiers complained that the counselors in charge of their terms of service were women. Sociologist Yagil Levy, commenting on the Zamir document, said that there is a critical mass of religious soldiers in the field who have intensified demands on gender culture in the army, and the officers are paralyzed in dealing with them. He wrote that, General Barbivai's promotion notwithstanding, "the status of women in the army has been declining. In the ensuing discourse, women are presented as an obstacle to modesty that must be minimized." Barbivai, he said, is "a general without female soldiers." Zamir warned that the army has to take measures to prevent "the takeover by religious radicalism" in the army.[24]

Barbivai, for her part, has actually been very vocal on this point and is one of the strongest advocates for the idea that Haredi induction must not come at the expense of women. "With the understanding that 30% of first-grade pupils in Israel are ultra-Orthodox, the army has to plan ahead and ensure its ability to draft both men and women in a way that will enable the army to carry out its assignments," she told the *Los Angeles Times.* "Combining the ultra-Orthodox drafts with meaningful service for women will take careful, wise implementation and require a balance between the draft and universal values of equality. These values go beyond the specific issue of religious men. The task is to create conditions that allow men and women to share any environment effectively, not only a combat environment."[25]

Despite this advocacy, the document was not met with tremendous enthusiasm by the military brass. Some accused Zamir of his own political motives upon retirement. "Where has he been the past four years?" one general asked. "These issues were under his jurisdiction." Others claim that the portrait he painted was not nuanced enough and did not take into account the variations of religious observance. And of course there were those who tried to paint moral equivalency between the desires of women to be equals and the desires of others to keep women out. "It's all political," one reserve officer said derisively, "with feminist professors on one side and rabbis on the other. We're talking about operational units. Can this work or not?"[26] So much for a moral code.

This religious radicalization is undoubtedly impacting army functioning too. According to retired Brigadier General Zeev Lehrer, who served on the chief of staff's panel on the integration of women, "There is a clear process of 'religionization' in the army, and the story of the women is a central piece of it. There are very strong pressures at work to halt the process of integrating women into the army, and they are coming from the direction of religion."[27]

"It is clear that the more religious men serve, the more of gender segregation practices we will see," Hadass Ben-Eliyahu said. "Not only separate units, but also separate tasks, what kinds of jobs are

open, entire units or structures that are closed to women."[28] All
of this will undoubtedly cause strain on the army functioning.
Creating separate, segregated units for the men requires increased
personnel and budgets, as well as allocated "gender-pure" spaces
for the men. This has an impact across the army—in the kitchen
and dining room, where staff have to run double shifts to accommodate men; in training, where staff have to rearrange schedules
around the gender of the teachers; and even in the setup of the
camp, where consideration has to be given to creating female-free
zones. This is a big, costly nuisance. But mostly, it creates a terrible
atmosphere for women who, regardless of their rank, knowledge,
and training, are relegated to the status of mere "women," the
ones who have to step lightly and dance around others, the ones
who cannot walk into the dining room or the classroom when
certain men are in there, the ones sectioned off and limited to
jobs that do not "interfere" with men's religious needs to dwell in
female-free zones.

There's another reason why the army's seemingly easy accommodation of the Haredim demands exists: the army culture, like
the political culture in Israel, had its own problem with sexism
before religious groups even entered the scene. Indeed, despite
the impressive advancement of women in the IDF over the past
twenty years, there are also troubling cases in which jobs and units
are closed to women, not for religious reasons but simply due to
perceptions about what women can or should be doing in this
world, such as the elite commando units, or *sayarot*, those famous
tight-knit groups in which Prime Minister Benjamin Netanyahu
and Chief of Staff Ehud Barak served and formed their own snug
relationship. Women can be accepted to some *sayarot* in order to

"assist" in combat. But the most exclusive and high-status positions are reserved for men.

The segregation of women and men arguably begins when youth are first recruited at the age of sixteen or seventeen. From the first interviews and selection process, young men and women are directed to different paths. Females have fewer options and certainly fewer high-power combat options than males. A young man who goes into intelligence may find himself being asked why he is going into a field that is meant for women. Entire committees and panels can be found without any women's presence. And when women are allowed into certain fields, it is often in teaching positions rather than actual combat positions—such as the case of the coveted paratrooper positions, where women are often parachuting instructors but are restricted from combat.

Of the 69 percent of positions filled by women, it is not clear how many of those are actually in coed units and how many are gender-segregated. It is also unclear what the implications of gender segregation are on women's advancement. History shows that there is no such thing as "separate but equal," and if those 31 percent of units not filled by women are the ones like the *sayarot*, which are most likely to dovetail soldiers into high-powered careers, then this segregation by gender may be extremely unequal. "All-male units usually have a higher status in the army," said Professor Yagil Levy in the symposium on gender and religion in the army.[29]

Still, the army at times makes bizarre decisions when it comes to gender segregation, such as allowing women to command ships but not be sailors, or to teach paratroopers but not be paratroopers themselves. This may have to do with fears of sexual abuse or misconduct, but the IDF keeps quiet on any explanation of the issue.

So while the army is still grappling with its own gender issues, pressure to integrate religious men into the army will only continue to create a whole new set of obstacles for women in an environment where they already struggle for equality. And in the tension between the needs of religious men and the needs of all women, we have yet to see whose interests will be served by decision-making in the IDF.

In the meantime, the government has been working in two opposite directions regarding plans to draft Haredi soldiers. On the one hand, the IDF released plans indicating that the army intended to recruit 3,000 to 5,000 Haredi soldiers per year for a total of 19,500 over five years—a small portion of the 37,000 to 54,000 Haredi men who have exemptions, but large enough that there will be accommodations made for their absorption.[30]

Separately, the State has been trying to use judicial means to halt the process. "A universal draft of Haredim is not necessarily in the best interest of the military," the State claimed in a brief filed in January 2012 with the High Court of Justice. The State said that the complex preparations required from the IDF ahead of the draft strains the military's current resources and that a larger draft "is not feasible and will hurt the military... Making the IDF divert such funds to facilitate this change will infringe on its ability to meet its primary missions and goals." According to analysts, the IDF will have to "build more dedicated bases, so to accommodate the Haredi soldiers' demand for the separation of men and women, as well as create new men-only battalions, for the same reason. Another challenge, according to the State, is the IDF's own ability to screen Haredi candidates—a process which also mandates the formation of all-male teams in every level of the induction bases: interviewers, doctors, placement coordinators, and so on."[31]

The greatest protection, then, that women have is the fact that, in this case, adapting the demands for gender segregation will not be financially feasible. For once, economic analysis is on the women's side.

"This is not an argument about pacifism," writes Linda Pressly of *BBC News*. "The point is that many ultra-Orthodox Jews believe passionately their place is in the yeshiva and not a secular institution like the army."[32] Pressly spent time inside a religious learning enclave in Israel to try to understand what the yeshiva students think about the army. The ensuing discussion between Haredi and secular Israelis is indicative of the deep tension in Israel over whether Haredi men should continue to be allowed to study Torah full time—and get paid by the government for this lifestyle—in order to evade army service:

> *Inside a yeshiva in the west Jerusalem suburb of Bayit VeGan, row after row of men and boys rock and chant, deep in their devotion to the Jewish holy book, the Torah. Those who continue to study over years and decades acquire status in the community.*
>
> *"We are continuing the way of the Bible," says one student. "The Jewish way, to be Jewish—this isn't just about genes or a nation, it's a religion. And the reason we are in Israel is because of the Jewish religion. Our right to live in Israel is because we are Jews.*
>
> *"So what secular people should respect, and understand, is that what we are doing when we study in the yeshiva is giving us all a right to be here."*

In other words, learning and piety are as essential to Israel as knowing how to handle a gun—and Yitzhak Pindrus, the deputy mayor of Jerusalem, agrees.

He represents the ultra-Orthodox community, about a third of the city's population.

"I think the people who are keeping us as a nation are my brothers, my brother-in-laws, my uncles, my father—the people who are sitting and studying."

Although Pindrus did military service himself, he is vehemently opposed to the compulsory draft being extended to ultra-Orthodox Jews. He says those who want to force the community into the army are trying to undermine their position in Israel.[33]

Meanwhile, the Haredi public and Haredi leadership continue to organize active protest—again. In May 2013, thirty thousand to forty thousand ultra-Orthodox Israelis gathered outside of the main army recruitment office in Jerusalem to protest the draft, and the demonstration turned violent. According to Asher Zeiger, writing for the *Times of Israel*, demonstrators were tossing garbage cans, throwing stones, and erecting human barriers around the building while reading from the book of Psalms about "annulling the evil decree." Nine police officers were injured, and the police in turn used smoke grenades to disperse the crowd.[34]

One of the issues that some Haredi leaders have focused on in their objections to conscription is that men will have to get physical exams by women doctors, exams that include a "testicle check." The Vizhnitzer Rebbe, Rabbi Yisroel Hager, told his students that they should protest induction at all cost, and if arrested, go to prison with "tambourines and dancing" rather than have any testicle check. The army has already agreed that only men will examine religious men, and in fact, Deputy Health Minister Ya'akov Litzman told Hager personally that this procedure will be changed for Haredi soldiers, even though separate medical exams for Haredi men would cost the IDF money. But Hager is unmoved and is allegedly demanding written agreement from IDF Personnel Branch Major General Orna Barbivai.[35] It's hard to avoid the irony that the rabbi is now insistent on receiving authority from the only female in the highest army leadership to protect his men from having to interact with women.

What is fascinating about this particular debate over medical examinations is that there seems to be no reverse indignation for women who must be examined by male doctors. As mentioned in chapter two, the Haredi community puts together an annual conference on gynecology and obstetrics in which women are not allowed to speak and must sit in the back. So there is this bizarre, disturbingly counterintuitive approach to body exposure in which women are told their whole lives that they have to cover up but for the most intimate issues must go only to male doctors, while men are absolutely forbidden from going to the opposite sex for intimate medical issues. In essence, it seems like another form of sexism, a constant "protection" of men from sexual contact with women and a disregard for women's well-being.

Meanwhile, there may be signs of awakening coming from female soldiers, especially religious ones. For one thing, religious women are not necessarily accepting as a given that religious observance means excluding women from the army. They are entering new jobs and defying convention. In December 2012, the army graduated the first female religious pilot-navigator. The army says that three times as many girls are attending the recruitment events for religious female twelfth graders than three years ago and that there is a 32 percent increase over the past four years in girls' enlistment.[36] Female soldiers as a group may also be among the first to fight religious radicalism in the army. On the holiday of Simchas Torah last year, when the army created a gender-segregated holiday celebration in response to the demands of religious soldiers, some one hundred female soldiers left the event in protest.[37] That's a hopeful sign that women in the army are starting to realize they may have power—the same kind of power that religious men have—to demand that their needs be met. The question is whether they use that power to protect the lives of women overall.

Part II

PRIVATE PROPERTY

*The Battle to Control
Women's Personal Lives*

Chapter 6
FAMILY MATTERS: THE FIGHT OVER FERTILITY

When Hollywood actress Noa Tishby returned home to Israel for a visit in November 2011, the local press badgered her about starting a family. "Only in Israel do people get into my womb," she replied.[1] Tishby's rejoinder not only helped her avoid answering personal questions, but also encompassed a sharp commentary on Israeli society. In Israel, even women who are accomplished professionals are expected to embrace, first and foremost, motherhood.

When it comes to reproduction, Israel is probably most recognized for its policies in fertility. In vitro fertilization procedures are free and almost unlimited in Israel (for women through age forty-five, for up to two "live births"), a policy that certainly provides some welcome assistance to young couples struggling to have a baby, as well as to single mothers by choice and other unconventional parents. In fact, Israel has the highest per capita use of IVF in the world. Government-subsidized HMOs spend some $57 million a year on fertility treatments, one of the costliest policies of the healthcare system. All this is because Israeli culture places a high premium on babies and families.[2]

But this value has both positive and negative aspects to it.

Fertility is valued, but family planning is not. Motherhood is supported and encouraged, but nonmothering women are culturally and economically marginalized. As Carmel Shalev and Sigal Gooldin wrote in a 2006 article in the journal *Nashim*, "While pregnancy and birth-related expenses have always been covered in Israel by the public health system and by social security, coverage for contraception and legal abortion is only partial. It seems there is provision for women's special reproductive health needs only to the extent that their role as mothers is reinforced."[3] Indeed, these notions that women should be having babies at any cost have significant implications for women's health, including pregnancy, childbirth, and abortion.

To make childbearing more attractive, Israel literally pays women to have babies, the more the better, in hospitals. Women receive "birth grants" for each baby. As of the end of 2013: 1,719 NIS (about $475 U.S.) for the first, 773 NIS ($215 U.S.) for the second, and 516 NIS ($145 U.S.) for each one after that, although for twins, it's 8,594 NIS ($2,400 U.S.), and for triplets 12,891 NIS ($3,580 U.S.). Israel also grants its citizens monthly stipends, "child allowances" for children, in which the figure for each subsequent child increases rather than decreases: for children born before March 2003, the rate is 175 NIS ($47 U.S.) per month for the first child, 263 NIS ($73 U.S.) for the second, 295 NIS ($82 U.S.) for the third, 459 NIS ($128 U.S.) for the fourth, and 389 NIS ($110 U.S.) for the fifth and any one after that.[4] This certainly offers some welcome relief for parents, who also receive fourteen weeks of paid leave from the state.

This may be a source of envy for American women, who struggle with problematic maternity leave, expensive day care, and other nonsupportive government policies for mothers. "Hey Marissa Mayer, ever consider aliya [emigration to Israel]?" shouted one Israeli blogger when the Yahoo CEO and new mother went straight back to work after her birth. "Here Marissa and all other Moms are mandated fourteen weeks paid maternity leave plus a host of other benefits. And in Israel maternity leave is law. It's non negotiable, part of our culture. And because of it, most Israeli babies get off to the best possible start, at Mommy's breast where doctors and psychologists say they belong."[5]

The culture in Israel toward fertility, even when it comes with patronizing mommy advice, definitely has its advantages. Hannah Katsman, who blogs at *A Mother in Israel,* posted "Sixty-Five Surprising Facts about Parenting in Israel"—which include not only "getting a check from the National Insurance Institute in the hospital after birth," but also more cultural practices like how strangers will offer to hold a baby in the park in order to help out a mother, how children often accompany parents to weddings and restaurants, and how taxi drivers and bus drivers will smile and joke around with strangers' children.[6] In Israel, "everyone" loves children—both the state and society.

Still, this pro-natalist policy is not without a catch. The creation of these policies in Israel go back to the 1950s, when the virtually all-male Knesset instituted several key pieces of pro-natalist legislation not so much out of concern for women but out of a desire to increase the Jewish population of the world. Considering the post-Holocaust reality of the time, this may have been understandable. More than six million Jews had been killed, so the prevailing feeling among Jewish leaders was that it was imperative to replenish the population as fast as possible. Israeli leaders and legislators may have had the best intentions for the Jewish people, but women's well-being was not necessarily part of their thinking. According to anthropologist Susan Sered, the political discourse at the time promoted the idea that women's bodies need to be controlled and regulated in service to the nation. David Ben-Gurion, Israel's first prime minister, placed motherhood as a woman's duty to the nation. "Any Jewish woman who does not bring into the world at least four healthy children is shirking her duty to the nation, like a soldier who evades military service," he famously declared.[7]

This kind of survivalist thinking still dominates much of Israeli policy making and thinking about women's lives and bodies. There is still a governing view that women have a national duty to procreate. Knesset discussions continue to rely on the idea that Jewish women must "produce sons" for the nation. As feminist scholar and sociology professor Yael Hashiloni-Dolev wrote, "A complex combination of factors, including identification with the collective goal of fighting the 'demographic threat' (that the country's Arab population might eventually outnumber the Jews); the need to 'make Jewish babies,' particularly in the wake of the Holocaust; and the threat of losing a child in war or in a terrorist attack are all said to have influenced Israel's pro-natalist culture."[8]

Another factor is Jewish tradition, which sees parenthood as a moral and religious commandment and still treats infertility as a severe disability. As Hashiloni-Dolev continued, "Women's infertility is an archetype of suffering in the Israeli/Jewish imagination. The duty to reproduce falls upon all members of society, including its highest religious authorities; the ideal of celibacy is absent from Judaism."[9] Yali Hashash, upon an examination of the issues of contraception and abortion, added, "Beyond national, political, cultural, and ideological agendas, the medical establishment in Israel has also acted in its own interests in increasing its professional power and influence by ever deepening the medicalization of reproduction."[10] As feminist sociologist Nitza Berkovitch also wrote, "The Jewish Israeli female subject is constructed first and foremost not as an individual or a citizen but as a mother and a wife."[11]

Even some of the policies aimed at protecting women can be a double-edged sword. Women in bureaucratic positions in the Israeli government are entitled to work "Mommy hours"—that is, to leave work an hour earlier than standard, at 4:00 p.m. This policy undoubtedly eases women's struggles with work-life balance and makes the public sector attractive for women workers. But this "special treatment" for women may also preempt equal treatment. "Absolute prohibitions of night work for women or against working overtime for pregnant women, originally contained in the 1954 Employment of Women Law, supposedly aimed at protecting women from work hazards that might harm their reproductive capabilities, had the impact of preventing women from entering more profitable occupations or increasing their income by working overtime," writes Ruth Halperin-Kaddari.[12] This, in turn, reinforced gendered notions of work, in which men receive promotions and raises while women go home to look after their children. The fact that the rule applied only to women—as opposed to, say, parents of both genders—also reinforced the notion that child care is only for women.

The good news is that, over the past generation or so, some of this has evolved. The 1988 Equal Opportunities law prevents discrimination in the workplace, offers protections for mothers, and transforms the absolute rules about working in pregnancy and motherhood into options for women. Women are still encouraged to work "mommy hours," but they can choose not to. A 1997 provision took the revolutionary step of enabling both fathers and mothers to take half of the parental leave—although less than 2 percent of eligible fathers actually do.[13] But as Halperin-Kaddari notes, changing laws do not necessarily lead to changing cultures. So pro-natalist policies and cultures remain in place, with the double-edged sword of encouraging working women to become mothers. And there are some other sides to all of this pro-natalist culture that are perhaps less known and can have damaging effects on women.

Ultra-Orthodox women are expected to have many babies in quick succession. Some figures show a fertility rate of 7.9 babies per ultra-Orthodox family, more than other Israeli women. I will never forget the time I was in the waiting room in a gynecologist's office, speaking with the ultra-Orthodox woman next to me. She was just over thirty and had six children, but she was there for fertility treatments. "Women my age have ten or twelve children by now," she told me. The idea of six children being too few— and the woman being in need of fertility treatments—strikes me as a lot of pressure. Haredi women are also taught to suppress their own personal doubts and fears. Qualitative research in the *American Journal of Medical Genetics*, which interviewed twenty-five Haredi women, showed that "when prenatal screening indicates a possible fetal anomaly," for example, or "when a disabled child is born, these women interpret the situation as a God-sent ordeal in which they are called upon to prove their trust and certainty in God's plan and to resist the uncertainties generated by the probability-based technologies."[14] This kind of attitude may have its charm and spiritual attractiveness, but it also places women in the difficult situation of never being able to say no to having a baby.

While some women cope well with large broods, others do not. The problem is that Haredi women who do not cope well do not necessarily have options. Former Hassidic woman Judy Brown recently wrote in an article titled "I'm a Mother, Not a Baby Machine":

> *My hell began not when I said I don't want to have more children; but when I said, begged, pleaded, cried to be allowed to have fewer children; when I asked to be allowed to take a break, not for a year, but five, because I knew that I could not function as a mother to three little ones, when I had to give birth to at least three more.*
>
> *My hell began when I said I want to be a mother, not a baby machine…*
>
> *The problem is too many children. And that after a lifetime of indoctrination it is nearly impossible for most women to real-ize that they can be good mothers with the maternal instincts we all share with three children and no more.*
>
> *They have a right to say, "Enough," after less than six preg-nancies. And that this does not make them a damaged person.*[15]

According to the organization Isha L'Isha ("Woman to Woman") that works on empowering women around fertility issues in Israel, Israel's pro-natalism does not take into account the heavy price that women pay in terms of their health, well-being, and quality of life. The lack of attention to women's health is even more pronounced in the Haredi community, where contraception is forbidden until at least one boy and one girl are born in a family, or perhaps two boys and two girls. "In this absurd reality that has been created, rabbis are unofficially dictating the policy of fertility in the State of Israel," says Dr. Hannah Kehat, whose organization Kolech is working on this issue in collaboration with Isha L'Isha, "whether via direct contact between rabbis and gynecologists or whether via legislative intervention." The male-dominant world of gynecology in Israel, which has an interest in promoting high fertility rates especially via reproductive technologies, colludes with rabbis who have a strong political interest in encouraging large families among their constituents. Rabbis and doctors talk over the heads of women, making decisions about women's fertility without bothering to include women in the discussion. The most publicly glaring case of this is the Puah conference, which I described in an earlier chapter. But this is not just a problem in the Haredi community. Even legislation aimed at fertility issues in the Knesset often takes place without consideration of the woman's own health.[16]

While the pressure on women is enormous, there is a striking dearth of policies protecting their health, which is vital to help them navigate the ups and downs of raising happy and healthy children. Having large families in quick succession can take an emotional, physical, and financial toll on them. Studies show Haredi women suffering from maternal exhaustion, uterine weakness, and even depression.[17]

The most comprehensive study on the issue of fertility and women's health in Israel was conducted by Hadassah Hospital among 45,000 women who gave birth to 125,000 children in Hadassah over thirty-seven years. The study showed clearly that mothers of five or more children have a shorter lifespan than other women and tend to suffer from other diseases including cancer, diabetes, and heart disease. Women with more than ten children have a 49 percent increase in the chance of premature death.[18]

Systematically isolating other variables, the researchers found that this single factor, the number of children a woman has, is directly and independently correlated with premature death among mothers. They concluded that in pregnancy, the woman's body undergoes dramatic physiological changes that drain her resources for the baby, which impacts her metabolism and shortens her life.[19] In other words, numerous Israeli women are literally dying from having too many babies, but this information is never shared with women planning out their lives.

Moreover, the earlier a woman with more than five children began giving birth, the more health problems she encountered throughout her life. A study done at Shaare Zedek Medical Center, which looked at 440,000 births between 2000 and 2005, found a connection between spacing between pregnancies and women's health. A space of less than eleven months between births results in higher rates of varicose veins, back pain, incontinence, Caesarean sections, postpartum depression, and, most alarmingly, risk of early death.[20]

Nevertheless, this knowledge about the risks of excessive fertility is not necessarily imparted to family-planning women. A 2010 study on Haredi women's attitudes toward fertility found that among Haredi women, there is often complete ignorance about the health implications and emotional impacts of pregnancy, birth, and fertility treatments, and that the primary influence on their decisions about fertility comes from religion alone.[21] The study, conducted by Kolech, Isha L'Isha, and the Authority for the Status of Women in the Prime Minister's Office, also found that Haredi women with "only" two children have high rates of depression, comparable to that of secular women who suffer from infertility. Finally, the study found that Haredi women expressed a striking disconnect between facts and perception: despite the scientific evidence and realities of their bodies, they saw themselves as getting healthier with more births, an idea that they justify using religion while ignoring medical facts.

The study concludes that there is no language at all in the Haredi world—and only a limited amount for the rest of Israeli society—for discussing women's physical and emotional health when it comes to fertility. Women are being encouraged to have many babies but are not being told what the risks are to their own bodies. "In all the frameworks—hospitals, medical clinics, fertility organizations—there is never a discussion from the woman's perspective," Kehat said. Organizations like Puah that spend millions of dollars advancing women's fertility and technologies and the way it fits into Halacha "do not have a booklet anywhere on the impact of these treatments on women themselves—on her physical, emotional, or financial well-being," Kehat told me in an interview.[22]

This lack of information for women is particularly acute when it comes to in vitro fertilization (IVF), a process that has the potential to offer tremendous relief for women who want to have children and cannot (and thus would likely be ostracized by their communities). But it's not without its downsides. It can be a physically and emotionally painful process, draining energy and resources, distracting people from the rest of their lives, straining relationships, and bringing increased risks for breast cancer.[23] Additionally this treatment can cause other side effects, including brain tumors, blood clots in the legs and lungs, headaches, abdominal pain, mood swings, and general discomfort. But IVF is practiced by some 17 percent of Haredi women, including women who already have a number of children. Women are allowed two "live births" resulting from IVF—precisely because lawmakers wanted to increase the population of the Jewish people—which means that women can get an unlimited number of treatments until they reach this goal.[24]

But while women are getting IVF like candy, nobody is discussing the downsides of all this technology. "Encouraging the intensive use of ART [assisted reproductive technologies], and downplaying the risks involved, facilitate the construction of biological fertility as compulsory and of infertility as an acute condition," Shalev and Gooldin wrote. But opponents of IVF regulations vehemently protest this stance. In one Knesset debate where some lawmakers suggested limiting the number of treatments per woman, a member suggested that this was equivalent to mass murder: "We are talking about at least 2,000 children that [will not] be brought into this world because of this decree... Do you know what you are doing here and what kind of a proposal this is? It is like sitting down and shooting around 1,000 or 1,500 children."[25] Needless to say, the proposal was eliminated and never heard from again.

There is also a particularly "Jewish" kind of assault on women's bodies through excess fertility treatments that affects women keeping Jewish law. Sometimes women who are considered infertile are actually perfectly healthy. This so-called infertility has nothing to do with the woman's body but with the way she practices Jewish law.[26]

It goes like this: the Torah prohibits sexual relations when a woman is menstruating. A married woman is expected to immerse in the *mikveh*, the ritual bath, after she finishes her period, in order to become "pure" again for her husband. However, over the course of centuries of evolution of Jewish custom, it has become the practice for women to immerse not immediately after menstruation but rather seven days later, following seven "clean" days. During all that time—the menstrual period plus the seven clean days, some two weeks out of each month—Orthodox husbands and wives are not allowed to touch, hold hands, kiss, cuddle, or sleep in the same bed. And of course, they are not allowed to have sex. These practices can put strains on women in their family planning since some women ovulate while they are forbidden from having sex with their husbands. In other words, women are forced into an artificial kind of infertility as a result of the practice. If they decide to have children—as religious women are pressured to do—they end up in the cycle of IVF with all its implications, despite the fact that their bodies are perfectly healthy.

It doesn't stop there. Dr. Daniel Rosenak, an Orthodox obstetrician in Jerusalem who advocates for a more lenient approach to the laws of ritual immersion in order to resolve this issue, adds that there are many other points of damage that come from forbidding immersion during ovulation: damage to women's dignity and even modesty through excess medical invasiveness of the IVF process, damage to women's emotional well-being stemming from excessive internal checking of one's own body, stifling her natural libido, and destroying the natural flow of intimacy within marriage. Thus he has started calling on doctors and rabbis to allow women to stop keeping the seven clean days. Dr. Rosenak's proposal is viewed by some Orthodox men as radical, in that it suggests that religious women revisit the way that they were taught to keep Jewish practice. However, what really makes it radical is that he suggests that women's real lives and experiences be part of the considerations of family planning and women's sexuality.[27] That kind of thinking—that women's perspectives count at least as much as Halacha—has been absent from Orthodox discussions.

The problem of intrusion into women's fertility isn't limited to Haredi or religious women. It also affects another group in Israel:

single mothers by choice. There is a growing movement of women who are unmarried but want to bring life into this world and therefore choose artificial insemination. But the rabbis of the religious gynecology institute Puah are unsatisfied with this practice, even though there is nothing halachically wrong with it. In order to combat this, they have decided to issue a halachic ruling forbidding it and instead recommend that single women freeze their eggs until they get married.

"Freezing eggs is a painful process, but that's not the point," Israeli musician Karni Eldad wrote in the Israeli news site *Ynet*. "We are willing to make sacrifices when something is important to us. But here, we are dealing with perfectly healthy women who do not need to endure a difficult and invasive medical procedure that causes excess ovulation and suctioning to overcome a problem that most religious people just think is a halachic problem."[28]

Israeli women—Haredi and secular alike—are starting to find their voices amid a pro-natalist, rabbinically controlled culture of women's fertility. They are starting to ask questions about the prevailing messages about women's bodies and starting to talk back to this culture.

Another area in which the state is able to invade women's sexual lives is around the issue of premarital sex. This will take a moment to explain, so bear with me. Although premarital sex between two consenting adults is not precisely against the written Torah, it is frowned upon. A prohibition worse than premarital sex, however, is for a man to have sex with a menstruant woman—that is, one who did not immerse in the *mikveh* after her period. (Notice that the prohibition is directed to the man.) So a single woman who chooses to have premarital sex, if she does not immerse in the *mikveh*, is primarily violating this prohibition of causing a man to have intercourse with a menstruant woman. Of all the ways in which Judaism condemns premarital sex, the most severe violation, so to speak, is the prohibition against copulating with a menstruant, the punishment for which is *karet*, literally "to cut off," or being banished from the Jewish life for generations. The sexual relationship itself, if neither party is married and the two people are not closely related, does not in and of itself have some kind of major punishment associated with it. It's simply considered unbecoming of members of a holy tribe. Not to dismiss the weight of this holiness—let's say, premarital sex, aside from the menstruation aspect, is considered *seriously* unbecoming.

Given the hierarchy around these different rules and regulations, and given the realities of modern life, biology, and the human condition, it should not be surprising that premarital sex is not unheard of in the Orthodox community. The choice to have sex while remaining religious places some complex dilemmas in front of single Orthodox women. Some single religious women who want to have sex but still keep the Jewish tradition will immerse in the *mikveh* so that they don't violate the law against impure (menstruant) sex. They may be compromising their perceived holiness, but at least they won't cause anyone to be fated to an eternity of spiritual banishment. We can understand why this is an attractive option, all things considered. It's easy to understand why some single women would rather avoid that fate even if they want to sleep with their boyfriends.

To understand how strenuous this whole issue can be on unmarried religious women (as opposed to unmarried Orthodox men, who may have sex as much as they want without anyone knowing about it), take a look at the following blog. It's written by an unmarried Orthodox woman who has been chronicling her struggles with total abstinence, what she calls "a little like living in jail":

> *Sometimes I think that if I do not have sex I will explode. Sometimes I think that if I do not find out what it feels like to have a man's hands on me, I will go crazy... Some friends have told me that they cry sometimes because they feel lonely, but no one else has told me that they cry sometimes because they are sexually starving. Maybe they just will not admit it... It is bad enough to be alone, but to be not sexual is almost as bad, and the two together is terrible. I have been on depression medication for a long time. I have had fantasies of killing myself. I have considered hiring a male prostitute and getting it over with. No, I have not tried either of those last two things,* chas vishalom. *But it shows how hard it is to be 34 and single and a nice Jewish girl. I cannot blame anyone who decides it is not worth it. To all the married people out there telling older singles that they should deny themselves, I wish I could respond "let he who is 34 and never been kissed cast the first stone."*[29]

Total abstinence can be very painful, so it's easy to understand why some women would want to go to the *mikveh* to be clean to have sex. There was just one problem: the state was standing in the way. So one woman decided to take the issue to court.

The case in question is of a young Orthodox single woman who had a serious boyfriend but wasn't yet ready to get married. She still wanted to have sex with him. She decided to use the *mikveh* so as not to violate the prohibition against having intercourse while ritually impure. Its punishment is the worst available, considered worse than death in many cases. Unfortunately, when she got to her local *mikveh*, the attendant would not let her immerse because she was not married. The attendants, it seems, were given strict orders by their superiors in the Ministry of Religion not to allow single women to immerse.

The woman decided to fight this and filed suit. In December 2011, the Center for Women's Justice (CWJ), a feminist legal organization founded by the brilliant Orthodox feminist lawyer Dr. Susan Weiss, filed a High Court petition on behalf of two single women barred entry to the *mikveh*. The petition, filed with the support of Kolech as well, called on "the rabbinate and local rabbinic authorities to issue a directive stating that *mikveh* attendants refrain from questioning *mikveh* users about purpose or status. A favorable ruling would allow single women, widows, and divorcées to immerse in *mikvehs*, and would cancel an existing policy that bars *mikveh* use by unmarried women."[30] According to CWJ:

> *The rabbinate's policy of limiting* mikveh *use to married women…violates the religious freedom and right to equal treatment of single women, widows and divorcées. This exclusionary form of religious coercion places a discriminatory wedge between married and single women, and between the orthodox and other religious streams. In addition, the present policy violates a woman's right to privacy…*
>
> *The bottom line is that we are asking State-funded authorities to refrain from becoming involved in women's personal reasons for wanting to immerse themselves in a* mikveh, *and to recognize that each woman has the right to choose for herself.*[31]

The petition was greeted with ire by some in the Israeli Orthodox establishment and as welcome news elsewhere. Rabbi

Dr. Haviva Ner-David runs Shmaya, a pluralistic *mikveh* in the Galilee, the only *mikveh* in which anyone can immerse for any reason, Jew or non-Jew, man or woman, adult or child, no judgments or gatekeepers in sight. (As a result, she receives zero funding from the state or municipality, not for electricity or for a salary.) She commented that the petition "highlights the difficulties faced by those whose approach to *mikveh* observance doesn't meet the narrow standards set by the Rabbinate. These Jews, who seek to observe a central Jewish tenet by engaging in the profound spiritual experience of immersion, can find themselves caught in a deeply troubling situation." She added that "A *mikveh* is a ritual tool that should be accessible to all. The *mikveh* always remains pure no matter who immerses in it, how he or she immerses, or when he or she immerses. That is one of the unique aspects of *mikveh*, one of its purposes. It changes the status of the person who immerses in its Living Waters but is not itself changed in the process. This characteristic of *mikveh* allows for it to be, in my opinion, the ultimate tool for pluralism and openness in the Jewish community. All is allowed, and everyone is allowed, and we can all share the same *mikveh*. What a beautiful thing!"[32]

Rabbi Seth Farber, whose organization Itim deals with conversion issues that also require the cooperation of state-funded *mikvehs*, commented on the CWJ petition: "I believe that what is really at stake is the question of power and particularly, the power of Jewish life. Mikvaot in Israel are built with public money and are overseen—at least in theory—by public institutions. But all too often, what goes on inside the mikve is not subject to any oversight... What's at stake here is not simply the rights of a number of single women. Who holds the power at the mikve is emblematic of who controls Jewish life in Israel. The time has come for the state to allow people to live full Jewish lives and not to put up obstacles in their way."[33]

In response to the petition, in May 2013, the Chief Rabbinate adopted a "don't ask, don't tell" policy about *mikvehs*, in which they accepted that women will be free to use the *mikveh* without being interrogated about their marital status or anything else. Deputy Minister for Religious Affairs Eli Ben-Dahan announced that the network of *mikvehs* run by local religious councils would permit immersion by non-Orthodox Jews. "Every Jew, from any stream, including the Reform and Conservative ones, will be able to immerse in a *mikveh*, even for the purpose of conversion," he initially said. He said the Ministry is "striving to foster competition in the delivery of religious services with the purpose of making them more efficient and user-friendly, for the benefit of all citizens. Religious services are there for all of Israel's Jewish citizens, and everyone should be able to utilize them. I would like to emphasize that these services are given in accordance with Jewish law."[34]

This was initially greeted as a huge victory for women's religious rights in Israel. "The State should not be in the *mikveh* business," CWJ director Susan Weiss, who represented the women in the lawsuit, posted on her Facebook page, commenting on the Ministry announcement. "If it is, then it must provide services to everyone. If the Rabbinate's conscience does not allow them to do this, administration of the *mikveh* should be transferred to a governmental apparatus with a clearer conscience."

Support also came from Rabbi Yuval Cherlow, a rabbi of the Tzohar rabbinic group that tries to present a more liberal-minded Orthodoxy. He said in a responsum that although "the halachic position is unequivocally against single women immersing...and I cannot permit that even if it will prevent a sin of *karet*, the *mikveh* is not just mine but is public property. And the question is whether women who do not think like the chief rabbis should be allowed to actualize their position… And anyway trying to prevent this by force will not help."[35] So even among religious leaders, there is a recognition that coercive control over women's sexuality is not a good thing.

However, the victory for women was short-lived, since Ben-Dahan quickly recanted his ruling—presumably in response to pressure from his rabbinical colleagues. "The *mikvehs* operate according to the law governing religious services, and will continue to function according to Jewish law," he said following the release of his first statement. "We are still far from the goal of State-funded *mikvaot* being open to all," Ner-David lamented. "The 'don't ask, don't tell' policy may solve the practical problem in some cases, but many additional practical problems remain painfully open. Moreover, it does not resolve the ideological problem, leaving discriminatory policy on the books."[36]

The state, then, continues to monitor women's sexuality and fertility, promoting marriage and birth while restricting premarital sex. There are two more areas of women's intimate lives where these disturbing policies find expression: contraception and abortion.

When it comes to contraception, Israel is in some ways ahead of America—and not just because it does not have to grapple with Paul Ryan's law for "personhood," which views an embryo as a full person and would thus render most contraception akin to murder. With the recent announcement that the "morning after pill" is available over the counter, Shari Eshet, the head of Israel's branch of the National Council of Jewish Women, tweeted, "This pill has been available over the counter for all ages in Israel for years. [It] never ceases to amaze me how liberal Israeli law can be on one thing and so uncompromising on others."

Still, as much as rabbis and political leaders will jump through hoops to encourage fertility, the opposite is true when it comes to contraception. The law may seem liberal, but its implementation certainly is not. According to Dr. Ronit Irshai, when it comes to matters related to modern artificial fertility, the rabbis are very lenient, but when it comes to contraception and abortion, they are surprisingly strict. "Sex without procreation is treated strictly; procreation without sex is treated leniently, on the premise that reproduction at almost any cost is the preferred value... This concept does not regard the value of woman as an 'end in itself' (in the Kantian sense); rather, it sees her primarily in her reproductive role—as a means." She then brings a ruling of Rabbi Yehuda Henkin on the issue of spacing pregnancies in which he says that women can use contraception "for the child's sake" but not merely to go out to work. In other words, women's primary job is to be a mother, and all other considerations—such as her own ambition, financial stability, or general well-being—are irrelevant.[37]

This idea, that contraception is not the "correct" practice for (married) women who should ideally always be trying to conceive, impacts state economic and medical policy. Whereas women receive free IVF treatments, contraception is not covered under the healthcare system. In other words, even though family planning has been proven to be supremely important in women's educational, professional, and economic advancement around the world, women in Israel are penalized for trying to take control over their own fertility.

Dr. Ilana Ziegler, executive director of the Israel Family Planning Association, notes that "A woman's having control of her own life is the first condition needed for a reduction in fertility... She needs economic independence, she must be able to make a proper living, she must be free to love, to build her own life, and her health— including the promise that the embryo she is carrying will be born a healthy infant and will continue to live or that she can stop her pregnancy if she so decides—must be guaranteed."[38] Yet women's overall health and well-being advancement, it seems, are not a priority for the health ministry or the religious ministry in Israel.

The disturbing exception to this practice of minimizing contraceptive use was discovered among Ethiopian Jewish women. An investigative report revealed in 2012 that Ethiopian women immigrating to Israel were forced to take contraceptives. After much denial followed by international outrage, Health Ministry Director General Ron Gamzu admitted that Depo-Provera, a hormonal form of birth control injected every three months, was given to Ethiopian women as a matter of policy. His statement came after Sharona Eliahu-Chai of the Association of Civil Rights in Israel demanded an immediate end to the injections and the launch of an investigation. "They told us they are inoculations," said one of the women interviewed by Eliahu-Chai. "They told us people who frequently give birth suffer. We took it every three months. We said we didn't want to."[39] This story is shocking by any standard, especially for its racial and ethnic overtones. But it is especially disturbing when compared to Israel's general policy about contraception. It is as if to say that the state wants white women to have lots of children, but black women not so much.

Still, it's possible that rather than view this story as merely an incident of racist shortsightedness, there may have been some rational thinking behind it. After all, if control over fertility is key for women's advancement, then it's plausible that the representatives of the Ministry of Health were trying to help the Ethiopian women learn about family planning. In theory, the idea that the state is supporting and funding women's contraception is actually a step in the right direction for women. The problem here is less about the issue of contraception and more about education, choice, and race. That is, the Ethiopian women were not given the *choice* about whether to take the contraception—presumably because they are black and therefore "other"—which renders the whole idea of progress moot. The women were treated as silent objects within a public policy of fertility. The process reinforced their powerlessness and the notion that their bodies are owned and controlled by the state.

In the meantime, perhaps the greatest victims of this idealization of the large family are Haredi women who have no language or information to understand their own subjective experiences of motherhood. Their bodies—more than those of any other Jewish women in Israel—are used as vehicles to advance the needs of the Jewish collective. Their own lives barely matter. While many Haredi women may not be interested in protesting this, one has to wonder about the women who do want to protest, and there certainly are some. What happens to these women who want to make different choices? What happens to a Haredi woman—or any Israeli Jewish woman—who wants to have fewer children, or perhaps none at all?

In Israel, childlessness by choice is virtually unheard of. And the woman who makes such a declaration in order to have an abortion may find herself being labeled insane.[40]

Ironically, while contraception can be hard to come by or greatly discouraged in Israel, Israeli women have an easier time obtaining abortions than women of other countries—certainly easier than women in some states in America. Abortions are mostly legal in Israel, with an estimated 20,000 legal abortions in 2011, according to the Central Bureau of Statistics.[41] Women who seek abortion also do not face the same obstacles that some American women face. There are no violent protesters outside of abortion clinics, no firebombs, and no ever-pending legislation to make abortion illegal. Instead, when it comes to abortion, Israel's policy toward women is a mixed bag. There are different, more subtle kinds of obstacles to women seeking abortion, especially those women who want to have complete control over their own decisions about fertility.

Israel's 1977 abortion law legalized the procedure while establishing some terms and conditions. The first major caveat is that women had to meet one of these four criteria to obtain abortions: (1) the woman is under eighteen or over forty; (2) the fetus has a serious mental or physical defect; (3) the pregnancy resulted from forbidden relations such as rape, incest, or adultery; *or* (4) the pregnancy threatens the woman's physical or mental health. (The law originally had a fifth criterion that allowed abortions for economic reasons, but it was abolished in 1980 as a result of pressure from religious parties who consider finances an illegitimate consideration in family planning.)[42]

In practice, these criteria make it much easier for unmarried women to have abortions than married women, according to Orly Hasson Tsitsuashvili, the director of Ladaat, an organization that promotes sexual health and provides family planning education and counseling. In fact, abortions are fairly common. Between 1980 and 1990, an average of 15,000 to 16,000 abortions were performed per year in Israel, corresponding to 18 percent of births in

Israel. By comparison, figures were 10 percent in the Netherlands, 32 percent in Sweden, and 70 percent in Czechoslovakia.[43] Abortions for married women whose pregnancy does not fit into the four categories, however, are illegal—even those suffering from poverty or struggling with large families. And a married woman who simply does not want a child or wants to control family planning certainly does not count.

However, Israel has one obstacle to abortion that doesn't exist in any other country: an abortion "panel." That is, in order to decide whether the woman fits the four criteria mentioned above, a three-person committee consisting of doctors and social workers must meet and approve all requests for abortions.

These abortion panels—there are forty-one across Israel—place women in a humiliating and unnecessary position of having to justify their body choices to a group of strangers, regardless of their and their doctor's views. "The fact that there is a panel is terrible," says Irit Rosenblum, the founding director of the New Family Organization that advocates for reproductive freedom. "It's completely chauvinistic, as if these panels know better than the woman what's good for her. And the panel puts women in a terrible position. Imagine a man facing prostate surgery being forced to stand in front of a panel asking if he should or shouldn't do it. If a woman decides to have an abortion, it should be up to her and her doctor to explore the issues and that's it... It's a relic from the Dark Ages."[44]

Despite the required review process, a vast majority of cases (98 percent in 2005) apparently receive permission from the appointed committee, and a doctor may bypass the committee in the event that an abortion must be performed to save a woman's life, as long as the doctors report the incident to the Knesset Health Bureau within five days of the authorization.[45] But these numbers may be inaccurate. Most family planning advocates servicing women believe that there are 50 percent more illegal abortions than legal ones—approximately 8,000 to 9,000 abortions a year. And the chances of not receiving approval—most common among those in the twenty to thirty-nine age group, women who are "supposed" to be making families—places women under undue strain and drives many to seek illegal abortions.

Illegal abortions, those that bypass the abortion panels, do not have the same connotation as illegal abortions in America. These are not back alley, coat hanger affairs, but more like under-the-state-radar abortions that usually take place in private, expensive doctor's offices available in Israel, although nobody knows exactly how many there are. Illegal "private" abortions generally cost more than the state-subsidized abortion, which range anywhere between 2,000 to 3,500 NIS ($500 to $1,000 U.S.), plus the woman's fee for the committee's review of her application, which costs around 360 NIS ($100 U.S.). Illegal abortions start at 3,000 NIS ($800 U.S.) and usually go higher. In addition, private abortions avoid bureaucracy and can be done within a few hours, whereas legal abortions may take a week while waiting for committee approval—a critical time period in early pregnancy. In other words, the privilege of privacy and full control over one's fertility is available only to those who can afford it.

"It's outrageous that women have to pay full cost for their abortions," Sharon Orshalimy, manager of the Tel Aviv Open Door Israel Family Planning Association, told us. "Especially since women who come to the public hospitals are usually the ones who don't have the means to pay. I don't understand the country's interest in making poor women who are already on welfare and don't want the baby have another baby."[46]

Also, abortions performed without panel approval are punishable by imprisonment for the doctor—although, in practice, this is unenforced, and activists agree that the panels are mostly a swiftly conducted formality. (In other words, bypassing the panel is a crime committed by the doctor, not necessarily by the woman.) Still, the fact that it's the doctor who is considered culpable reinforces the idea that women cannot or should not decide for themselves what is best for them regarding their pregnancies. "Until fairly recently, women were considered by the medical establishment to be a kind of inventory, a piece of property that can't think for herself," Rosenblum added. "We still have remnants of the perspective that she can't decide for herself. Hers is the only voice that should count here, but she is discounted."[47]

Interestingly, there are certain cases in which abortions are fully paid for by the State. To Israel's credit, severe cases such as incest and rape are state-funded. This may reflect a compassion for the woman that is arguably rooted in Jewish law, which, unlike some American laws on the issue, sees abortion as the correct action in these kinds of cases. This is because Jewish law is governed by the principle that if a fetus is "pursuing" the mother—that is, threatening her life—then the pregnancy should be terminated.

The government also pays for abortions for women serving in the army or under the age of twenty (for nineteen- and twenty-year-olds, they must meet one of the other criteria), who also do not need to notify their parents—making abortion the only medical procedure that does not require parental consent for minors.[48] Significantly, however, this service is not available for women doing national service (*Sherut Leumi*), the voluntary alternative to army service usually reserved for religious young women. This exemption is likely because the religious community sees abortion as not relevant or applicable, but it means that a religious young woman has to pay for her abortion while her secular soldier counterparts do not. So secular young women are effectively "allowed" to have abortions but religious women are not. There is a hidden message here about sexual agency as well. Religious unmarried women are assumed to be sexually inactive and thus shouldn't ever need an abortion. This policy therefore penalizes sexually active religious women for their perceived promiscuity.

The key point is that the abortion law is an attempt to regulate women's sexuality and family planning. Interestingly, the law seems eager to promote motherhood while eliminating "incorrect" motherhood and sexuality—pregnancies in women too young, too old, unmarried, victims of violence or incest, while impeding "correctly" married women from managing their fertility. To combat this, some married women lie to get the abortion, telling the panel that they are single. Others go through the system as best as they can and face the consequences.

"Ruti," a thirty-eight-year-old accountant, had been married for two years when she became pregnant. She knew all along that she did not want children. "I just do not see myself as a mother," she told my colleague Dr. L. Ariella Zeller and me as we were researching this issue, some six months after her abortion. "Some women get all soft and wistful when they see babies. I don't. It doesn't do anything for me. And I don't think I would be a very good mother." The decision to end the pregnancy was clear to her, but not to her doctor. "He looked at me like I was crazy, like he had never heard of a woman who doesn't want children. He would not help me, he would not give me information, he did not tell me what to expect or what the procedure entails. Nothing." Ruti went to the hospital with no information about what to expect and no professional support. And then, before they could begin, she was sent to the panel.

Ruti's abortion was approved by the panel, but under the category of "mental disease." "The doctor told me that I needed to get psychological help, because there's no such thing as a sane woman who doesn't want to have a baby," she painfully recalled.[49]

Since a "correct" Jewish woman in Israeli culture is a birthing mother, Ruti's paradigm of a woman who does not want children simply doesn't exist in Israeli society, law, or medicine. Doctors, social workers, and the law view her as a strange anomaly, almost a freak of nature. As Rebecca Steinfeld wrote in *Haaretz*, "Facing an abortion committee can be a shameful experience." Steinfeld cites medical sociologist Yael Hashiloni-Dolev who told her that the committee is "a 'ceremony of shame and guilt' in which women have to 'confess their sins or explain very intimate details about themselves to total strangers.' Health journalist Judy Siegel-Itzkovich said in 2009 that she thinks 50 percent of abortions performed illegally are women seeking to avoid this embarrassment."[50]

Unlike the United States, where the discussion of abortion is quite public at times, in Israel, abortion is simply not discussed openly, a situation that can have some dire consequences for women there.

"Most Israeli women have a very vague idea or even have no idea of the extent of legal abortion in Israel," says Dana Weinberg, founding director of Women and Their Bodies, an organization that advocates for women's empowerment over sexuality and fertility. "We get so many calls from women in Israel who have unexpected or unwanted pregnancies and are unaware of their choices... And the information is very limited—it's very hard to get information on abortion and that's why it was very important for us to put all of this information in English, Hebrew, and Arabic on our website."[51]

Educating women about abortion is a key component of family planning. Social worker Joanne Zack-Pakes, who served as director of the SHILO Family Planning Educational and Counseling Center in Jerusalem for sixteen years (now known as Ladaat) and currently counsels independently on abortion issues, described the irony of the situation in Israel in which educated modern women are not familiar with the obstacles to getting an abortion in Israel. When her organization ran a training program for professional women in Haifa to volunteer at a hotline on these issues, she was surprised at the lack of awareness. "The women, all professionals in the field, did not have a clue what the abortion law was in Israel," she told us. "So if you have knowledgeable educated feminist women who do not know the abortion law, the mainstream population certainly does not know it."[52]

The problem is that this lack of public discourse about women's reproductive freedom and choice means women are not properly educated about family planning, a significant issue in women's economic, political, and overall well-being. As the United Nations Population Fund argues, "The ability of women to control their own fertility is absolutely fundamental to women's empowerment and equality. When a woman can plan her family, she can plan the rest of her life. When she is healthy, she can be more productive. And when her reproductive rights—including the right to decide the number, timing and spacing of her children, and to make decisions regarding reproduction free of discrimination, coercion and violence—are promoted and protected, she has freedom to participate more fully and equally in society."[53] Clearly, getting educated about processes of abortion thus has benefits not only for women, but also for Israel more generally.

Women's lack of knowledge also creates another problem: the easy entry of religious antiabortion groups using inflammatory religious rhetoric to prevent women from having abortions. The right-wing newspaper *Israel Today* announced in 2011 that "Israel still has an abortion problem"—that is, that there are "too many" abortions in Israel. "Since the founding of the State of Israel in 1948, more than 1.5 million babies have been aborted—more than the number of Jewish children killed in the Holocaust. Going by current birth rates, had those children been allowed a chance at life, there could be 5 million to 10 million more Israelis today," the author writes, fueling the idea that it is the job of Jewish women to have as many babies as possible because of the Holocaust. The paper also announced that it will be partnering with the antiabortion group Be'ad Chaim to reduce the number of abortions in Israel.[54] Antiwomen, radical religious ideas are thus spreading into mainstream Israeli discourse.

An organization that Americans would staunchly deem pro-life called Efrat can be seen and heard all around Israel, on billboards, in newspapers, and in radio spots. "Are you pregnant and don't know what to do?" the announcer innocently asks. "Call us!" But the only solution that Efrat offers is to convince women to have the baby, even if the pregnancy is unwanted, unhealthy, or dangerous. Efrat uses outrageous language to attract attention, like an ad on the front page of the *Jerusalem Post* that reads: "Efrat's success: The Health Ministry reports [a] 19% decrease in [the] number of abortions! But 150 unborn babies are still aborted every day. Tens of thousands of children have been already saved by Efrat. Become a partner to save even more." The goals of the organization clearly have more to do with the (male) founder's political agenda than with women's well-being. "In memory of the over one and a half million Jewish children who perished [in the Holocaust]," the Efrat materials read, "[Herschel] Feigenbaum founded EFRAT, to increase the Jewish birthrate in Israel."[55] Women seeking abortions are thus compared to Nazis, threatening the Jewish people with extinction.

In the worldview of Efrat, an organization established by religious men with strong ties to Republican senators and Haredi rabbis, women's bodies serve the Jewish collective. But this is only one face of the organization. To the broad Israeli public, Efrat tries to come across as a type of Planned Parenthood organization, seeking to "assist" women who are considering abortion. Indeed, according to Ruth Tidhar, MSW, assistant director of Efrat and the only woman listed as senior staff of the organization, Efrat is simply providing "information." This "information" includes one million pamphlets distributed each year that describe the early development of the fetus. "A woman who has an abortion is going to feel a lot of sorrow afterward from it," says Tidhar, admitting that she herself never had an abortion. "You want to have an abortion—fine. But just know that 90% of the women who have abortions are really sorry about it afterward." Efrat's unfounded claim that almost all women regret abortions—like their fabricated statistic of 28,000 illegal abortions in Israel each year—fuels a bizarre rhetoric quite unlike anything heard in America. "You have to write this," Tidhar told us. "That we're out of this American pro-choice/pro-life box. We're something else altogether. We don't do lobbying, we don't do legislation. We are the real pro-choice. We are giving women a real choice."[56] Or so Efrat claims.

Hedva Eyal, coordinator of the Isha L'Isha reproductive rights project, shudders at this analogy. She shared with Dr. Zeller and me an incident when a couple approached them for guidance in having an abortion. The couple had originally called Efrat for help, not knowing that Efrat was an antiabortion group. They subsequently received persistent phone calls from an Efrat volunteer, recounting horrific stories about what would happen if she had an abortion. The woman called Isha L'Isha crying and traumatized. "They eventually stopped hounding her, but meanwhile we have a traumatized woman on our hands," Eyal said.[57]

The work of Efrat finally came to public attention in October 2012 when eighteen-year-old Raz Attias was killed by police after planning a double suicide with his girlfriend. According to Raz's mother, three activists from Efrat who called themselves "pregnancy guards" sat with the girl at the hospital, telling her not to have an abortion. Tidhar categorically denied that Efrat had any contact with the girl.[58] Efrat came under public attack following these events. Nevertheless, Israel's chief rabbis came out with a letter of public support for Efrat, praising them for preventing the "killing [of] fetuses, which is like actual murder."[59] Shortly thereafter, the Jerusalem Conference decided to award the prestigious "Jerusalem Prize" to Efrat. "We found it especially necessary to award them the prize this year because of the unfair opposition from the public and media over the past year," David (Dudu) Sa'ada, director of sponsoring organization B'Sheva, explained.[60]

Perhaps most disturbing is the financial aspect of this story. While Ladaat, the pro-choice organization, is operating on an annual budget of $150,000—none of which is allocated for advertising—Guidestar Israel shows that that Efrat is working off a $4 million budget, all from "private donations," including approximately $300,000 for advertising.[61] This glaring economic disparity is also gendered: the Efrat board and senior staff are predominantly male, while the Ladaat staff and board are predominantly female. This has implications not only for advertising, but also for reaching women. Only six hundred women come through Ladaat's doors each year (to get free counseling or visit a clinic with a doctor who provides gynecological exams and discusses and dispenses birth control information and samples), while Efrat has some two thousand volunteers who spend their time speaking to women, sometimes seeking them out, and sometimes even standing outside the Ladaat office in the center of Jerusalem. It is hardly surprising, then, that while Efrat claims to have helped three thousand to four thousand women a year, Ladaat's numbers are going down. It is almost as if there is an unofficial battle over the pregnant womb, and thus far, Efrat is winning on all fronts.

Meretz Knesset member Zahava Gal-On is almost a lone soldier on the legal battlefront for women's reproductive rights. The only Knesset member over the past decade to try to do away with the abortion panels, she proposed a bill in 2006 that would remove the four preconditions for abortion and leave the decision up to a woman and her doctor.

"The bill seeks to create a new discourse around pregnancy and abortion that is not about motherhood but rather about equality and women's rights to control their bodies and their fertility," Gal-On told me, "one in which the woman is at the center. I wanted to advance a change in the societal ethos via legislative action."[62]

Gal-On's attempt to bring the issues to the public light with her proposal to cancel the abortion law failed. Surprisingly, even some feminist lawmakers voted against it. The reason seems to be that they are afraid of the religious parties and the possibility that by undoing the abortion bill, abortions will become harder for women rather than easier. "Nobody wants to wake a sleeping bear," said Joanne Zack-Pakes of the Israel Family Planning Association. "It is so tied up with coalition government and the religious having such power. The professionals are often worried if we bring it up to the foreground and bring it up to the press because they are afraid it'll get more restrictive. So therefore everything is hush-hush around abortion."[63]

Feminist legislators may be justified in their fears of the religious parties. Then Chief Rabbis Shlomo Amar and Yona Metzger wrote in opposition to Gal-On's proposal that the "killing of fetuses in their mothers' wombs" is akin to "murdering souls" and "delays the redemption," introducing a language that had until this point mostly been absent or under the radar. Two years later, in 2007, Shas MK Nissim Zeev proposed an opposing bill to make late-term abortions illegal. "What is happening in Israel is murder, every day," he told the press following his proposal. His party leader, Eli Yishai, supported him, saying, "I know some people think he's being extreme, but I want to tell you honestly and personally, that children in the womb are expecting us to be brave. Other countries in the world have laws that are stricter than this. Even France." Meanwhile, Rabbi Eliyahu—the "Rishon L'Zion"—wrote in support of Zeev that "millions [sic] of children have been cut down alive since the state [of Israel] was created" and compared it to what the ancient Egyptians did to Jewish babies. "There, too, there was a panel of doctors who decided that it was okay for the king to kill Jewish children." Eliyahu also attacked the midwives and the doctors, who he accused of being murderers, and argued that this is not only about the commandment to "be fruitful and multiply," but also about bringing the redemption closer.[64]

Meanwhile, Irit Rosenblum, in collaboration with Meretz MKs Nitzan Horowitz and Zahava Gal-On, has proposed a revised abortion bill, but it seems to be lost in a pile somewhere in the Knesset, and the ruling party has expressed intentions to leave it there for the time being. A Knesset committee debate initiated by Gal-On on the subject of canceling the abortion committees was deferred indefinitely.[65] And so the issue lingers.

While some religious leaders are trying to introduce radical concepts about abortion to the Israeli public, religious women are quietly having abortions. Dr. Jordana Hyman, an ob-gyn who treated religious women in Israel for many years, said, "Religious women are having abortions. Haredi women are also having abortions. Usually they involve a rabbi in making the decision. I have seen women terminate a pregnancy because of an unintentional pregnancy in a case of severe postpartum depression. I have had patients consider abortion as an option, mostly ultimately not going through with it, and have spoken to their rabbis at their request."[66] In other words, religious leaders may want to control women's bodies, but some women are protesting via abortion.

There are also economic reasons for religious women to have abortions. Religious Jewish women, for example, not only face excessive pressure to have large families from a young age, but are also more likely than other Israeli women to be poor. Where religious neighborhoods such as Bnei Brak and Meah She'arim are also the poorest—an estimated one in four ultra-Orthodox children lives under the poverty line in Israel—the absence of education for family planning can have severe socioeconomic implications for both women and the community at a whole, such as poor nutrition, health, and educational opportunities. Abortion as family planning is also a way to be a little less poor. No wonder Efrat entices pregnant women with a package that includes a monthly $300 stipend, basic baby supplies, and diapers for a year. Efrat is effectively bribing women to have babies, and these financial incentives can have a very powerful influence on both poor women and religious women. But this is only a Band-Aid solution. The long-term consequences of having an unwanted baby include a lifetime of financial, emotional, physical, and psychological stress, all of which ultimately threaten women's well-being.

Statistics about the number of religious women having abortions are difficult to obtain. Orly Hasson Tsitsuashvili, the executive director of Ladaat, told us that one out of six women who come to Ladaat are religious, most of whom are "young and married but not ready to have a child yet. It's family planning."[67] She also notes that most have not used birth control pills properly, reinforcing the idea that family planning is not properly taught in Israel, especially not in the religious communities. The incidence of abortion among religious women demonstrates a lack of balanced education about fertility and family planning. And as we know, education about family planning is strongly correlated with women's health, education, and overall well-being.

Meanwhile, there are signs that perhaps Israel's abortion policy may be changing. On January 5, 2014, the Israeli cabinet approved a law making abortion free for all women ages twenty to thirty-three. An announcement about a newly amended healthcare package included funding for more than six thousand women seeking to terminate their pregnancies, at the cost of 16 million NIS ($4.6 million U.S.). The funding will primarily benefit single women, young women, and women carrying illegitimate babies. *Times of Israel* columnist Debra Kamin, commenting on this change, wrote, "The number of nations that now take a stance as liberal as Israel's on abortion can be counted on one hand."[68]

But others disagree with that assessment. Rebecca Steinfeld responded in *Haaretz* that the claim of Israel being one of the most liberal countries in the world on abortion is wishful thinking. "Despite the positive elements, women in Israel must still surmount a series of obstacles to obtain legal abortions: criteria, committees, and campaigning anti-abortion organizations," Steinfeld argued. "In order to fulfill the criteria, some women are forced to lie, especially married women, who must claim they're mentally ill or pregnant due to extramarital sex. This can have dangerous repercussions given that religious authorities have exclusive jurisdiction over marriage and divorce in Israel. It's not surprising that most women undergoing illegal abortions are thought to be married women aged nineteen to forty. This goes to show that requiring women to fulfill certain criteria can compromise their honesty, further undermine their marital rights, or risk their health."[69]

Still, the legislation does not eliminate the abortion committees, and it does not silence the critics. Dr. Eli Schussheim, chairman of Efrat, was quoted as saying that the new rule is like "stealing… from sick people…and giving the money instead as a prize to six thousand negligent women."[70] Nevertheless, women in difficult situations with unwanted pregnancies now have a slightly easier time getting the abortions they need.

The pressure on Israeli women—especially religious women—to have many babies without considering the impact of these decisions on their own health has many troubling, long-term consequences for women.

Certainly Israel's overall pro-natalist culture has advantages for Israeli women. One only has to compare the status of motherhood for the working Israeli woman and the working American woman to realize that the idealization of motherhood comes with some great perks. Women are literally paid to have babies and to look after them, and Israeli culture is overall very friendly to children.

However, Israel's idealization of motherhood needs to take into account maternal health, which in many cases it does not. Rather, women often become objectified in the medical establishment, frequently considered vehicles for producing the next generation rather than whole people with whole minds.

Chapter 7

A NOT-SO-PERFECT UNION: MARRIAGE, DIVORCE, AND THE ENDLESS SUFFERING OF CHAINED WOMEN

Languages reveal a lot about the culture to which they belong. Some of the most informative parts of the language and the culture(s) in which it is spoken are often the hardest to translate. For example, the fact that there are fifty-three different words for types of snow in Inuit tells us how important snow is in Inuit culture.[1] The common Thai word tɕāj has no single-word equivalent in most other languages, but it means "sincere kindness and willingness to help others, even before they asked, without expecting something in return." It's the same for the Swedish *mångata*, "a roadlike reflection of the moon in the water," or the Greek φιλότιμο, "friend-honor," "to respect and honor your friends, the quintessence of Greeks."[2] These words are like linguistic secrets: they reflect unique elements of their culture that no other culture can quite emulate, at least not in a word.

Hebrew, too, has a word that is untranslatable. When I first learned this, I was excited at the prospect that my beloved language also has something special—until I discovered that the untranslatable word is not a source of honor or pride but rather a source of shame. The untranslatable Hebrew word is agunah, which most literally means a "chained woman." An agunah is a woman who is stuck in a marriage that she has already exited because her husband refuses to grant her a divorce, something notoriously unique to Jewish life. There doesn't seem to be a one-word linguistic equivalent to this in other languages or societies, and that, in and of itself, is telling of the values of Jewish culture.

The problem of the agunah in Jewish culture has existed for two millennia. It is based on the original Torah, which states that divorce happens when a man gives his wife a writ of divorce—known as a *gett*—and thus releases her. Rabbis over the generations have interpreted this to mean that only a man can "give" a *gett* or, effectively, initiate a divorce. (Although, interestingly, historical evidence suggests that this was not always the case. Documents from the Cairo Geniza show that in fifth century BCE Elephantine, women could initiate divorce and give their husbands the *gett*.[3]) Starting in the Mishnaic and Talmudic periods from the second century forward, when the oral rabbinic law was codified, the standard law became fixed that divorce takes place through the actions of the man onto the woman—even against her will—and not in reverse. As the Babylonian Talmud clearly states, "A woman is sent away [by her husband] whether she wants to be sent away or even if she doesn't want to be sent away, a man sends away his wife only if he wants to."[4] Today, Jewish women are fully dependent on the will and volition of their husbands in order to exit marriage.

"Rachel," a forty-eight-year old mother of five living in an Orthodox neighborhood of Jerusalem and a long-time colleague and friend of mine, faced this exact conundrum. A social worker by profession, she had been married for seven years and had five children when she decided she wanted to get a divorce. Her husband was verbally and emotionally abusive, yelling at her if the house wasn't spotless, throwing the dinner she cooked into the garbage if there was something he didn't like about it, and maintaining complete control over finances to such an extent that she wasn't allowed to go to the supermarket by herself. His abuse was often couched in smiles and tenderness, of the "Don't you worry about the shopping, dear; I'll take care of everything for you" variety. Only twice did he actually hit her, and she tried to dismiss it as an aberration. It took her years to understand that even when it's couched in smiles, his ultimate need to control her was bad for her. It wasn't until a friend said to her, "You know, Rachel, this is abuse," that she realized something was very wrong in her marriage and she decided to leave.

She and her husband tried court-mandated counseling for over a year, but nothing changed. Her husband, a statuesque, eloquent, and well-dressed ultra-Orthodox man who worked as a kashrut supervisor in a food company, had strong ties to the rabbinic judges and was able to easily manipulate opinion and rulings in his favor. He also emotionally manipulated the children and worked hard to turn them against her. After six years of trying to get divorced, her lawyer advised her that if she wanted freedom, she had to be willing to give her husband whatever he wanted. He demanded not only money, but also custody of the children. Despite several psychologists' opinions that the children should be with the mother and not the father and that the husband was abusive and unreliable, the lawyer advised that she give up custody in exchange for receiving her *gett*, advising that she could fight that later. She had already been an agunah for six years and was trapped. So she followed his advice and received her *gett* but lost her children. Ten years later, she is still struggling to get her children back.

This imbalanced Jewish divorce system has been problematic

long before the creation of Israel, since the times that the Jewish oral law was codified in the first centuries of the Common Era. The Jewish legal books are replete with discussions of divorce that acknowledge unequal exit power from marriage. The 1,500-year-old Talmud responds to the question about what happens when a man refuses to grant his wife a *gett* with the solution, "You force him until he says, 'I want to.'" The Talmud also promoted a certain degree of compassion toward unhappily married women, which many scholars consider evidence that the rabbis were themselves ambivalent about their own sexism. In fact, the Talmud offered a list of reasons why a woman should be entitled to get divorced. Some are amusing, such as the husband works in a tannery and always smells like leather; some are painful, such as he is infertile. (Significantly, though, domestic violence and unfaithfulness don't make the list of objectionable traits.) The rabbi credited with offering the most far-reaching solutions to women's suffering in his time was the early eleventh-century rabbinic leader Rabbeinu Gershom (Gershom ben Judah, 960–1040), who instituted what turned out to be a radical innovation meant to protect women. He issued an edict banning polygamy as well as divorce against the woman's will. At the very least, a woman could not be thrown out of her marriage on a whim, and her husband had to treat her like his one and only.

Although Rabbeinu Gershom's edict giving women some volition in divorce is still valid today, obstacles remain. For one thing, a man can get out of listening to the edict through a little loophole called the "letter from one hundred rabbis." A man who wants to divorce his wife against her will, or alternatively who wants to take a second wife without bothering to divorce the first, can get one hundred rabbis to sign a letter releasing him, and he's fine.[5]

This isn't as hard as it sounds, and each year, several men in Israel get out of having to divorce their wives this way, able to start new marriages while their wives are still stuck in the first one. "Every year, the chief rabbis sign twenty to twenty-five cases enabling men to take second wives," said veteran lawyer and agunah activist Sharon Shenhav of the International Jewish Women's Human Rights Watch. "We had a case where the husband would only concede to the *gett* if his wife gave up all her rights to the apartment. She refused and he was allowed to take a second wife. The man claimed that he wanted to fulfill the mitzvah of procreation and since he had only daughters with his first wife, he had not fulfilled this mitzvah. His first wife was fifty-six years old and could no longer bear children, so he was permitted a second wife."[6]

In addition to the one-hundred-rabbis loophole, even if it means committing polygamy, Rabbeinu Gershom's edict left in place the larger problem with Jewish divorce: men still ultimately have the final and authoritative say in the matter. Moreover, the sensitivity that earlier generations had to women's marital limbo went away just a century after Rabbeinu Gershom. Another medieval rabbi named Rabbeinu Tam (Rabbi Jacob Ben Meir, 1100–1170), issued a ruling that a *gett* that is coerced is invalid. This one ruling, which was later accepted and adopted by major rabbinic leaders from the Middle Ages through modern times, effectively negated whatever protections women had accumulated until then.

This ruling—compounded by a follow-up ruling by the Maharshdam (Rabbi Samuel ben Moses de Medina, 1505–1589) that says men's demands in exchange for a *gett* should be adhered to, whatever the cost—causes enormous suffering to Jewish women for a number of reasons. They make rabbinical judges afraid to put pressure on men to release their wives, worried that such a divorce would be considered invalid anyway. After all, if a divorce is not valid and a woman remarries, it's as if she is committing adultery or bigamy, and any children she has in that second relationship will be considered *mamzerim*, illegitimate Jews, ostracized from the community. The rabbis are so worried about creating *mamzerim* that they would rather be "cautious" and keep women as agunot.

These opinions, some nearly a millennium old, astonishingly keep women chained in unwanted marriages indefinitely. "With all the confusion, conflicting opinions, hesitation, conservatism, and dissonance with modern conceptions of marriage and divorce in these ancient, holy texts," veteran agunah activist Dr. Susan Weiss and journalist Netty Gross-Horowitz write in their book *Marriage and Divorce in the Jewish State*, "the rabbis sitting on Israeli rabbinic court tribunals approach divorce claims with more reverence for them [the texts themselves] than for the plight of women denied a divorce. Rather than make decisions that may challenge what they see as immutable, divine rules or the opinions of revered rabbinic authorities, the rabbis cajole and delay, hesitant to issue decisions of any kind, particularly ones that may interfere with a husband's 'free will.'"[7]

The result of all this is a Jewish divorce system that often leaves women stuck in unwanted marriages with no viable or foreseeable exit. These women, these agunot, live lives in limbo, neither married nor divorced, unable to move forward in their lives, build families, or just be free. A woman who ignores the law and builds a family renders her future children *mamzerim*, cut off from the Jewish people for generations. Moreover, considering how vulnerable women are when they seek divorce—they risk either becoming a chained woman or a woman cut off—the system is ripe for abuse and extortion. Men who seek to hurt their wives or control them forever need not reach for a gun or a knife. They have the *gett* as a weapon for potentially perpetual abuse. A man who wants to benefit from this system need only make some demands from his wife—financial, emotional, or otherwise—in return for granting her a *gett*, and he will undoubtedly be the only winner, because under the current Jewish divorce system, he has all the leverage. He holds her freedom in his hands.

Although agunot exist all around the world—in the United States and Canada, 462 cases of agunot were recorded in the past few years—the system in Israel is infinitely worse for women.[8] This is because, in Israel, every single case of marriage and divorce is controlled by the state rabbinical courts, a system largely managed and maintained by ultra-Orthodox rabbis at the expense of Israeli taxpayers. According to the 1953 Rabbinical Courts Jurisdiction (Marriage and Divorce) law, these courts have sole judicial power to make decisions with respect to issues of marriage and divorce for Jews living in Israel, and all marriages and divorces will be according to Torah law. That is, under their jurisdiction, there is essentially no such thing as "civil divorce" or "civil marriage." That means that for a Jewish Israeli to be registered as married or divorced in Israel, one has to go through this state-controlled, ultra-Orthodox system, which, as Weiss and Gross-Horowitz write, "foster[s] a culture of extortion in Israeli rabbinic courts, where contested divorces are not solved by pressuring stubborn and recalcitrant husbands to give the *gett*, but by pressuring women to give in to their husbands' terms."[9]

"The problem of agunot has always existed, but as religion has become more strict and fundamentalism has grown, as it has around the world, so too in Israel," says Robyn Shames, director of the International Coalition for Agunah Rights (ICAR). "In addition, ultra-Orthodox men discovered that the State of Israel provides well-paid jobs for people like them, and as a result the rabbinical court system has gone from being run by moderate Orthodox rabbis to being run by ultra-Orthodox men who are themselves becoming increasingly fundamentalist." Shames argues that the entire system of having a state system of rabbinical courts is flawed. "At one time in history, rabbinical courts were part of the community, the rabbis knew the people who stood before them and there was more humanity, more connection. Today, since the state has taken over the job of running rabbinical courts, the rabbi is not part of your community, and he doesn't even feel anything toward you because the ultra-Orthodox have their own courts. It's not even their own people who come to them. So there's this distance between the rabbinical judges and the people coming to the court. The judges don't feel any great affinity toward the people standing before them, they don't feel some great urgent need to solve their problems. They don't see them as 'their people.' So they feel very free to be strict because they don't feel the 'tears of the agunah' as rabbis once did."[10] Put differently, the state ownership of the rabbinical court has effectively transformed a communal institution to a state bureaucracy, with all that entails.

The precise number of agunot in Israel is hard to obtain. In part, this is because there is no clear definition of who qualifies as one. Women's rights' organizations cite an estimated 10,000 agunot living in Israel today.[11] However, for many years, then-head of the Jerusalem Rabbinical Court Rabbi Eli Ben-Dahan (now deputy religious affairs minister) denied such figures, claiming that only a few dozen cases exist. In 2009, Ben-Dahan claimed that there were 180 agunot, using a vague definition that in order to be an agunah, one's divorce case must have been open for at least two years and not resolved. Ben-Dahan also outrageously claimed in 2006 that there were more recalcitrant women than recalcitrant men and argued that many of the open cases were simply about financial disputes, with no evidence to back this.[12] What really puts his claims to doubt, however, is that two years after he said that there were only 180 agunot, he announced that the Rabbinic Court Special Task Force managed to free 292 women.[13] One has to wonder where all those extra agunot suddenly appeared from.

Meanwhile, veteran legal scholar and agunah activist Professor Ruth Halperin-Kaddari disputes the courts' method for calculating this figure because it fails to account for all the cases in which women cave in to extortion pressures in order not to become an agunah, or women who decided not to divorce at all in order to avoid the situation entirely. Halperin-Kaddari estimates that, when calculated that way, there are one hundred thousand women in Israel who fit into the category of agunah.[14] Perhaps the most accurate figure being floated around is this: from 1995 until February 11, 2008 (more recent figures were hard to come by), a total of 40,541 divorce cases did not end in divorce, including cases that the rabbinic courts referred to as both "active" and "inactive" (with inactive cases being those the court closed).[15] Although these are not all necessarily agunah cases, it seems that this portrait is indicative of some of what is going on in the rabbinical courts in terms of dragging out cases without the women even being aware that they are becoming agunah.

Statistics are also hard to obtain because the rabbinical courts keep notoriously poor records; there are no regular protocols, and the court only has a scribe summarize hearings, sometimes very cryptically, with decisions that are several lines long. The makeup of the judges' panel can be changed without warning, and new judges can then go and start proceedings from square one, asking to see papers and hear testimonies that are many years past. Women are often very frustrated when decisions are randomly overturned because there happens to be a new judge on the case. Months and even years can pass between court hearings, and there is no accountability or even apology for this.

In effect, there is no state oversight into the rabbinical courts. "Three quarters of what transpires can be left out of the final protocol," one activist said. "It is not like civil court where everything has to be transcribed. There are no rules and there is complete disorder." She described a situation in which a woman's nose was broken by her husband in the rabbinical court and the incident was omitted from the protocol. "What goes into the protocol is very subjective," Shenhav notes. "It is not actual testimony and it cannot be appealed."[16] In another case, brought by Weiss and Gross-Horowitz, a woman's husband illegally recorded her walking around at home when she thought she was alone under the pretense that she was having an affair, which was never substantiated and she consistently denied. The rabbinical judges spent fifteen minutes viewing footage of the woman walking around in her underwear. Mortified, she sat there, the only woman in the courtroom, in what Weiss and Gross-Horowitz call a "sex trial" and was completely helpless as her privacy was totally and unjustifiably violated. Even though the rabbinical court system is paid for by taxpayers—and more importantly controls the lives and personal status of all Jews living in Israel—the state seems to have no mechanism for regulating its tangled bureaucratic infrastructure. The rabbinical courts seem to follow their own rules.

On top of all that, the rabbinical court is often a sexist place to begin with. There are no female judges; judges' panels are all male. The court reporters, clerks, and even the janitors are men.

When the clerks schedule hearings, they tell women to come "modestly dressed."[17]

In addition, it wasn't until 1994 when the Supreme Court forced the rabbinical courts to allow women to have religious pleaders—the equivalent of a lawyer—that any women with power appeared in the rabbinic courtroom. For a few years, Sharon Shenhav was the only woman on the committee to appoint rabbinic judges, representing the Israel Bar Association. And for about ten years, Dr. Rachel Levmore was the only woman working on the administrative side of the rabbinical courts, as part of the "Agunah Unit" in the Directorate of the Israeli Rabbinical Court in Jerusalem. But for many years, except for the women pleaders, there were no women with any power inside the system at all. In August 2013, four women were added to the committee to appoint religious judges—a huge achievement that came about thanks to the efforts of the activists described in this chapter.

The fault here, it should be noted, is not only with the rabbinical judges, but also with the secular powers that be, which empower the rabbinic patriarchy to work solely for their own political goals. The general absence of women on the committee to appoint rabbinic judges is a case in point. The committee has twelve seats, almost all of which end up going to men—some are seats for city rabbis, who are by definition men; some are seats for certain cabinet ministers, who are usually men; and some are seats for Knesset members from religious parties, who are also only men. There is only one seat available to women, and that is as the representative of the Israel Bar Association.

All of this makes it very difficult to assess what is really happening in the rabbinical courts—and especially difficult to garner accurate information about what's happening with women and divorce there. When I was involved with the Jerusalem-based agunah rights organization Mavoi Satum, we focused less on the precise number of agunot and more on the risk factors that all Jewish women face when trying to divorce in Israel—that is, the way we viewed it, the act of refusing to give one's wife a *gett* is an act of abuse and control, the last in a long series of abusive behaviors. We were surprised to discover in one of our early years that 100 percent of all cases that were referred to us at Mavoi Satum were of women who had been emotionally and/or physically abused in their marriages. (We used to cite 96 percent just to be on the safe side, but we never encountered that imagined 4 percent.) That's when it began to occur to us that the agunah issue has to be viewed in the larger context of spousal abuse. An agunah is not just someone who is denied divorce; it would seem that an agunah is, by definition and by practice, an abused woman.

It is a well-documented fact among domestic violence workers that the moment of exit is the most dangerous moment for an abused woman. For a man whose entire life is based on hurting and controlling women, the moment she says, "I'm leaving," the man can flip out. It is no wonder that many of the women killed in Israel by their domestic partners were killed *after* they filed for divorce. Put in this context, we can understand what *gett* recalcitrance is about: it's the last stand of an abusive spouse bent on having ultimate control of his wife. He does not need a gun or a knife to hurt her, because he has the *gett*.[18]

Given the power that Jewish law gives to husbands, and given the dynamics of domestic abuse in which abusive men will look for any means to control their wives, especially at the moment when the woman is about to exit, the risk of Jewish women becoming agunot is very high. I would argue, as Mavoi Satum does, that one in seven married Jewish women—the rate of spousal abuse in Israel—is at *high* risk of becoming an agunah.

Significantly, research shows that Jewish women around the world are likely to stay three times as long in an abusive relationship as non-Jewish women. Abused women in America stay on average two to four years, for a whole host of emotional, psychological, financial, and even logistical reasons. Leaving an abusive man takes courage, not to mention fortitude, careful thought, and practical planning.[19]

In the Jewish world, women stay on average eight to twelve years. This should raise a huge red flag in the Jewish community, which should be asking itself why this happens. How does the Jewish community socialize women into marriage? What is it about the way Jewish women are educated that makes them believe that abuse is somehow okay, that staying with abuse in marriage is the right thing to do? Why is it so hard for so many Jewish women to come to the understanding that they do not have to stay with an abusive spouse? According to feminist philosopher and author Susan Moller Okin, unequal exit power in marriage can have a devastating impact on women and in all likelihood contributes to the dynamic which keeps Jewish women in abusive marriages.[20] Ruth Halperin-Kaddari similarly argues that the agunah situation has a residual effect on all marriages, making women afraid to try to leave even when they want to.[21] What is truly horrifying about this situation is that Israel remains perhaps the only country in the Western world in which abused women are left in marital limbo. In other parts of the world, evidence of abuse in marriage is automatic grounds for divorce. In Israel, abusive men are given the ultimate power over their wives.

Helen, a forty-nine-year-old nurse and army officer who lives with her two children in the Jordan Valley, waited eight years for her husband to give her a *gett*. Although she says he showed no signs of violence when they met at the age of twenty-six and for the two years that they were dating, he eventually became so violent during their ten years of marriage that the police ordered him to stay away from the house and brought criminal charges against him. He was actually convicted of abuse for threatening to murder their two children. When he was forced to leave the house, he did so only after he took a hammer and destroyed it—every last bit of it, including floors and walls. For all these crimes, he received a sentence of six months of community service. Here is how Helen tells her story:

> *The process in the rabbinical court was a joke... As a woman, I'm nobody. The rabbis coddled my husband. They offered him money from the "agunah fund." "Maybe you should give her a gett?" they would suggest. They wouldn't force him, of course. Half the hearings he never showed up to. The process was ridiculously slow—a pathetic hearing every six months. My husband wouldn't show up, and there were no fines, no arrest warrants. He was forgiven, no big deal. Next time. That's how gently they dealt with him. And I'm just a piece of trash. They didn't even talk to me. They talked to my lawyer. I was a nothing, I was like air. I could come or not come, it didn't matter, it was like I wasn't even there.*[22]

Helen was thirty-eight years old when she applied for a divorce and was hoping to be able to rebuild her life. "I wanted to get married again, have another child," she said. "They took that from me. The rabbinical court stole that from me." Despite the intense religion-driven pro-natalism in Israel (see chapter six), rabbinical courts are not rushing to free agunot so that they can build the families that they want.

Even though she is a secular woman, Helen did not just want to live with a man without being married, because "I won't just bring a man into my house and live with him and my two children. That's not my educational standard. It's not my value system. I wouldn't do it." Plus, it should be noted that if the rabbinical court finds out that a woman who is still married is sleeping with another man, she is, according to Jewish law, permanently banned from ever marrying that other man. No such sanctions apply to men who commit adultery. Even if a man marries a second woman and has children with her, there are no consequences. The children are not even considered illegitimate. That particular status is reserved only for women who find another man—even a woman who has been waiting for a rightful *gett* for years.

Helen eventually got her *gett* thanks to the work of women's advocacy organizations, like CWJ, Mavoi Satum, ICAR, and Yad L'Isha, a legal aid center. Her attorneys hired a detective who found her husband trekking in Thailand for a year. He was brought back to Israel, and only after her lawyers had him arrested did he decide to give her a *gett*. Apparently, sitting in jail was the pressure he needed. Meanwhile, according to Susan Weiss and Netty Gross–Horowitz, "the halls of the religious courts are full of powerless women. Nobody is listening to them. Resignation and apathy reign."[23]

It's not all bad news though for these chained women. Since the 1990s, agunah activists have been working on various aspects of legislation to protect divorcing Jewish women in Israel. One of the first key pieces of legislation is based on the idea that men may be inclined to grant a *gett* if the right pressure from the right people is applied. The 1995 Law of Sanctions gives power to rabbinical courts to apply force to recalcitrant husbands, including revoking drivers' licenses, passports, and professional licenses—such as a license to practice medicine—and even putting a man in jail. To pass this law, agunah activists exerted many efforts on advocacy work vis-à-vis rabbis, literally getting rabbinic approval for the use of sanctions. Many rabbis agreed, although some still do not. As such, there are great disparities in how this law is applied in Israel. In Haifa, for example, Chief Rabbi She'ar Yashuv Cohen is a great supporter of women's rights, and the courts under his authority regularly and effectively use the sanctions to free women. Elsewhere in Israel, sanctions are barely used. So while this became the first real leverage that divorcing women have, it is used inconsistently and can be hard for the women to enforce if their rabbinical courts don't support it.

In 2011, over fifteen years after the Law of Sanctions was enacted, a new bill was proposed that would *force* rabbinical courts to use sanctions against recalcitrant husbands, regardless of whether they agreed with it. The bill, proposed by MKs Otniel Schneller (Kadima) and Zevulun Orlev (Habayit Hayehudi), would require the courts to initiate a hearing and get the process moving within thirty to ninety days if the court had previously ordered the husband to give a *gett* to his wife. The bill also mandated that the courts must track the *gett* process with precise recording of dates and regular convening of hearings. Shas legislators worked to block the bill, but it passed in 2012.[24]

On other fronts, the sanctions continue to be used in many

rabbinical courts, even if not all rabbinical judges choose to use them, and even when they do, the sanctions are not always effective. Some men would prefer to stay in jail for years rather than give their wives a *gett*. One man, Avraham Yihye, notoriously stayed in jail for thirty-three years until he died rather than grant his wife a *gett*. He was known to have told his wife that she would be a widow before she would ever be a divorcée.[25] (Life in prison apparently wasn't so bad—he got free room and board, some new friends, and eternal control of his wife.) Another man, Shai Cohen, was in prison for six years, and on the day in 2013 that he was brought to court to finally give the *gett*, he escaped from the bathroom window, causing a huge and futile police manhunt, because the rabbinical courts are powerless against recalcitrance.[26] In another twisted story, the state banned one recalcitrant husband from being allowed to buy a plot in a Jewish cemetery in Israel—although, if he is willing to give up the *gett* only after he dies, the wife won't need it anymore, because she'll be a widow rather than a divorcée.[27]

As we've seen, the rabbinical divorce court system as it was established encourages men to extort their wives. One key example is the Property Relations Law (1973), which ensured that property division rulings can only take place once a divorce has officially been granted, giving recalcitrant husbands the tools with which to extort their wives financially in exchange for the *gett*. A man can very easily say, "I won't give you the *gett* until you give me what I want in the divorce settlement." One key piece of legislation to try to reverse this, the Law of Division of Property proposed by Knesset Members Michael Melchior (Labor-Meimad) and Zevulun Orlev (National Religious Party, predecessor to the Habayit Hayehudi party), passed in 2008, reverses the process of division of property, so that courts can create divorce settlements before the *gett* process. This eliminates the dynamic of extortion from the *gett*-giving process.[28] This was a long time coming: women's organizations had been trying to reverse the original law of division of property since it was passed in 1973, but it took nearly four decades for them to gain strength over the opposing religious legislators. Mavoi Satum director Batya Kahana-Dror, who worked closely with Melchior and Orlev on the legislation, said that the law "corrects the balance of power between husbands and wives and amends a grievous wrong."

Women's groups continue to advance legislation to help free agunot. One bill currently being worked on hopes to fix the "race to the courthouse." Although the *gett* can only be given under the jurisdiction of the all-male judges of the rabbinical courts, the 1953 Rabbinical Courts Jurisdiction law gave civil courts authority to decide all other aspects of the divorce process, such as child custody, alimony, and the division of property. Consequently, wherever divorce was filed for first became the deciding court. In effect, because the rabbinical courts tend to be favorable to men, what often happens in Israel is a "race to the courthouse," with women racing to file first in civil court, likely to rule more in their favor, and men racing to file first in rabbinical court. This system only exacerbates the already trying process of divorce. One woman, whose story Weiss and Gross-Horowitz recall, spent nineteen years being dragged back and forth in a ping-pong of a divorce case, including one court revoking a *gett* that was already given.[29] Her suffering was a result not only of her husband's recalcitrance, but also of an ongoing competition that the rabbinical judges have with their civil counterparts. Under the new legislation, the family courts would automatically be in charge of all items other than the *gett*.

In one of the biggest legislative victories, MK Aliza Lavie (Yesh Atid) and MK Shuli Mualem (Habayit Hayehudi) advanced a bill—the first bill to be proposed in the current Knesset, which also signaled cross-partisan collaboration on women's issues—that would force the Committee for the Appointment of Rabbinic Judges to reserve four seats for women. There are currently no women on it. Significantly, although Mualem's own party failed to support her, the bill actually fulfills the demand of the High Court and the Attorney-General from earlier in the year to ensure adequate female representation on this committee. "It's incomprehensible that women not only cannot be religious judges but cannot influence who the judges are," Justice Minister Tzipi Livni said. Haredi MKs, on the other hand, were unmoved. "This bill says something that, if it were said about the (secular) courts, would cause outrage—that there is not true justice in the rabbinical courts," MK Ya'akov Margi (Shas) said.[30] Having women on the committee that appoints rabbinical judges is the first step—though hardly sufficient in itself—to bring gender equity to the divorce process in Israel. Even though there are still no women rabbinical judges, and even though women still lack the most basic right of being able to divorce of their own volition, at the very least, this move gives women a small but powerful role in speaking out for justice for women.

Despite these advances, the system remains fundamentally flawed because men have all the leverage in the divorce process and women have none. But Susan Weiss—as a lawyer, agunah activist, and CWJ director—is trying to shift that balance.

Weiss had an agunah client we'll call "Yael" who experienced some unexpected travails.[31] In the midst of an exhausting hearing, her husband made an outrageous demand: "Give me 100,000 NIS and I'll give you the *gett*." As she sank in despair and anger, the rabbinical judges surprised her. "How much of that can you give?" they asked her. Not knowing what to respond to this request for extortion, she threw out some random figure. "We can put in another 10,000 NIS," the judges replied. The money, they said, comes from their "agunah fund," a stash of funds ironically named that is used not to support agunot but to pay husbands in exchange for giving the *gett*. The rabbinical court is literally paying off recalcitrant men to divorce their wives, CWJ argued. It seems recalcitrance is a lucrative business.

The pleader in the courtroom was shocked that this was going on—but now had proof that there was something desperately wrong with the system. Following this and other similar events, the CWJ brought a High Court petition asking that this "agunah fund" be declared illegal. The funds—the exact amount of which remains unknown, as do their financial sources—were originally intended to be allocated for investigators to locate recalcitrant husbands who disappeared and to pay for issues that may have to be settled outside of Israel. In practice, the CWJ argued in their petition, since the early 1990s, the funds have been used primarily to pay off demands by husbands in exchange for the *gett*.

The rabbinical court defended the practice by saying that they were releasing agunot, not promoting extortion. In the end, the High Court accepted the arguments of the rabbinical court and determined that the practice is mostly fair and just, barring a few minor issues. One is that a woman should be added to the committee that oversees the funds, and the criteria for determining how the money is spent need to be formalized and made transparent. Also, the High Court ruled that the amount should not exceed 10,000 NIS ($2,600 U.S.) per case, except for "special circumstances." Although there are small victories in this decision—the inclusion of women on committees and a general cap on spending for recalcitrant men—overall, this decision was met with disappointment by women's groups. The High Court failed to acknowledge the presence of extortion in the divorce process and the role of rabbinical courts in advancing that dynamic. The rabbinical courts are "giving recalcitrant husbands a prize rather than a punishment," attorney Frances Raday said in dismay.[32]

A more significant strategy of using lawsuits to help redress the agunah injustice, which is also being spearheaded by CWJ, is filing tort lawsuits for damages incurred to agunot during their years of suffering. This particular strategy aims to redress the underlying gender imbalance in Jewish divorce by giving women some kind of financial leverage to use against their husbands. This strategy has met with some major successes. In 2004, the Family Court awarded damages of 425,000 NIS ($110,000 U.S.) to a woman for *gett* recalcitrance. In 2008, the Family Court also ruled that a man's recalcitrance causes undue suffering and is thus a cause for damages even when the rabbinic court has not yet "ordered" the husband to divorce his wife and awarded damages to the wife in the amount of 550,000 NIS ($140,000 U.S.).[33] In another case that year, a woman was awarded 680,000 NIS ($200,000 U.S.) in damages[34]—an award that was maintained on appeal in 2011, creating a new level of judicial precedent protecting women.[35] In 2010, the Family Court awarded 600,000 NIS plus $15,000 in damages for recalcitrance and repayment of money that the woman paid to her husband in exchange for the *gett*.[36]

The fact that women can now sue for damages changes the power balance in divorce and provides women with some much-needed leverage that has been missing in the Jewish divorce system for so long. It also forces the rabbinical court to acknowledge that this is a process that causes unnecessary harm to women. Finally, it may provide some much-needed relief to agunot and potential agunot by scaring men into giving the *gett*. In short, it changes the rules of the game.

CWJ has some other creative strategies for using the civil court system to make changes in the rabbinical courts. In 2008, CWJ sued the rabbinical court administration for issuing a tender for the job of legal assistants that allowed only men to apply. The Labor Court ruled in CWJ's favor, although the absence of women employees in the rabbinical court remains a major issue.[37]

Also, in 2010, the Family Court voided clauses in divorce agreements, authorized by the rabbinic court, in which a mother waived her parental rights in exchange for the *gett*.[38]

This is quite significant because often women abdicate custody in exchange for their own freedom and then struggle to regain parental rights vis-à-vis the state social welfare authorities. This is still relatively new, so it's difficult to know how it has affected divorces in Israel so far. But this ruling, like the damage lawsuits, has the potential to change the rules of the game.

Overall, there are many activists seeking creative strategies to alleviate the agunah problem—some twenty-seven organizations are members of the umbrella group ICAR, the International Coalition for Agunah Rights—and some of these strategies are starting to bear fruit. Still, the underlying injustice and the untenable power that the rabbinical courts have been granted by the state continue, and a permanent, far-reaching solution has not yet been implemented.

In some ways, the agunah problem is really only the symptom of a bigger problem in Israel. Around the world, the issue of agunot affects only religious Jews who choose to abide by Halacha, and the solutions available conform to that, such as halachic prenuptial agreements and conditional marriage. Indeed, Beit Hillel, an Orthodox academic institution, announced that they support the use of prenuptial agreements to free agunot.[39] Although this announcement is better than nothing, the cry is rather weak and late in coming against the backdrop of crowds demanding actual systemic reform. Here's why: prenups do not actually free agunot; rather, they potentially can prevent women from becoming agunot in the future—though that's not a certainty—and prenups definitely do not alter the entire patriarchal structure of the divorce system or address the problem of Orthodox control over marriage and divorce in Israel.

By contrast, there are civil options available around the world that are not used in Israel. As Weiss and Gross-Horowitz point out, civil courts in New York, Canada, South Africa, England, and Scotland have all implemented regulations and laws to protect agunot in different ways.[40] France, for example, was the first country to allow agunot to sue their husbands for damages, and courts in other places have found creative ways to force men to pay for turning their wives into agunot.

These developments all illustrate that the problem in Israel is not only about Jewish law, but also about an absence of protections for women via civil law. The problem is worsened by the profound lack of choice for people seeking a divorce: no one has a choice about whether to abide by the religious system. It is the only system available to use in order to officially obtain a *gett*. To counter this, more and more Israelis are choosing to opt out of the entire rabbinical court system and get married outside of Israel. By getting married outside of Israel, they are never officially "married" in Israel and therefore wouldn't need to get officially divorced there—at least in theory. Cyprus, it seems, has become the preferred destination for this. But even for those Israelis, they may run, but they cannot always hide.

Just ask Vered Shavit. She did everything she could to avoid the rabbinical court. She got married in Cyprus and then had a non-Orthodox, nonrecognized ceremony. By all accounts, she should not have been considered married in Israel. But when her husband left her, he decided that he wanted to get a proper divorce anyway and opened a file in the rabbinical courts. The couple was not even technically married according to the rules of the rabbinical court, because Reform rabbis are not recognized as rabbis in Israel. But that didn't stop the court from demanding that she get a *gett*. In the end, she couldn't avoid the system. She made a video about it, "dancing on the steps of the rabbinical court," just to have a final say.

Ultimately, the agunah issue is just one aspect of the deeper problem in Israel, which is the absence of civil marriage and civil divorce in Israel. This is arguably the greatest injustice to women, because it forces all Jewish women to go through a system that could permanently trap them in unwanted marriages. In fact, it's unfair to men also in that it deprives men of options and religious freedoms as well. Weiss and Gross-Horowitz make a very strong case that the current divorce system in Israel violates a whole series of human rights and civil rights, including the right to freedom of conscience, the right to equal treatment under the law, the right to privacy, the right to due process, the right to property, the right to liberty, and the right to marry.[41] They also argue that the lack of separation of religion and state and the inordinate power given to religious judges are at the root of women's suffering, as well as the suffering of converts and non-Orthodox Jews in Israel, which we will examine in the following chapter.

Overall, the agunah problem represents such a terrifying threat to women's civil liberties in Israel that even after writing this chapter and working on this issue for nearly twenty years, I still find myself shocked by it. Certainly there are some compelling partial solutions in play that use legislation, tort law, and Jewish law to provide some kind of prevention, protection, and leverage to women. But these are not comprehensive enough and have not yet addressed the systemic gender imbalance that rests at the core of this issue and continues to threaten the well-being of Jewish women.

Chapter 8

THE OFFICIAL JUDAISM: BLACKLISTS, BASTARDS, AND THE CONVERSION PROBLEM

When "Michal" was getting divorced from her then-husband "Avi," she had no idea that the threat of becoming an agunah would become the least of her problems. In fact, she was about to embark on a saga in which her entire identity would be revoked from her, in which she would lose her earnestly acquired status as a member of the Jewish people. With the story of Michal, the rabbinical courts took on a brand-new role: the power to determine who is and isn't Jewish, not only among those who are born Jews, but also among those who converted decades or generations ago.

Michal, who officially converted to Judaism in the 1990s (by the Special Rabbinic Court for Conversion in Israel, headed by Rabbi Haim Druckman), had been married to an Israeli man, Avi, for fifteen years when they decided to get divorced. The divorce was amicable, and when they walked into the Regional Rabbinic Court in Ashdod with a signed and authorized divorce agreement, they assumed that the rest of the process would be a quick formality. They were both ready for Avi to give Michal the *gett* and for both of them to move on with their lives. As they were about to begin the ceremony, the rabbinic judge, Rabbi

Avraham Atiya, suddenly asked Michal two completely unrelated questions: "Do you use the electricity on Shabbat?" and "Do you go to the *mikveh*?" Michal had no idea that her impromptu answers would become a nightmare for her, as the court was about to retroactively nullify her conversion and render her children blacklisted too.

"Michal had no idea what was going on," explained Rivkah Lubitch and Susan Weiss of the CWJ, which represented Michal.[1] "In the hearing room, the rabbinic judge did not say one word to Michal asserting that he was contemplating the validity of her conversion." Michal spent months waiting for her final divorce papers to come in the mail. Instead she received a forty-six-page ruling that contained mostly issues irrelevant to her divorce. But it held one key sentence for her: that her conversion fifteen years earlier was invalid and that her children's names were put on the "ineligible for marriage" rabbinic blacklist. It's astounding that in this day and age, they could even do that.

The rest of the document was equally as irrelevant to the divorce process and reads like a political-religious manifesto about the validity of conversions performed by Rabbi Druckman, Rabbi Avior, the military rabbinic courts, and Rabbi Yisrael Rosen. (It is worth noting that the rabbinic court Rabbi Druckman was heading was established by Prime Minister Ariel Sharon, under the auspices of the Prime Minister's Office, and answered directly to Chief Rabbi Shlomo Amar.) This "Special Court" under which Michal was converted apparently had sidestepped the jurisdiction of the rabbinical court (though the rabbinical courts do not have the authority to rule on conversions anyway).[2] "Matters of conversion" are not part of the jurisdiction accorded to the rabbinic courts by statute, and that apparently made the rabbinic judges in Michal's divorce case upset enough to use her application for divorce as a platform to put up a fight about it.

Most Israelis and Americans would undoubtedly be shocked to learn that the State of Israel keeps a blacklist of "those ineligible to marry" there for various reasons. Certainly Michal was shocked. This list includes people who are considered *mamzerim* (bastards), women whose *gett* is in the process of being considered for being overturned (somewhere between being an agunah and a divorcée), and converts who conversions are considered in doubt by the rabbinic court. The idea that there is such a thing as a list of people who are not allowed to marry violates every notion of what it means to live in a civil society. I cannot imagine how Americans or anyone else would react if such a list was found to exist in their country, if a person were to discover on the day that he or she goes to register to get married that he or she has been blacklisted and is simply not allowed to marry. Michal was beside herself with dismay.

CWJ helped fight this. The organization represented Michal in her appeal to have her conversion reinstated. But her situation went from bad to worse. At her hearing at the High Rabbinic Court in July 2007, she and Avi were interrogated at length— together and separately—and in great detail and intimacy about their religious observance: Did they keep the Sabbath properly? Did they separate meat and milk properly? Did they keep the commandments about refraining from sex while she was menstru-ating properly? They asked Avi about his religious studies and his family's religious history. When he left the room and Michal was alone, she was interrogated about her upbringing, her personal life, her family relationships, and eventually about her conversion.

"When did the robe cling to your body?" they asked her. They were referring to her immersion in the *mikveh*, where nothing but a slinky robe and lots of water separated her body from the eyes of the three male rabbis who were watching. A convert to Judaism must immerse in the ritual bath completely naked in front of three witnesses while taking on the commitment to the Torah. But since women are not considered valid witnesses (!), in many cases, the conversion takes place with men "sort of" watching. In order to protect the woman's modesty, she wears a very loose-fitting robe over her otherwise naked body while they "witness" her immersion. (Like a domino effect, or perhaps more like a multi-car accident, one sexist practice seems to beget others.) Michal explained to the rabbinical judges how embarrassed she had felt to stand in a room with three rabbis in a robe that clung tightly to her body. This apparently bothered the judges, because if the robe was clinging to her body when she was supposed to be "naked," that would have rendered her conversion invalid.

Michal's conversion was indeed confirmed by the Court headed by Rabbi Avraham Sherman to be "in doubt" and her children were to be registered on the marital blacklist. The reason given was that Michal had not adequately kept the command-ments *after* her conversion—that is to say, she wasn't religious enough for them—a ruling that has appalling ramifications for Jewish people around the world. After all, the implication is that converts are never fully Jewish. At any moment in their lives, a rabbinical judge can decide that the convert is not religiously observant enough and therefore no longer considered Jewish. Moreover, in a ruling that reveals the blatant political agenda behind this entire episode, the High Rabbinic Court added that all of the conversions performed by Rabbi Druckman since 1999 are invalid. They also wrote that municipal marriage registrars have the authority to refuse to register a convert for marriage if the applicant does not appear to be religious, thus giving bureaucratic clerks the power to demolish a person's entire identity with a little sideways glance and swirl of the pen. In one swift movement, this outrageous ruling called into question millennia of Jewish practices.

"This whole notion of retroactive cancellation is anti-halachic," said Rabbi Professor Daniel Sperber, a leading expert in Halacha and Talmud and veteran practicing Orthodox rabbi in Jerusalem. "Just think about what it means. It means that a genuine person who wants to be converted can never be sure of his own future. Because in five or ten years, some *beit din* [rabbinical court] for some reason will say, 'No, we are going to cancel it retroactively.' Modern Orthodoxy cannot countenance such an attitude." Instead of shutting out true believers, rabbis, he said, are supposed to "struggle to find a livable, equitable, humane, compassionate solution [for them] within the parameters of Halacha."[3]

The court's judgment caused something of an outcry in Israel and in America from both religious and secular groups. Rabbi Druckman, himself an American-born, right-wing Orthodox rabbi with a strong following in the Orthodox community in Israel, understandably came out with very strong language against this ruling—which he said "should be torn up"—as well as against the rabbis who issued it. (He stopped short of demanding that their rabbinical credentials be retroactively invalidated.) "There is no law in Halacha dictating police observe if converts are *Shomer mitzvoth* (Torah observants)," he said.[4]

Even the American Orthodox rabbinical umbrella group, the Rabbinical Council of America (RCA), took an unusual step and publicly criticized this ruling, saying that they were "appalled" by the ruling and calling it "beyond the pale of acceptable halachic practice," because it creates a "massive desecration of God's name" and "a reprehensible cause of widespread conflict and animosity within the Jewish people in Israel and abroad." The RCA, as well as Sephardic Chief Rabbi Shlomo Amar, called for a "thorough review and repudiation" of the rabbinical judges involved.[5] This clearly shows the disconnect between American and Israeli views on Judaism and Jewish law.

Of course, others were nonplussed. Rabbi Barry Freundel, head of the conversion committee of the RCA, downplayed the significance of nullifying conversions. "It isn't as if there is a huge group of would-be converts with nowhere to go," he said. "They can go to any court or authority who accepted them as Jews before. In fact, there are very Haredi rabbis whose conversions were nullified," and Rabbi Freundel has reconverted some of them.[6] But even though he may have made them Jewish again, the whole system is still shaming and humiliating to converts.

On the other side of the spectrum, advocates for religious pluralism—that is, those arguing that non-Orthodox and non-religious Jews have equally legitimate Jewish identities as Orthodox, observant Jews—were horrified at the implications for the many converts living in Israel. In particular, there was concern for immigrants from the former Soviet Union, some forty thousand of whom are not observant, and another few hundred thousand who are not considered halachically Jewish and are waiting to be converted in an Orthodox way. Rabbi Seth Farber of the organization Itim, which, among other things, helps Israelis from the former Soviet Union navigate the rabbinical court system, wrote in 2012 that "there are more than 330,000 immigrants from the former Soviet Union who aren't considered

Jewish by the rabbinate and cannot be married or buried in Israel as Jews."[7]

"How did rabbinic judges manage to convince us all of a new law—that it is possible to cancel conversion?" asked Rivkah Lubitch of CWJ, representing Michal. "This scare campaign has to stop, and with it all the relentless digging into the private lives of people by rabbinic judges who sit on the official courts of the State of Israel and collect a salary paid from taxpayer money."[8]

The overturning of conversions soon became a maelstrom. Druckman's conversions of some five thousand soldiers on behalf of the IDF were also asked to be overturned, and the State Attorney sided with the Rabbinic High Court. "All the conversions that take place in the IDF are legally questionable," said Yochi Gnessin, who represented the State Prosecutor in front of the Supreme Court hearing asking to invalidate conversions of IDF soldiers, in effect turning them from Jews into non-Jews.[9] Around the country, marriage registrars were making Israeli citizens' lives impossible by refusing to register converts considered not observant enough, and rabbinical courts continued to revoke the conversions of converts who sought a divorce. Shortly thereafter, Druckman was forced into an early retirement.

In the meantime, the whole system has stalled. In 2011, the state's Conversion Authority performed just 4,293 conversions, compared with 8,008 in 2007.[10] In 2012, the number was up slightly to 4,645 conversions, but still a major slowdown.[11] On the issue of conversion, Israel is stuck. Israel, the only Jewish state in the world, the country established as an asylum for all the Jews in the world looking to be part of the Jewish sovereign country, is trapped—held hostage by religious extremists standing at the gates of the nation and deciding who is in and who is out.

As for Michal, her life was turned upside down by the ruling. But while her story catapulted the issue into the public eye, she is one of tens of thousands of women whose lives are impacted by these turns of events. One fact that is often overlooked by many reports on conversion to Judaism is this: the majority of converts in Israel are women, including some 80 percent of converts from the former Soviet Union (FSU).[12] That's because Orthodox Judaism believes in matrilineal descent, which puts far more pressure on non-Jewish women who marry Jewish men to convert to Judaism than it does for men in the same situation.

Michal's story shows that as issues of divorce, conversion, and ritual immersion overlap, the humiliation of women is multiplied. Women disproportionately converting means that women are being unnecessarily pressured into proving their Jewishness. In this process, women's bodies are overly scrutinized and invaded by the male rabbinic establishment, in charge of the entire process from the *mikveh* to the rabbinical court, as they attempt to "prove" a woman's Jewishness. In some cases, this completely ruins women's lives. The gender imbalance in this entire system is scathing to women.

In addition, the impact that Michal's story has on people getting married in Israel is terrifying. As journalist Yair Ettinger wrote, the entire system of rabbinical courts is a political battle between rabbis over who has more power. He said that the rabbis of the cities of Ashdod, Rishon LeZion, and Ashkelon, for example, do not recognize state-sponsored conversion, so converts who want to register for marriage in those cities will be told that they are not Jewish.[13]

As the Rabbinic High Court ruling demonstrates, the municipal marriage registrars—often ultra-Orthodox, taxpayer-supported bureaucrats appointed through backdoor measures—have this untamed and unregulated power to turn away couples that wish to marry if one member of the pair is deemed not truly Jewish. In order to "prove" their Jewishness, couples are sometimes asked to bring copies of their grandparents' ketuboth, a religious marriage contract, documents that are often difficult or impossible to obtain (especially if the grandparents are no longer alive or weren't married in Israel).

The marriage registrars will often take their powers even further and question people who they suspect may have ancestors who converted. In some cases, if couples cannot produce both of their grandparents' ketuboth, even though they themselves are Jewish and always considered themselves Jewish, they may be asked to produce a photo of the grandparents' Jewish graves. This is why getting married in Israel "sometimes means hiring a detective," as Daniel Estrin wrote in *The Atlantic*. "Jews who want a marriage license must first prove they are Jewish in accordance with Orthodox tradition, which means they need to have been born to an uninterrupted line of Jewish mothers. Such a pedigree can be difficult to prove, especially for the children of Israel's largest immigrant community, the former denizens of the Soviet Union, many of whom spent years obscuring their Jewish roots to avoid discrimination. Enticed by lax immigration policies, these émigrés flooded Israel two decades ago and gave birth to children who now are beginning to seek marriage," but don't have any of the required documentation or qualifications to show they are indeed Jewish.[14]

This sudden insistence on "proving one's Jewishness" is possibly a result of a panic at the influx of a million immigrants from the FSU, but possibly just a power struggle between the Haredi leadership and the State of Israel over control of the religious bureaucracy. "Across thousands of years of Jewish history, seldom did a person need to prove to be a member of the tribe," Estrin notes. In any case, the situation has become a nightmare for many people who are, for all intents and purposes, fully Israeli—people who pay Israeli taxes, serve in the Israeli army, speak Hebrew, keep Jewish holidays, and who know no real life other than their lives in Israel—but who are suddenly asked to prove their Jewishness when they decide to get married as Israelis.

This unregulated power of the marriage registrars often targets the weakest members of society—especially immigrants. But the power wielded by the marriage registrars also affects everyone else, even some unsuspecting, Israel-born Jewish Israelis. For example, male priests—*kohanim*—are forbidden according to Jewish law from marrying women who are converts or divorcées. That's fine if a woman's status is known, but in Israel's current atmosphere, where everyone's Jewishness is under question, this can be impossible to determine. Such was the case with a friend of mine, a *kohen*, who was engaged to be married to a woman who thought she was Jewish. Her mother had converted, and she was born after the conversion. But because the rabbis were in doubt about the mother's conversion, they made the bride convert again, just to be safe. As a result, when she went to register to get married to her *kohen* fiancé, they were barred from getting married, because as a "convert," she was no longer eligible to marry him. Well, they got married anyway, but not in Israel, and he is no longer considered to be a *kohen*. He had to renounce his heritage because the registrars had excessive doubt in the people standing before them.

Some of the people destined to suffer most—the ones marginalized and most invisible—are the so-called *mamzerim*, the aforementioned people literally blacklisted by the rabbinical courts and unable to marry. There are some four thousand people blacklisted secretly—and the list is growing. Since most people do not even know this exists, there is no way for them to know that they are blacklisted until they go to register to be married.

Rivkah Lubitch, a religious pleader and activist, has been tracking the growth of this list and says that there has been a nearly threefold increase in the number of *mamzerim* on the blacklist over the past two years, for reasons unknown to anyone aside from those who control this list. Lubitch, one of the most vocal advocates for *mamzerim* in Israel, opened up a blog, "*Mamzerim Hakodesh*" ("holy bastards"), about "real people, real problems" that discusses stories of *mamzerim*.[15] One story, which she shared with her *Ynet* audience, is about the daughter of an IDF widow whose first husband was killed in battle. The mother had received permission at the time from the IDF chief rabbi to remarry, but when the daughter went to register for her own marriage decades later, the registrar in charge was unsatisfied with the evidence of her father's death—after all, his tank was burnt so badly that his body was barely identifiable. The registrar concluded the soldier's wife should not have been given permission to remarry, and hence the daughter is possibly a *mamzer*, and she was refused permission to marry.[16]

Lubitch writes, "*Mamzerim* are people who suffer indescribably throughout their entire lifetimes for something they didn't do. They were born into a situation of shame, embarrassment, rejection, and shunning. And they transmit this status on through the generations, until they assimilate (if it is even possible to assimilate, when the lists in the rabbinic courts are computerized). The reason that the public doesn't know about this phenomenon is because their shame is so great that they hide their story so that no one knows that they exist. In this matter the rabbinic court cooperates beautifully with the *mamzerim*. Everyone keeps quiet."[17] This problem may exist around the world, but it is only in Israel where *mamzerim* are being systematically shunned, argues legal scholar Professor Pinhas Shifman. *Mamzerim*, like agunot, have been around for a long time, and the millennia-old halachic system treats them as stuck, even when solutions exist (Shifman, like Lubitch, proposes several solutions).[18] "It is our opinion that Israeli women fare worse than their Diaspora sisters," write Weiss and Gross-Horowitz, "since all of them, whether or not they are religious, must marry in accordance with ultra-Orthodox rules."[19]

Irit Rosenblum, founding director of New Family, which advocates for freedom of marriage and divorce in Israel, argues that Israel must remove powers from the rabbinic bureaucracy and redefine the concepts of marriage and family. "The absence of separation of religion and state in Israel means that households that fall outside the recognized definition of 'family'—namely, a man and a woman of the same religion married by the requisite Orthodox rites—are discriminated against in recognition, rights and benefits," she wrote. "Issues of 'personal status' remain the domain of religion, and there is no civil marriage, divorce or protection of human rights befitting the diverse society that is Israel."[20] Indeed, the fact that so many people in Israel are barred from realizing their own dream of establishing a family with the ones they love—people who may not even know that they have that problem until they try to get married—constitutes one of the most jarring violations of civil liberties in Israel.

It can be fairly summed up that the marriage and divorce system in Israel is a mess. The system, which was perhaps a well-intentioned model of protocols that sustained small Jewish communities in the diaspora, does not work as a system within a democratic state apparatus. When ancient traditions are suddenly imposed on an entire populace without question, when freedom of choice is systematically removed, and when the rules are embedded in an inflexible law that is upheld by ultra-Orthodox bureaucrats, the result is a disaster. That is the situation in modern-day Israel. The system is desperately calling out for reform.

In addition to the people marginalized by the system—immigrants, converts, *mamzerim*—there is another large group of Israelis who are also completely delegitimized within this system: non-Orthodox Jews. Among American Jews, this represents the overwhelming majority of Jews—some 80 percent to 90 percent are not Orthodox.[21] And yet, the fact that around the world, Orthodox Jews are a tiny minority does not stop the State of Israel from empowering Orthodoxy with a stunning amount of control over the lives of Jews in Israel and elsewhere. David Breakstone, vice chairman at World Zionist Organization and active member of the Masorti (Conservative) movement in Israel, wrote about what happened when his son, Yair, fell in love with a woman who was not considered Jewish by the State and asked her to marry him.

> *"I want to so much," Veronica responded hesitantly. "But I'm not sure you will after what I'm about to tell you."*
>
> *Yair looked at her quizzically.*
>
> *"I'm kind of not Jewish," she stammered.*

Veronica, it turns out, is one of those 300,000 immigrants from the former Soviet Union who arrived here under the Law of Return as a child of a Jewish father and a non-Jewish mother.

Though she came at the age of 12, received a Jewish education in an Israeli public school, celebrates the Jewish holidays with family and friends, and served in the army, she...knew that when the time came, she would be denied a Jewish wedding. So when Yair proposed to her, she trembled with dread.

It's not that Veronica didn't want to convert. But in an earlier installment, she discovered that the doors of the rabbinical courts were closed to her, as she was unable to commit to a strictly Orthodox lifestyle, including the stipulation that she date only observant men. Still, she was not prepared to relinquish the profound tie she felt to the Jewish people and the Jewish state. For his part, Yair couldn't imagine having anything less than a traditional Jewish wedding, nor could he conceive of having non-Jewish children.[22]

Breakstone arranged for his future daughter-in-law to be converted by a Masorti rabbinical court. She underwent a process of learning and studying—along with her adoring fiancé—and "emerged from the *mikveh* with tears in her eyes," Breakstone writes. She received a conversion certificate that is not recognized by the Chief Rabbinate. "So the Jewish wedding they had their hearts set on would have to be performed by a Masorti rabbi. They would be married in the eyes of God, but not of the Jewish state. And a generation from now, when their children are ready to be wed, the story will repeat itself." Breakstone's experience demonstrates that the rabbinic control over the entire apparatus of marriage, divorce, and conversion in Israel can potentially affect all Israeli Jews and in fact all Jews in the world.

Ultimately, this antiquated system for marriage and divorce leaves many people in Israel stranded, according to Rosenblum. "Matters of personal status have an impact on every sphere of life in Israel, from the partner you can marry, to the authority that can marry you, your rights in divorce, fertility treatments, adoption, abortion, taxation, maternity rights, power of attorney, inheritance, and more," she writes. "While demographic and social changes have revolutionized the face of the family, the law has not evolved to meet the complex new reality. In Israel's nearly 65 years of statehood, our society has diversified, but our family law is still frozen in time. I estimate that today, only 58 percent of households meet the de-facto formula for family, leaving the remaining 800,000 units without the full recognition and protection of law."[23] In short, it is proving increasingly more difficult to have a marriage or divorce recognized as legitimate there.

No wonder many Israeli couples are running to Cyprus to get married. Indeed, between the years 2000 and 2006, 12 percent of all Israeli marriages took place abroad, most in Cyprus. Of those Israelis who married abroad, only a third are couples in which both spouses are registered as Jews. The rest are couples who would have a terrible time trying to get married in Israel today.

"Israeli family law is a peculiar institution indeed," write Weiss and Gross-Horowitz. "The official marriage and divorce laws seem to be standing obdurately, and purposely, out of sync with modern behavior, harking back to a fundamental, patriarchal family order in which men take women and send them away according to their own terms, and women have very little, if anything, to say about it."[24] The story about marriage, divorce, and conversion in Israel points out not only the lack of some basic civil rights in Israel, but also the ways in which these practices adversely and disproportionately affect women.

Michal's story, which brought the cancellation of conversions to the public eye, was particularly enraging to the large FSU immigrant community in Israel, represented politically by the Yisrael Beiteinu Party. MK David Rotem of Yisrael Beiteinu fought back by introducing his own bill. The Rotem Conversion Bill addressed the needs of people whose fathers are Jewish (and therefore are Israeli citizens)—but whose mothers are not and are therefore not recognized as Jewish by the rabbinate and cannot get married in Israel. It proposed that people be allowed to choose where and with which rabbi to register their marriages—based on the assumption that they would be able to find one in Israel outside their own cities who is more sympathetic and broad-minded (an assumption since contested).

The reasoning behind the bill is that when it became clear to the rabbi of Ashkelon that all his residents were going to Tel Aviv to get married, market forces would be put to work. The power of competition would kick in and entice rabbis to be more responsive to the needs of their populaces. But the bill also gave municipal rabbis the power to create conversion courts and gave the chief rabbi power to approve all conversions, both of which could trip up immigrants as well. Thus while the bill aimed to find a solution for converts and immigrants, it contained some major flaws.[25]

Understandably, the Rotem bill brought about a firestorm in the international Jewish community. The Orthodox community was surprisingly supportive. The RCA in particular, which was very worried their own Orthodox conversions were being overturned in the State of Israel, saw this as a great solution. In a released statement, the RCA wrote that the Rotem bill resolves the conversion crisis by "significantly expanding the number of local rabbinical courts for conversion, so as to facilitate conversion in accordance with the relevant requirements of Jewish law and ethical sensitivity. It also prevents retroactive revocation of conversions by third parties. And not least, it has the support of Israel's official rabbinate."[26]

While the Orthodox community in Israel and North America largely applauded the Rotem bill, the non-Orthodox Jewish community in Israel was less enthusiastic. This is because the bill would completely exclude non-Orthodox conversions in Israel and give the Chief Rabbinate, for the first time, ultimate and official authority over any and all conversions by anyone. Moreover, the stipulation contained in the bill that conversion would be recognized only if the convert "accepted the Torah and the commandments in accordance with Halacha" remained problematic for non-Orthodox Jews whose reading and understanding of Jewish practice is not necessarily an Orthodox one.

Perhaps most significantly, the bill would overturn the 2002 High Court of Justice ruling that required the Interior Ministry to recognize converts of all denominations, whether their conversion was performed in Israel or overseas. This is a big change that the Masorti and Reform movements in Israel spent many years working on. Since the 2002 ruling, non-Orthodox converts abroad may make aliyah under the Law of Return (even over protestations from the official rabbinate), and non-Jewish Israeli residents who undergo a Masorti or Reform conversion in Israel may change their registration to "Jewish" in the Interior Ministry.

The Rotem bill would cancel all that. As Rabbi Andrew Sacks, the head of Israel's Masorti movement, argued, the Rotem bill "would potentially eliminate the progress made by the Masorti and Reform Movement in the area of conversion thus ensuring a true monopoly. Far better would be to privatize the official Rabbinate and allow all streams equal access."[27]

Rabbi Uri Regev of Hiddush accused Rotem of "knowingly and deliberately acting against the Jewish people…by kneeling to the Chief Rabbinate and Haredi politicians, and crowning them as responsible for conversion in Israel." American Jews got involved too. Jerry Silverman, president and CEO of the Jewish Federations of North America, wrote to Prime Minister Netanyahu, saying, "We are deeply shocked and disappointed to hear that the bill will suddenly be presented tomorrow in its current, highly problematic format without any input from… Diaspora communities," and added that he was concerned about "significant damage that such a bill could cause to ties between Israel and Diaspora Jewry, at precisely the time when we are all working so hard to build bridges."[28]

"Where is the protest? Why do we blindly accept the decree that only a man and a woman of the same faith and nationality can wed in Israel?" wrote Irit Rosenblum, founding director of New Family Organization in Israel. "Why do we let the Chief Rabbinate decide which Jews can marry other Jews or anyone at all? Why do we let the rabbinate ordain an elite clique of male Orthodox clergy while marriage by rabbis from other streams is illegal? Why do we accept that adherents of faiths not recognized in Israel, or that don't meet the religious definition of any faith, are 'religion-less' and can only marry one another?"[29]

Perhaps unsurprisingly, the Rotem bill did not withstand all this outrage. It is currently stuck in an interministerial committee, and in the meantime, the Knesset has been reelected—although Rotem retains the powerful position of chair of the Knesset Constitution, Law, and Justice Committee. Meanwhile, a more sinister side of Rotem's motives emerged in early 2014 as Rotem let slip that he doesn't really consider Reform Jews to be Jewish.[30] This comment raised the ire of non-Orthodox Jews, caused another brief explosion in Jewish identity politics, and reminded the general public about how high the stakes are in this whole game. While most Israelis are glad that the Rotem bill has been filed in a drawer somewhere, the entire story illustrates just how desperately a solution is needed to the ultra-Orthodox domination of all matters related to conversion and marriage in Israel.[31]

Perhaps the most obvious takeaway from all these nightmare stories of marriage, divorce, and conversion in Israel is this: Israel needs to institute a process of civil marriage and divorce. Calls for civil marriage—that is, marriage that is not dependent on a religious authority to be deemed legitimate but can be conducted via secular or simple bureaucratic means—have been growing in Israel over the past decade or so, getting louder and stronger as each story of marriage injustice emerges. MK Yair Lapid won a tremendous victory in the 2013 elections in large part because he was in tune with the growing segment of Israel that is looking for an alternative to the Orthodox monopoly on personal status issues. As an indication of how central the issues of marriage, divorce, and conversion were in the elections, here is a transcript of an ad campaign by the Sephardic ultra-Orthodox Shas Party against the FSU dominant Yisrael Beiteinu Party, an ad that caused an uproar:

Groom: "Marina, what is the fax for?"

Bride: "Beiteinu sent it, a wedding present."

Groom: "How nice of him. But what the hell—a fax?"

Bride: "To receive permission."

Groom: "Permission for what?"

Bride: "From 1-800-convert."

Groom: "1-800-convert??"

Bride: "*Da*, you call 1-800-convert and receive permission."

Groom: "Wait, you aren't Jewish?"

Bride (brandishing a freshly issued "certificate of conversion"): "I am now!"

This ad implies that Yisraeli Beiteinu is "giving away" conversion certificates to FSU immigrants—as if to suggest that FSU immigrants are not "truly" Jewish but simply become Jewish the way some people go to the dentist or order flowers. The ethnic overtones are particularly jarring, and it's hardly surprising that the FSU community in Israel responded with horror. Seth Farber, one of the strongest advocates for FSU converts vis-à-vis the rabbinate, responded to this spot with anger. "This ad campaign is a slap in the face for immigrants from the former Soviet Union" and added that "the Torah mentions thirty-six times the prohibition of denigrating converts." He also did not mince words for the Sephardic chief rabbi, who he said "is a signatory to every conversion certificate in the State of Israel, [and] is allowing the party with which he identifies to belittle people who passed the state conversion system and people who are currently stuck in that system due to its intolerable bureaucracy."[32]

Well, Shas paid the price for this ad. In the 2013 elections, Shas was excluded from the coalition—for the first time in thirty years—in large part because of the rise of the pluralistic Yesh Atid

Party led by Yair Lapid. Lapid won a surprising nineteen seats (out of 120) and was the most coveted coalition partner for Netanyahu. But Lapid's condition was clear: no ultra-Orthodox parties in the government. Public sentiment was clear: people are tired of ultra-Orthodox control over their private lives.

The ultra-Orthodox monopoly over marriage and divorce also affects a large portion of Israelis, not just converts and immigrants. Irit Rosenblum estimates that 42 percent of family units fall outside acceptable family unions according to definitions of the rabbinical court. "Religious jurisdiction over personal status means that their union, and any children born into it, is discriminated against," she writes. "In a nation where every citizen's personal status is determined by archaic, all-male religious bodies, inequality is ingrained in the very institutional fabric of life... Couples yearn in vain for civil unions and the legislature is silent. Loving couples of different religions can't form families in Israel, and the legislature is silent. Same-sex couples can't marry, and the legislature is silent. Religious institutions impose their laws on the entire population—including people of different religions and foreign citizens—and yet the legislature remains silent. What is equality if nearly half of Israel's families are outside of the consensus?"[33]

The lack of marital freedom in Israel makes it one of the worst countries in the world when it comes to that topic. Hiddush conducted a cross-country analysis of marital freedom around the world and gave Israel a score of "zero"—the only Western country to receive that grade. "The study shows that freedom of marriage prevails in 93 (48%) of the world's countries. There are partial restrictions on marriage in 56 (29%) countries and in 45 (23%), including Israel, there are severe restrictions on freedom of marriage. Thirty-three of the 45 countries that received the grade '0' (severe restrictions) are Islamic countries," the researchers wrote. This puts Israel in the same category as fundamentalist dictatorships and Muslim countries, as opposed to liberal democracies where citizens have options for marriage. "In general, stable democracies provide their citizens with a wide variety of options for marriage," the report continues. Hiddush Chair Stanley P. Gold said, "Our hope is that [this research] will assist in promoting a policy change in Israel that will bring forth freedom of marriage. It is universally recognized as a major human and civil right and should be a nat-ural implementation of Israel's own Declaration of Independence, which promises freedom of religion and conscience."[34]

Calls for civil marriage in Israel have started to emerge from the non-Haredi Orthodox community as well. Hebrew University law Professor Pinhas Shifman, a longtime advocate for finding halachic solutions for agunot, published a book that advocates for a comprehensive system of civil marriage and divorce in Israel and critiques the Orthodox monopoly in Israel on moral as well as on religious grounds.

Americans too are joining the protest, demonstrating that ultra-Orthodox control of marriage not only threatens Israelis, but also Jews around the world. For example, Nancy Kaufman, CEO of the National Council of Jewish Women, published a vigorous essay calling for an end to the Orthodox monopoly on Jewish marriage in Israel. "Creating a mechanism for civil marriage in Israel and sanctioning marriage under alternative religious avenues is paramount to the future of the Jewish state. Such measures will not only deepen respect for Jewish and religious diversity, they will enhance the principles of democracy in Israel and strengthen the ties between Israel and world Jewry," Kaufman wrote.[35]

Civil marriage, which was not conceived when the Jewish state was established in 1948, is clearly a growing need in Israel, where ultra-Orthodox control of all matters relating to marriage, divorce, and conversion poses a major threat to the rights and well-being of so many people—women, converts, immigrants, and Jews in general in Israel and around the world.

There are indications that legislators are paying attention to these calls for marital reform, though effective solutions have yet to be officially proposed. Religious Affairs Minister MK Naftali Bennett (Habayit Hayehudi) and his deputy Eli Ben-Dahan (who used to be the head of the Jerusalem rabbinical court) announced in May 2013 that they were "making history" by pushing forth marriage reform legislation to make marriage and divorce in Israel easier and force rabbinical courts to be more receptive to Israelis of various statuses and situations. The new regulations, called the Tzohar Laws for the group of Tzohar Orthodox rabbis who aim to be more "open" and "friendly" rabbis (non-Haredi Orthodox), would allow couples to register where they want, "thus creating a healthy competition among religious councils," and preventing them from "being held hostage to any one religious council" based on where they live. The new laws would also begin to officially recognize weddings performed by Tzohar rabbis.[36] This would take power away from ultra-Orthodox rabbis and make room for non-Haredi Orthodox rabbis, but obviously that only addresses a small part of the problem.

Still, journalist Yair Ettinger, writing in *Haaretz*, called the reform "revolutionary," even if it doesn't solve all the problems and leaves an enormous amount of power in the hands of Orthodox rabbis:

> *It's true the Chief Rabbinate will continue to have exclusive authority to perform weddings for Jews within Israel's borders and*

that civil marriage is out of the question. But if the reform goes through, the revolutionary and vital concept of competition will enter the religious-services picture here for the first time. It means competition among rabbis, competition among religious councils, competition for citizens, men or women, when they are about to marry—and competition for their registration fee. This revolution, which will require most of the religious councils to travel decades forward in time, takes into account for the first time the fact that there is more than one way to be Jewish (for now that way is Orthodox; recognition of the other movements will have to wait). The Haredi Ashkenazi rabbi of Ashkelon can provide excellent services to some of his city's residents—Haredim, for example— while others, say from one of the surrounding kibbutzim, might wish to receive services from a religious Zionist rabbi.[37]

Still others are less impressed. Rabbi Gilad Kariv, executive director of the Israel Movement for Progressive Judaism, said in response that "the only revolution that can cure the religious services crisis in Israel is annulling the Orthodox monopoly and giving the Jewish public in Israel a real option to choose between communities, circles, and different denominations in Judaism."[38] In the meantime, the reforms are on hold as Justice Minister Tzipi Livni, one of a handful of women in the cabinet, vetoed them. She was accused of being "political"—taking revenge against Ben-Dahan's party Habayit Hayehudi for having previously vetoed a bill her party submitted—or maybe she just thought it's a bad bill. This bizarre story, which may have something to do with politics and bedfellows, is not over yet.[39]

In any case, these proposed reforms ultimately maintain the status quo in which the Religious Ministry controls marriage and divorce, even if "friendly" Orthodox rabbis are in charge. In fact, Bennett and Ben-Dahan seem to have their eyes on even more ways for the Religious Ministry to control people's lives, and some are scary. This is perhaps most evident in the quiet manner in which the Religious Ministry established an "Education Authority" to "connect Jews to their roots and strengthen their Jewish identity." That may sound lovely on paper, but in fact, considering that the only model of "Jewish" that is recognized by the Ministry of Religion is Orthodox, and considering that the announcement included plans to hire "yeshiva students who 'live' Judaism"—and, by the way, are all male—the program borders on forced indoctrination. It's not enough that the all-male, all-Orthodox Religious Ministry and rabbinate control people's lives, especially women's. Now they are going to spend more taxpayer money to convince people that this is all good and beautiful. They call it education, but it sounds more like a political marketing campaign using tools of informal education.[40]

Ultimately, this proposal represents another dangerous intersection of religion and state in Israel. Yet, it is couched in the language of "reform" and "education" within the religious ministry. It begs the question about whether the entire institution of a state-backed religious authority can ever be a safe institution in a democratic state. What is clear is that the Religious Ministry has no plans to recognize the legitimacy of any marriage, divorce, or general lifestyle other than its own.

One of the interesting outcomes of these discussions is the emergence in Israel of a growing group of people who are Orthodox but not ultra-Orthodox. The group, most prominently represented by the Tzohar rabbis and the religious Zionist parties, has struggled over the past generation or so to find its voice and identity amid growing religious fundamentalism. When Naftali Bennett came along in 2013 and rebuilt the Habayit Hayehudi Party, it gave non-Haredi Orthodox Jews—Religious Zionist or modern Orthodox Jews—a new vigor. This new vigor has focused in large part on rabbinical politics in Israel and especially the recent election of new chief rabbis in Israel.

In July 2013, the two chief rabbis completed their ten-year fixed terms, and their successors were chosen by a special 150-member electoral assembly of political appointees. During the period leading up to the election, the Tzohar rabbis launched a massive public campaign to install Rabbi David Stav, the founder of Tzohar, as the next chief rabbi. They argued that if the chief rabbi position was held by a more open, modern, and liberal-minded rabbi, all these issues of marriage, divorce, and conversion would be resolved. Stav, the fifty-three-year-old municipal rabbi of the town of Shoham, speaks fluent English, wears a knitted skullcap, prides himself on the fact that his children serve in the army, and talks about the importance of rabbis being able to hear the voices of the Israeli people. "Most rabbinical appointments are political appointments," Stav told a Jerusalem crowd in early 2013 as part of his campaign trail. "A rabbi has to be appointed by the community, has to know the community, and is responsible to the community. Today, the rabbis are not appointed by the people who they were meant to serve."[41] For many non-Haredi Orthodox Jews, Stav represented a beacon of hope.

Stav actively campaigned on Israelis' discontent with the system of marriage and divorce in Israel. In his paid advertisements, he cited a figure of 30 percent of Israelis who get married out of Israel in order to avoid contact with the rabbinate. Some people were hanging their hopes for rabbinical reform in Israel on Stav's election to chief rabbi. Indeed, when Religious Affairs Minister Naftali Bennett announced during the chief rabbi campaign that he was going to institute a series of reforms in rabbinical councils that I mentioned earlier—some of which came straight from Stav's campaign speeches, such as giving people freedom to choose which registrar to use in order to create competition and forcing clerks to adopt better customer service—many Israelis responded with enthusiasm. Even the Masorti movement initially expressed excitement about this, as did members of Yesh Atid, Bennett's secular coalition partner.

But others were not convinced that even if he were elected, change would be significant. In a leadership colloquium conducted by the American Jewish Committee (AJC) in New York in November 2012 on the subject of the role of the Chief Rabbinate, calls to disband the Chief Rabbinate altogether overtook the calls to reform it from the inside. Barry Shrage, president and CEO of the Combined Jewish Philanthropies of Greater Boston, said, "The Rabbinate is a thoroughly political institution, and the Haredi parties are growing stronger. The founding fathers of the United States understood that when religion gets involved with politics it becomes corrupted, and therefore they protected religion from politics through the First Amendment."[42]

American Jewish historian Jonathan Sarna called for the adaptation of a free-market capitalist approach to religion in Israel. "Although proponents of a Chief Rabbinate say Orthodoxy will lose if it is not protected, Orthodoxy might actually win in a religious free market. And if it doesn't win, it doesn't deserve to." Susan Weiss completely concurred, calling for an end to the Chief Rabbinate. "The rabbinic courts should be privatized, all conversions should be recognized…and the state must recognize civil marriage."[43]

Rabbi Uri Regev agreed with Susan Weiss. "Israel needs to deal with basic rights, personal-status issues, and conversion," he said. "Israel ranks at the bottom of world democracies when it comes to religious freedom. There is no other democracy where citizens can't marry civilly."[44] "The system has become bankrupt," he later told reporters. "The Chief Rabbinate has become a threat to the State of Israel and to the Jewish people. It should be abolished."[45]

Despite these objections, Tzohar continued its campaign. Rabbi Yuval Cherlow, one of Stav's colleagues at Tzohar who was also at the AJC colloquium, found himself trying to defend the institution of the chief rabbis and convince everyone that Stav would be a different kind of chief rabbi. "The very existence of the State of Israel and its relationship to the rest of world Jewry rests on the Jewish character of the state. Taking that away will diminish the importance of Israel for all Jews," he argued at the AJC colloquium. He also said that "the Chief Rabbinate serves an important function as the gateway to Judaism for converts... Rather than giving up on the idea of kingship altogether, the Torah prescribes ways to limit his power."[46]

Dr. Steven Bayme of the AJC and leading academic Dr. Dov Zakheim actually supported much of what Cherlow said. "Calls for the abolition of the office remain unlikely to be realized in the near- to mid-term future," they later wrote. "The fundamental challenge therefore entails abolishing the coercive power of the Chief Rabbinate, most notably with respect to the crucial issues of personal status— marriage, divorce, conversion, and burial."[47] In other words, since the office of the chief rabbi isn't going away any time soon, the best people can aspire toward is that the new rabbis will be less "coercive"—which means either be more "friendly" or simply have less power.

What is interesting about all these public discussions about marriage, divorce, and conversion is that the underlying gender issue is often left out. The fact is that we are talking about issues that disproportionately affect women. It is primarily women who are stuck in unwanted marriages that the rabbinical courts will not release. An overwhelming majority of those seeking to convert are women, and it's women's status that determines the Jewishness of the next generation. At the same time, the rabbinate itself is completely dominated by men. As long as the Chief Rabbinate is an Orthodox institution, there will never be a woman in that position or anywhere near it, making policy or halachic decisions, speaking in public, airing opinions, or in a position of status or authority in the Ministry of Religion. Consequently, women are disproportionately impacted by an all-male rabbinate and have zero decision-making authority on any level in the institution. In other words, through these institutions, the State is funding exclusive male power to control women's lives.

To understand how impossible it is for women to try to reform this system on their own, it's important to explore how deeply this issue runs. The institute of the Chief Rabbinate in Israel, no matter how "friendly" it may portray itself, is a strictly patriarchal institution. No women are allowed to be rabbis; hence, no women can be anywhere in the institution or even be consulted as rabbinic or halachic authorities on any issues.

There's more: even on the 150-person committee to elect the chief rabbi, which consists of seventy rabbis, mostly from Israel's biggest cities and towns, and eighty "public representatives"— mayors, Knesset members chosen by committee, and heads of local religious councils—there were exactly two women: Netanya Mayor Miriam Feirberg-Ikar and Herzliya Mayor Yael German. "It's as if there is no understanding that chief rabbis have to be acceptable to the ethnically and religiously diverse public, not to mention half the population, which is female," wrote Liora Minka, chairwoman of the Emunah National Religious Women's Organization, one of a group of women's organizations that petitioned Attorney General Yehuda Weinstein to add women to the committee.[48] (This is not to be confused with the committee that appoints rabbinical judges—a committee of twelve that had zero women until the court forced the inclusion of four women in August 2013.) "Precisely because [the Chief Rabbinate] is a religious body, which keeps women out of the decision-making centers and public positions, there is great importance in ensuring their representation in the assembly for choosing the heads of that body," the petition says.[49]

As a result of this pressure, MK Eliezer Stern (Kadima) introduced a bill to increase the size of the 150-member committee to 200 and reserve 20 percent of the panel for women. Shas and United Torah Judaism used whatever power they had to block the bill, because adding more votes would dilute their own power and increase Stav's chances of getting elected. Even the religious Zionist party Habayit Hayehudi was opposed to the committee expansion, as well as to Stav, who is too liberal for them. In June 2013, it was announced that ten women were added to the committee—better than zero but still a small representation. And anyway, it was to put women in place to vote for the "best" man, not to ever vote for a woman. So even this victory was bittersweet.[50]

In any case, Stav lost the election. The new chief rabbis are Rabbi David Lau, son of former Chief Rabbi Yisrael Meir Lau, and Rabbi Yitzhak Yosef, son of former Chief Rabbi Ovadia Yosef. Change seems farther away than ever.

Nevertheless, there is some good news. Feminist activists and advocates for religious pluralism in Israel continue to fight for change.

The CWJ managed to help Michal by appealing to the High Court of Justice to overturn the decisions of the Ashod and High Rabbinic courts that ruled against her and declare that those courts had acted outside of their jurisdiction. In 2009, the High Court of Justice recommended that Michal be sent back to the Tel Aviv Rabbinic Court to review the original verdicts. The Tel Aviv Rabbinic Court subjected Michal to another round of intense interrogations as trying as the ones she endured at the hands of the Ashdod and High Rabbinic Courts. Thankfully, the outcome this time was different. Nearly a year later, they issued their ruling that Michal's original conversion *was* valid and that she and her children are Jews. In response, CWJ is challenging the whole idea of overturning conversion and has filed a petition claiming that courts should not be able to do this at will. CWJ, as well as Michal and countless other Israelis, anxiously await the answer to this critical appeal.

Meanwhile, the CWJ and other grassroots advocates continue to seek new ways to protect women and their statuses in Israel. In 2012, CWJ celebrated a legal victory for a woman who had been blacklisted by having the court annul her first marriage. This was good news for the woman, although Rivkah Lubitch, who was representing the woman, points out that the process of solving one case at a time rather than looking for systemic solutions is not necessarily helpful. She suggests adopting an approach that says to Israelis (or perhaps even to all Jews) "we are all *mamzerim*." With that, she says, "the matter is finished. The only ones who are not *mamzerim* would be converts who have newly joined the Jewish people. But, since a convert is anyway allowed to marry a *mamzer*, the problem is resolved and *mamzerim* may marry anyone." Lubitch argues that other solutions to the *mamzer* issue are available without having to blacklist anyone too.[51]

Another interesting development is that the government issued permission for the first time to register intermarried couples as married by having people declare themselves "without religion." In May 2011, the late author Yoram Kaniuk, who was married to a non-Jew, was the first to register as "Israeli" rather than "Jewish."[52] Although this does not help people who would like to call themselves Jewish or who are marrying other Jews, it is a first small step toward civil marriage in Israel.

But there are still many more reforms to come. Irit Rosenblum of New Family is leading the charge for the passage of a Basic Law that would recognize all forms of families and parenting constellations and establishes a system of civil marriage for any two adult, single partners. "For all those forbidden to marry by the rabbinate, for all those couples struggling to have children, for all those couples who can't legalize their love, and for all those struggling for their human rights in the face of discrimination—it's time to act," wrote Rosenblum. "On family justice, the silence of the legislators is deafening."[53] And CWJ launched a new campaign on Facebook that suggests alternative candidates for the office of chief rabbis of Israel—including three women. "Through this campaign, we hope to highlight how problematic the present selection process is as well as to raise important questions regarding the institution of the chief rabbi itself—do we really need a chief rabbi? And why can't the rabbi be female or from a denomination other than Orthodox?"[54]

As with other issues, this chapter in Israeli history is hardly over. In fact, this story is literally unfolding as I write. But as we will see in the final section, what seems clear is that for the first time, all of those who are speaking out, blogging, commenting, posting to Facebook, and expressing a different vision for religion and state in Israel are finally starting to have an impact on policy makers and lawmakers.

Part III

VOICES OF CHANGE

Chapter 9

THE LITTLE GIRL WHO MOVED A NATION: HOW NA'AMA MARGOLESE BECAME A FACE FOR CHANGE

When eight-year-old Na'ama Margolese walked to school one warm day in September 2011, she likely had no idea that she would be starting a national furor. The slight, soft-spoken, long-haired girl from Beit Shemesh, Israel, wearing a long skirt and sleeves past her elbows, was just like almost every other child starting the second grade—excited to see her friends, anxious to meet her new teacher, lugging her heavy knapsack. What she was not expecting was that she would be confronted with jeering men hurling eggs and tomatoes, screaming at her and her friends with insults such as "shiksa," "*gevalt*" (a Yiddish exclamation of surprise or incredulity), and "sluts." Poor Na'ama, who was also spat on by the protesters, came home from school, terrified to go back.

The reason for the Haredi outrage, which was aimed specifically at unsuspecting and vulnerable elementary school girls, was that local Haredi leadership lost a municipal battle to prevent this particular school, the Orot Banot State Religious Girls' School, from opening. Though the school was religious, the Haredi community still did not want a non-Haredi school in such close proximity. Located between an ultra-Orthodox neighborhood of Ramat Beit Shemesh and the more modern-Orthodox neighborhoods of Beit Shemesh, the school marks a spot where Haredi sprawl was stopped in its tracks by more moderate religious groups. But nobody expected the Haredi community to take out their rage on little girls.

The police did not react to the harassment at first but then began video recording the violence. Enraged parents, in the meantime, began to figure out how to organize, opening up a Facebook page and toying with ways to take back their own streets. Rabbi Dov Lipman, an American resident in the town who a year later would become a Knesset member described as "ultra-Orthodox," was active with the parents, exemplifying how the extremists are considered radical even within ultra-Orthodoxy—yet they still have so much power, as radicals often do.

On the first day back to school following the Jewish holidays in October, the violence escalated as demonstrators threw a nasty stink bomb through a window of a third grade classroom. Police made a rather weak effort to intercede, and video footage captures the police politely explaining to protesters that they cannot scream and yell in front of the school. When this proved ineffective, police finally used the threat of riot control equipment—stun guns—to force them away from the school. The Haredi protesters eventually dispersed, shouting "immodest girls, get out" and "tell your parents you don't want to study here" and "we won't stop until this school is moved!"[1]

The turning point in this story, which gives the episode a different ending than so many other encounters with religious extremism in Israel today, came when Na'ama Margolese unwittingly became the face of the struggle. A Channel 2 television news report on this series of events captured Na'ama walking to school one day with her mother, Hadassa Margolese, bent over Na'ama's sobbing and trembling little backpacked figure, gently urging her to come with her to school. Little Na'ama was simply petrified to walk down the street, and for good reason. The sheer terror is audible in Na'ama's pleading of "No! No!" as her mother softly asks her if she wants to walk down the street with her to school. When the video went viral and the rest of Israel saw that a perfectly innocent little girl was absolutely terrified to walk down her own street, the country woke up. In a follow-up story, Haredim were also shown attacking reporters. The Haredi insistence that these little girls were "immodest" began raising questions about their fascination with the perceived sexuality of little girls. Israelis began wondering whether there is an element of pedophilia in the whole concept of Haredi men rioting about little girls, which ignited outrage. The truth of the situation was suddenly clear: Haredi thugs have been taking over the streets of Israel and ruining people's lives, and nobody was doing anything about it.

Another aspect of the televised story that captured Israel's attention was the fact that Hadassa Margolese, the thirty-two-year-old Chicago native, was wearing a skirt and hat—so-called modest dress of the religious world. Suddenly, it became clear to Israelis that the violence was not about actual values and ideals but about seeking total control. "The surprising part of the story is the fact that the Haredim weren't protesting a school where young secular girls run around in halter tops or cut-off shorts," wrote Allison Kaplan Sommer, one of the leading journalists following the story as it unfolded for the *Jewish Daily Forward*. "Their problem was with a modern Orthodox, in Israel known as national religious, girls' elementary school located on the outskirts of their neighborhood. The school, Orot, has had an adjacent religious boys' school, Orot Banim, which the Haredim have lived next to comfortably for the past two years. But the girls' school has been specifically targeted because, they say, modestly-clad religious girls age six to eleven playing in their field of vision is inappropriate."[2]

"This latest skirmish underlines the fact that whether it is school buildings, the *mikveh*, or segregation on bus lines, it is increasingly the national religious community that is now on the front lines when it comes to fighting extremism in religion," Kaplan Sommer wrote in another post. "In neighboring Jerusalem there is a history of national religious neighborhood being overwhelmed by Haredim, which resulted in the national religious residents eventually giving up and moving out."[3]

Na'ama Margolese's story sparked serious concern around the world too. As the international media began widely covering the story and criticizing the severe oppression of women and girls there, Israelis sat up and listened. The Beit Shemesh mayor ordered signs taken down that call for gender segregation on the streets and announced plans to install security cameras around the city in order to catch the thugs, and Prime Minister Netanyahu responded by declaring his commitment to fighting gender segregation.[4] A Facebook page dedicated to "protecting little Na'ama" garnered over ten thousand followers. Na'ama's mother became a local and national hero, fielding calls from reporters and politicians and becoming the unofficial leader of the movement to stop violent radical religious takeover of the streets. "The exclusion of women from the public sphere makes my blood boil. They (Haredim) are trying to take us back to dark eras; this is a grave injustice," Hadassa Margolese said.

Israeli politicians were jolted from their previously passive stance on these issues too. "The demonstration today is a test for the people and not just the police," Israeli president Shimon

Peres declared. "All of us…must defend the image of the state of Israel from a minority that is destroying national solidarity and expressing itself in an infuriating way." Opposition leader Tzipi Livni condemned "the extremist elements that are rearing their heads and are trying to impose their world view on us," NBC reported.[5]

But the Haredi men, for their part, seemed unmoved and perhaps even bolstered. Haredi thugs attacked reporters and municipal workers taking down signs and continued to stand outside the school, yelling and spitting. An estimated three hundred Haredi men gathered two days after the news report, throwing rocks and yelling insults like "Nazis" at the police. In response, the New Israel Fund coalition of some thirty organizations—both religious feminist and religious pluralism organizations—initiated a major protest in Beit Shemesh.

"Who's afraid of an eight-year-old?" the Israeli headlines blared in anticipation of the protest. Thousands of people from around Israel descended on Beit Shemesh—a town of some eighty thousand people that sits between Jerusalem and Tel Aviv—including many secular Israelis who would have never imagined themselves coming to this town with its reputation for being ultra-Orthodox, even if it began as a mixed-secular town and still has large pockets of non-Haredi populations. Facebook statuses and Twitter feeds were full of people asking for directions and joking about the influx of secular Tel-Avivians on this religious town. Signs held by protesters read "Free Israel from religious coercion" and "Stop Israel from becoming Iran."

This protest, Israel's first mass demonstration against the increasing waves of Haredi violence against women, was remarkable in its strength and diversity. There were speakers representing a range of organizations, Knesset members from five different political parties—including three women, two of whom are heads of their respective parties—and citizens religious and secular who have become symbols of the struggle against the removal of women from the public sphere. This was a watershed moment when large numbers of Israelis from all social sectors began to wake up to the real threat of religious radicalism.[6]

Throughout the event, there were ongoing calls from the crowd for the Haredi Beit Shemesh Mayor Moshe Abutbul to resign. "You destroyed this city," protesters called out during a speech he made about his intentions to put violent citizens behind bars. Several speakers and many signs referred to the current plans to build thirty thousand new housing units exclusively for Haredim. There is no obvious gender issue in the housing plans, and the fact that this was a theme of the event suggests that many people came to protest the seeming Haredi takeover of the city and blamed local and national politicians for that.[7]

Another major theme of the event was a protest of religious extremism in Israel generally. MK Tzipi Livni was probably the most outspoken about this, when she veered from gender altogether and started talking about settler violence against IDF soldiers. "People will ask, what's the connection between all these issues?" she said, just as I was thinking the same thing. "I'll tell you: we are fighting for the nature of our country, our democracy, our Judaism."[8]

This is undoubtedly true, but it would have been nice for her to stay more focused on the gender issues—especially given the fact that Knesset Member Limor Livnat, the speaker who came after her, recently accused her of "just discovering women's issues, only realizing now that she's a woman when elections are imminent."

Indeed, what the rally did not quite do is send a message about the real issue at hand—i.e., violence against women carried out by Haredim with official or unofficial governmental sanction. Lili Ben-Ami, founder of the Lobby for Gender Equality, was live blogging a gender count of speakers. "First speaker, representative of [organizers] Be Free Israel: a man. Second speaker: Beit Shemesh resident, a man. Third speaker, also from Be Free Israel: a man. Emcee for the evening: a man. Waiting for a woman to speak." The overwhelming majority of speakers, in fact, were male.[9]

Interestingly, the first woman to speak was Hadassa Margolese, whose voice was the one that rallied the whole nation. She walked onto the stage with a man who spoke after her. Then, when the emcee invited Hadassa to light a Hanukkah candle, the man took the candle out of Hadassa's hands and made the blessing, as Ben-Ami noted.

Three more organizations were represented by male speakers, and a fourth man who started the Facebook page for the event also spoke. Then a man and a woman representing the citizens of Beit Shemesh were invited to the stage—the man grabbed the microphone and spoke, saying, "Our women are the best!" And then the two walked off the stage before the woman uttered a word. Another male Beit Shemesh resident was called onto the stage and said, "The daughters of Israel are modest, and they must not be harmed."[10]

Eventually, Knesset members Livni, Livnat, and Shelly Yachimovich provided a female presence—and Yachimovich was notably the only person onstage to use the word "feminism"—but nevertheless the message came through loud and clear. "The event proves well that the exclusion of women is deeply rooted in Israeli society, in all its sectors," Ben-Ami concluded.[11] I agree.

Some of the outrage was clearly not about defending equal rights for women. In fact, there is a lot of antireligious sentiment driving much of this, which signifies an awakening of an Israeli secularism that is fed up with religious coercion. The *Ynet* reporter covering the event even called it the "protest against religious coercion" and not the protest against violence against women.

It seemed like even though Israelis were starting to wake up to the threat of radical religion, they did not necessarily understand that the issue here was about violence against women. It's not just the Haredi community that has a problem with sexism, but it's much easier to point the finger elsewhere. Men dominating women takes place everywhere. And at this crucial moment of women's protest, men were stomping on women as well.

Nevertheless, this was still an important, hopeful first step. That was in December 2011. It was a protest on its first legs, and women—especially religious feminist women—were pushed aside in a way, as they almost were with Women of the Wall as well. But since then, things have been shifting. Religious feminists and secular pluralists have started to work in tandem on a range of issues, and all are realizing that the religious radicalism that threatens the entire Israeli population has women in its crosshairs. As the movement starts to coalesce, so does the vision of the future.

Interestingly, in the numerous places in Israel where a radical religious misogyny has been gradually creeping into public spaces and threatening to ruin many lives, the people on the frontline trying to stop the spread of these practices and ideas are often religious women. What's unique about these women's religious feminist perspectives is that they do not see religion in and of itself as an evil thing. Instead, they are fighting a sharp battle to protect the integrity of their religion while removing the forces of radical misogyny that pervert it. This is a tricky position and one worth emphasizing. It is easy to look at these problems and dismiss all of Judaism or all of Israel as the root problem. But that would be wrong. Even within ultra-Orthodoxy, there are calls for more compassion and gender inclusion. Whenever I post an item on Facebook about something awful happening in the ultra-Orthodox world, several ultra-Orthodox friends gently remind me that not all ultra-Orthodox people are like that. In turn, I concur and remind them how important it is for people like them to speak up and fight back, not only for women overall, but also for themselves. That is the key to resolving the problems facing women in Israel—and women the world over. It is about taking a stand and saying to those who threaten women, their families, and their values: *This violent behavior is not what it means to be a person living in the path of God.*

To understand why this is happening and why it's critical to encourage, it's helpful to learn a bit from scholar Martha Nussbaum's analysis of feminist social change within traditional societies. She did a lot of work in India working on empowerment with women in a very traditional society and wrestles with these issues of change from within and moral relativism. She asserts that while an appreciation of "ethnicities" often leads to the adaptation of a stance of moral relativism, secular feminism can also be patronizing to traditional women. She argues for the adaptation of a certain set of universal values, which she conceptualizes in terms of "human development," that need to be demanded across cultures. These values, which include issues such as bodily integrity, bodily health, emotions, life, and affiliation, are denied to women in often extreme numbers. So, for example, she argues that to talk about a practice such as genital mutilation as "cultural" is a misuse of ethnic appreciation that leaves women suffering. Similarly, she writes that practices of domestic abuse and marital rape should not be looked at as cultural but as negations of fundamental human capabilities, leaving women to lead lesser lives. It's about working to repair injustices while respecting women's very real and treasured connection to tradition and religion.[12]

However, religious feminists cannot fight this battle alone. The greatest successes in the fight against this spread have been when religious feminist women join forces with proponents of religious pluralism in Israel. This was the pattern with the segregated buses: religious women such as Naomi Ragen were the first to start speaking about the problem and then worked with IRAC and NCJW to coordinate "Freedom Rides" and judicial action. As a result, there was a significant reduction in the number of segregated lines, from over two hundred to less than fifty in 2013. This was also the pattern with the removal of women's faces from billboards in Jerusalem: religious feminist Jerusalem Councilwoman Rachel Azaria worked with religious feminist organization Kolech to protest, but it wasn't until they joined forces with Rabbi Uzi Ayalon of the Masorti movement and created a mass alliance of protest groups that real change took place. Today, Jerusalem has begun restoring images of women on the street and in brochures, giving them a public face again. Women of the Wall is probably the best example of a movement that began as a religious feminist activity—women's prayer groups are the epitome of religious feminism in action—and evolved into a unique amalgam of religious pluralism and Orthodox feminism that was key in bringing about the involvement of liberal American voices and creating real awareness and change. It is this strategic alliance between religious pro-women voices and the voices of religious pluralism in Israel and abroad that forge a powerful force to halt the spread of the violent, devastating, misogynistic religious radicalism there.

IRAC and Kolech epitomize this. These two organizations have collaborated on key initiatives in almost every area of gender and religion described in this book. The two groups have conducted research on gender segregation in the public sphere, have brought key legal petitions on issues such as the Kol Berama radio station, and have sat together to plan mass protests. They have drafted legislation together and have presented at the Knesset together. Both Anat Hoffman of IRAC and Dr. Hannah Kehat of Kolech have separately described to me the power of this collaboration in strategic, pragmatic, and ideological terms.

For the Orthodox community in particular, there is an important lesson here. For once, Orthodox women activists are going where Orthodox men have always been afraid to go. There is this nagging irrational fear among many Orthodox rabbis and leaders that sitting together with leaders of other Jewish denominations will cause them to lose their own legitimacy and identity. It's rather like a "cooties problem," where Orthodox rabbis think that collaboration with non-Orthodox Jews will taint them. One of the great contributions of Orthodox feminism is a release from this "cooties" fear. Orthodox feminists are choosing to focus on what needs to get done and are collaborating with people from all around Israel—non-Orthodox Jews as well as non-Jews—to accomplish these important societal reforms. What's most ironic is that these partnerships that Orthodox rabbis seem to be allergic to are in fact reflective of one of the fundamental tenets of the Jewish faith and culture. They are profound reflections of a vision of a better society, exemplifying *tikkun olam*, the Jewish value of social justice, "repair the world."

This is precisely what happened in Beit Shemesh in what ended up being one of the most important moments of protest in the struggle against religious radicalism in Israel. It was a turning point in the struggle, when both secular Israeli activists and religious feminists realized that they needed each other to make real change. Certainly there were some issues of women being kind of "pushed aside" at the rally. But ultimately, the women leading the fight kept pushing and brought about change.

Today, things are quiet around the Orot Banot school, what has been described as "a tenuous calm." There were no incidents of violence at Orot Banot for school year 2013–14, and construction is taking place for a community center meant to serve *all* population sectors. Of course, some of this work remains gender-segregated: a dialogue group for men called "Be a *mensch*" brings together all-men's groups from different social sectors, while an all-women's film group called "Wonderful Women" works with women from different sectors.[13] Still, this is all a good start.

Meanwhile, although there are some signs of hope, for the Margolese family, it may be too little, too late. The family has decided to leave. "It wasn't so much the Haredi men that have pushed me over the top as my own neighbors," Hadassa told me. There is a sense, she said, that even though people like the results she achieved, they would like her to pipe down.[14]

The tension came to a head around an issue having nothing to do with the school or with Na'ama. Hadassa wrote an article in which she criticized the attendant in her local *mikveh* for being too invasive, controlling, and frankly immodest by, among other things, glaring at her while she immersed without ever looking away. For writing this article, Hadassa got called many names and an entire article was written about her afterward, accusing her of being immodest and provocative and not sufficiently religious.

"It's time for a new start," she told me, "which will be good for Na'ama also." Na'ama only wanted to know if when she moves, it will be reported on the radio.

Around the same time as the Beit Shemesh protest, other movements of protest were starting to bubble to the surface. In that same month, some five hundred people gathered in a park across from the Mashbir mall in Jerusalem's city center on a cool Wednesday night. The event, called "Singing for Equality," was an outdoor concert with many female singers to protest the increasing gender segregation in Israel and the exclusion of women's images and voices from public spaces and events. Organized by Yisrael Hofshit, the concert/protest was conceived a mere five days earlier around the idea of "sounding women's voices" in Jerusalem, where their words have been largely silenced. Even with only a few days to prepare, colorful and elaborate posters stood erect as part of the stage stated, "Good morning Israel, the time has come to wake up and get back the Israel we lost."

Achinoam Nini, the recording artist better known as Noa, was among the performers who took the stage at the concert. "You want to know why I'm here?" she told my friend and colleague Dr. Ariella Zeller who interviewed her after the concert. "Everything that I've learned about Judaism, learning in yeshiva in the States—first in SAR Academy and then in Ramaz, where I had wonderful experiences—everything that I know to be important to Judaism is being destroyed by some radicals. They've interpreted the Judaism that I know and love in a way that I feel is erroneous and unintelligent, and I'm here to fight against that."

She continued, "We are now fighting for the identity of this country as a Jewish democracy. What kind of Jewish democracy it's going to be. And I'm fighting it for the kind of Jewish place I want my children to live in. I don't want to leave and I don't want to succumb to radical extremism."[15]

There was a mix of young, middle-aged, and old, religious and secular and in between, at least half Hebrew-speaking with a strong presence of English, and rabbis of multiple denominations. Absent from the crowd were members of the Haredi community.

And there was singing. The evening began with the eleven high school students in the conservative Masorti movement's NOAM choir called Shirat Machar, Sing for Tomorrow, who sang a medley of Shlomo Artzi songs. One of the singers, sixteen-year-old Hadas Bandel from Jerusalem, told us, "People my age, in my generation, don't know what is happening. They know in Jerusalem there is a problem with the buses and they are making the girls go to the back, but nobody is really aware of what is going on. At school I was telling everybody to come tonight. People were staring at me. They were like, oh I didn't know what was happening."[16]

The event was sponsored by Be Free Israel, formed a year earlier to advocate for separation of religion and state and against religious coercion in Israel. Mickey Gitzin, the thirty-year-old executive director of Be Free Israel, commented, "Women are back in the public sphere in Jerusalem."[17] The New Israel Fund also gave support to the event and ran a campaign with the posters "Women Should Be Seen and Heard," which was prominently placed at the rally. Shira Ben-Sasson Furstenberg, a religious feminist coordinator of Religious Pluralism grants for the New Israel Fund, brought her entire family to the rally, including her three children. She described what was happening in Israel as "the snowball effect," where it started with one segregated bus line and then became streets, clinics, women's faces, and women's voices. "Where will it go next? And we need to stop it. I can't even say it's small because it's not small anymore."[18]

The event marked a key moment in the emergence of a strong voice of secular Israeli protest, the assertion of a secular-democratic vision for Israeli society.

There was a strong showing of the Israeli Conservative (Masorti) movement as well. Rabbi Uri Ayalon of the Jerusalemites movement said, "Equality between men and women is nonnegotiable."[19] Rabbi Barry Schlesinger, the rabbi of Moreshet Avraham Congregation, Orah Lipsky, also from Congregation Moreshet Avraham in Jerusalem, and Rabbi Andy Sacks, director of the Rabbinical Assembly in Israel, were among the Masorti people in the crowd.

Significantly, there were also noticeable clusters of religious people who came to promote not only democracy, but also a vision of religious life.

Shira Ben-Sasson Furstenberg added, "I know people in America sometimes say, 'Well, this is Israeli stuff, it's not appropriate to get involved'…and I say it is appropriate for you to get involved because it's about you and it's not just about the Jewish state; it's about the Jewish people and it's about our values and our Torah— it's backward. Take a picture, put it on our website. Talk to your rabbi, talk to your congressman."[20] To wit, when Hillary Clinton commented about gender segregation in Israel earlier that month, the blogosphere was aflame.

Achinoam Nini also urged Americans to get involved. "I think that American Jews should wake up and smell the country," she said. "There is not going to be any place to come back to on holidays or on summer vacations if this place is going to turn into a Taliban Jewish state. We're well on our way to doing that. And we are isolating ourselves, building walls again. We're building a ghetto here rather than opening it to the rest of the world. I think that American Jewry should take a stand and say we don't want this. This is not the homeland we dreamed about… Take a stand to create a real free and open democracy for all of its citizens."[21]

Miri Shalem, a long-time resident of Beit Shemesh, was particularly struck by the ways in which increasingly radical enforcement of religion has affected the women in her community. As the director of the local community center of Ramat Beit Shemesh—that same hotbed of religious radicalism that sparked the initial protests against the Haredim's maltreatment of those poor schoolgirls— Miri has encountered women who she says suffer from what she calls "religious abuse." "All the pressure on 'modesty,' the pressure to stay out of the public sphere, the physical violence that surrounds them—it has an impact," Miri, herself a hair-covering Orthodox woman, told me.[22] She has been working on helping Orthodox women heal from these issues for a decade, using the extraordinary medium of dance as reparative therapy.

It started with what she calls a "discotheque for religious women." For ten years, she has been running an evening of dance—"not Hasidic dancing, not the kind of dancing you would do at a religious wedding," like "Hava Nagila," "but real dancing to the kind of music we love." The evenings, for women only, have given Orthodox women a safe place where they can unravel some of the troubling messages about the female body that surround them. "Dance gives women an opportunity for self-expression," she says, "in a way that nothing else does."[23]

The religious women's disco brought about two other major developments. One was the first ever all-women's dance festival in March 2011 that Miri helped organize. An unexpectedly huge turnout of eight hundred women came to a small moshav, Tzora, right outside Beit Shemesh, where they watched an endless stream of all-women dance troupes. "They were the highest level of dancers," said Miri, still astonished at the enormity of the event two years later, "but they only dance in front of women."[24] This was the only time an all-women's dance event of this magnitude had been staged, but Miri reports that there is a thirst for more. "It was such an incredible success, that I get calls all the time from different places in Israel to talk about it and help other groups produce similar events," she says.[25]

The festival led to the second major event, which was the first ever religious women's flash mob in Beit Shemesh. "I saw women's desire to dance and I saw a need to take it a step further," she said. "With all the issues of segregation surrounding us, all that women are going through, I saw this thirst in them. The dancing did something." And so in January 2012, Miri put together a women's flash mob on the streets of Beit Shemesh. Some 250 women and girls of all ages—many wearing religious attire, some wearing jeans—can be seen dancing with passion, joy, and gusto to Queen's "Don't Stop Me Now."[26] "So many women have told me that the video makes them cry," she said. "To see all these women dance like this—we're so used to hearing about women being oppressed, and this is just completely the opposite. It's invigorating."[27]

The response to the flash mob was more than Miri anticipated.

With 200,000 views on YouTube, Miri started getting requests for women's flash mobs for different causes. Since then, she has created women's dance flash mob videos for breast cancer awareness, agunot, and One Billion Rising, and several more projects are in the works. She started an organization called Women Dance for Change, which looks for ways to use dance to advance social causes for women. "The woman's body suffers all kinds of oppression," she said. "There is religious oppression of 'modesty' and segregation, compounded by physical and sexual violence that many religious women suffer. They often have nowhere to turn and no language to understand their experience. The tool of dance is therapeutic, learning to use the body for positive things." She adds that the experience of dancing in public counteracts the impact of all the pressure on public gender segregation. "Using the body in a public space improves women's self-confidence and helps promote the feeling that you don't have to hide your body but you can use and it can be seen in a public space."[28]

When all is said and done, however, dance is just dance, and women have to go back to their regular lives. So in March 2013, Miri, the serial innovator, started a new center, Merkaz Lema'anech—literally "the Center for You" (using the singular female form of "you")—that offers a whole range of counseling to women to help them improve their lives. This includes career counseling, self-presentation, emotional therapies, and more. The counselors, all women from the area, most Orthodox, offer very discounted rates to women to ensure that clients will come. In the few months that they have been operating, they have received over a dozen women a week seeking help, mostly Haredi—and the number is rising rapidly. "These women are in crisis," Miri says, "because they got married young and had lots of babies in quick succession. They are now in their thirties or forties and they have no idea what they want out of their lives. They have to figure out ways to earn a living, but they have no training. Nobody has ever helped them figure out how to lead their lives. It was just, get married young to a nice yeshiva bocher and have lots of babies. Nobody gave them the life skills to figure out their lives beyond that."[29]

Miri Shalem, the forty-three-year-old mother of four, who is working on a master's degree in gender studies at Bar-Ilan University, is definitely a woman to watch. She is one of a handful of Orthodox women in Beit Shemesh working toward gender change from within.

Another fascinating development is among Haredi women seeking political positions. The ultra-Orthodox religious parties have never allowed women on their Knesset party lists, but until this past election, it did not seem to bother anyone. But those days could be gone. In the 2013 elections, a group of women's organizations brought a High Court petition demanding that parties that do not have equal gender access for all should be declared illegal. Although the petitioners' request was ultimately rejected—Haredi politicians arguing strongly that "women's place is different; men have one role and women have another" won the case—the events garnered some crucial attention. One woman in particular took notice, and took action. Esty Shushan, a Haredi journalist who writes for the ultra-Orthodox site *Kikar Hashabat*, decided that she had enough of women's exclusion from the halls of Haredi power and started an online campaign *Lo Nivharot, Lo Boharot*: "If we can't be elected, we are not voting."[30] That is to say, Haredi sisters, do not vote for Haredi parties that exclude us.

"We're good enough when they need us to help them get elected, but we're not good enough to be elected ourselves?" her Facebook page, which got over one thousand followers within weeks, calls out. In a column in *Ynetnews*, she wrote: "The Haredi politicians don't even bother trying to justify women's exclusion from the party lists based on Halacha, because there is no halachic prohibition against women running for the Knesset. They admitted that it was 'social codes' that send me, the Haredi woman, away from the Knesset, away from decision-making, away from anything valuable, toward some other place. Who knows, to the kitchen, to the sink, to the hairdresser, or the devil knows where, 'behind the scenes' as [Aryeh Deri's wife] Yaffa Deri calls it."[31] She points out with irony that Shas has no problem sending women in front of the cameras to justify sending women behind the scenes.

A thirty-five-year old mother of four from Petah Tikva, Shushan spent the entire election period writing and campaigning online to try to get Haredi women not to vote for Haredi parties that exclude them. "Haredi women can lead, develop careers and support their families," she wrote. "Haredi women can be found in every industry today, in decision-making positions. But being a Knesset member is the one job that is reserved for Haredi men only. Yet this job has the most decisive power in society."[32]

Indeed, it is interesting that the system of Haredi men studying and receiving government stipends instead of working has actually created an entire culture in which Haredi women have become the main breadwinners in many households. Much like nineteenth-century *shtetl* life, in some places where Jewish men are steered away from "secular" studies, the women pick up the slack in the business and professional world. Haredi women, some argue, have more opportunities for professional, career, and academic advancement than do Haredi men. And even though the "double shift" of being breadwinners and mothers to large broods can be draining, there is also something empowering for a woman to know that she can support her own household. In the religious Zionist world, where rabbis can still be heard calling to forbid women from working outside the home altogether, one might argue that women are less empowered than the ultra-Orthodox women who manage powerful careers to feed their families.

Shushan argues that the strength of Haredi women is what truly scares the Haredi politicians and businessmen. "They want women to be educated from birth not to [aim for] places where they can have real power," she writes, arguing that Haredi men interested in maintaining their own power work hard to convince women not to *want* to go into politics. "They have the audacity to tell us what we want without even asking us, and [have] created mechanisms to ensure that we won't be able to have our voices heard. They sell us this bitter pill that this 'preserves our femininity.' In practice, they're still stuck in archaic ideas that are exploding before their own eyes."[33]

Unfortunately, Shushan's efforts did not seem to impact the 2013 Knesset elections. Both ultra-Orthodox groups, the Ashkenazi United Torah Judaism Party (UTJ) and the Sephardic Shas Party, did quite well for themselves: UTJ even went up by two seats from the previous election (from five to seven), while Shas stayed steady at eleven seats.[34] However, the movement seems to have taken roots in another way: for the first time, three Haredi women announced that they were running in their municipal elections in November 2013.

In May 2013, a Haredi woman named Shira Georgi announced that she was running for municipal council in her hometown of Safed, a city in northern Israel with a very large Haredi population.

In response, she was inundated with mail, including some of the less pleasant variety. Shas council member in Safed Rabbi Zeev Shavavo told reporters, "Women are not options for Shas voters. Their place is at home, with the children. It's not for naught that there are no [Shas] women in the Knesset or municipalities. It was the decision of [Shas spiritual advisor] Rabbi Ovadia Yosef who believes first and foremost in women's modesty." The mayor of Safed threatened to go to the late Shas spiritual leader Rabbi Yosef to prohibit Georgi from running, to which she responded, incredibly, "I'm not asking for his permission."[35]

Shira Georgi won in the election, becoming the first woman on the Safed municipal council in some twenty years. Racheli Ibenboim, a twenty-eight-year-old Gur Hassid and executive director of Meir Panim, a large charity organization providing meals for poor and homeless people in Israel, announced that she was running for the Jerusalem council, number three on the Habayit Hayehudi Party list. However, she was inundated with threats against herself and her family, including threats of "excommunication," which can be devastating in the Gur community. So she pulled out of the race.[36]

A few days after Georgi announced that she was running for Safed city council, another Haredi woman took up the call. Ruth Colian, a Haredi mother of four who was active in Shushan's campaign to get women not to vote for Haredi parties, announced that she was running for a seat on the Petah Tikva city council as an independent and not as a Shas representative. According to reports, Colian said that Shas has "no choice" because women in the city have "nobody to turn to." She also said she was "inspired" by Georgi's decision to run.[37]

Unlike Georgi, however, Colian lost. The fact that she lost may in fact point to some even more disturbing processes of religious radicalization in Israel. According to blogger Hannah Katsman, one of the reasons she lost is because of the aggressive campaigning of a religious kabbalistic cult called Bnei Baruch (also known as Arevut, Kabbalah Laam). In addition to promoting the exclusion of women in society, the group also allegedly has some very shady practices in issues of money, power, and mind control. Katsman has been working on exposing their practices, as well as those of other ultra-Orthodox cults. The group surprisingly garnered four seats out of twenty-seven in the Petah Tikva municipal election, thanks to what Katsman calls "a sophisticated campaign with programs for kids, clean-up projects, and so on," which is why, she says, "it's especially important to get the word out about what this group actually does," that is to say, it runs a cult for the purposes of advancing its own power and money.[38]

Despite these mixed results, change may just be afoot in Israel when it comes to women, religion, and power. The most interesting changes are undoubtedly those that come from within the religious world. But none of the public consciousness-raising would have happened without the tireless activism of nongovernmental organizations (NGOs), some religious and some secular, on behalf of gender change. Some of the most powerful forces for change have been around judicial and legislative action. Throughout this book are examples of NGOs pursuing legislative and judicial actions in order to promote change, some of these with great impact. Below are a few examples:

- **Segregated buses.** IRAC and Kolech led the lawsuit against the Ministry of Transport, which eventually made segregation illegal. Today, every bus has a sign saying that women can choose to sit where they want. Bus drivers comply because they know they can be fined a month's salary if their buses are found to have segregation.

- **Women's faces on Jerusalem streets.** The campaign of the Jerusalemites changed the policy of showing women's faces on billboards in Jerusalem. Even the Jerusalem municipality has restored women's faces to many of their printed materials, such as the brochure for the Jerusalem marathon.

- **Gender segregation on the streets.** IRAC filed another lawsuit against the Netanya Chevra Kadisha on behalf of a woman who was excluded from delivering a eulogy at a funeral. As of publication, the lawsuit was still pending.

- **Rock throwing in Beit Shemesh.** Beit Shemesh resident Nili Phillip is leading a class-action suit against the municipality of Beit Shemesh to hold them accountable for the fact that women are being hurt by rock-throwing Haredi men. It is up to the municipality, they argue, to take down signs saying women cannot be on certain streets and to protect women. The lawsuit is pending.

- **Women's voices on the radio.** Kolech and IRAC are in the midst of a 104 million NIS ($30 million U.S.) lawsuit against the broadcasting authorities to protest the practice of the Kol Berama radio station excluding women's speaking and singing voices. Kol Berama is at risk of losing its license. The lawsuit may also pave the way for similar actions in other areas.

- **Civil marriage and divorce in Israel.** Several organizations are pushing for civil marriage and divorce in Israel—including New Family, Hiddush, and Be Free Israel, among others. The Masorti Movement is also pushing to have non-Orthodox marriages recognized as valid. Public sentiment is undoubtedly increasing in support of this movement and the possibilities are encouraging.

- **Information about fertility treatment risks.** Kolech is also pushing for legislation to create and enforce procedures in which couples must be fully informed about all the risks involved in fertility treatments. Also, before undergoing hormonal treatments, doctors must rule out all other potential factors, including "infertility within Halacha"—that is, that the woman is perfectly healthy but ovulates during her seven "clean" days.

- **Race to the courthouse legislation.** ICAR is pushing for legislation that would change the system of divorce in Israel to eliminate the so-called race to the courthouse.

- **Women as directors of rabbinical courts.** ICAR is also promoting a bill to change the current law that says that the executive director of the Rabbinical Courts—an administrative position, not a rabbinic one—has to be an ordained rabbi, meaning an Orthodox rabbi. This excludes women as well as non-Orthodox Jews. Changing this law would open up at least one position of authority to women.

- **Challenging the abortion panels.** MK Zahava Gal-On is spearheading legislation to make the abortion panels obsolete.

- **Challenging the rabbinical courts' jurisdiction over conversion.** The Center for Women's Justice is awaiting a decision on their appeal to the High Court of Justice challenging the right of the rabbinical court to overturn conversions.

- **Reform in the "services" of the Religious Ministry.** The Religious Ministry has responded to public pressure by beginning to institute reforms in the way the clerks of the Religious Ministry relate to the public, including allowing for some free market competition by allowing people to choose which city to register for marriage in. Although these proposed reforms contain some problematic elements as well (such as a proposal to make it an arrestable offense for non-Orthodox rabbis to perform weddings!), the fact that there is any proposed reform on the table points to the impact of social pressure and the fact that this entire issue is arguably in the midst of major transition.

The organizations working on these actions—IRAC, ICAR, Kolech, CWJ, Hiddush, New Family, and others—are in many ways the future of Israel because they are protecting the core democratic value that is key to Israel's identity. These activists are forcing Israel to reshape how basic human rights are protected, ensuring that Israel remains committed in law and in practice to all the important freedoms that are at risk of being lost. The outcomes of their work will likely determine how religion and state play out in the unfolding of Israel's culture and identity and what real life will look like for Israelis.

Perhaps the most inspiring story of change within this book is the story of Women of the Wall. When I began the chapter about WOW, the story was so bleak that it was painful to write. Women were being arrested every month based on an interpretation of a Supreme Court ruling that made no sense, enforced by a religious bureaucrat who controlled the Jerusalem police and, through them, these women's lives. All of this was happening despite storms of local and international protest. As WOW experienced setback after setback, its story easily could have turned into one of despair and desperation, of twenty-five years of struggle in which the situation for women only got worse.

Yet during the very months that I was writing this book, remarkable shifts began to happen. Prime Minister Netanyahu actually responded and appointed international Jewish hero and icon Natan Sharansky to find a solution. And Sharansky rolled up his sleeves and got to work. That was the first sign that something had changed, that somewhere in the corridors of power, someone realized that the voices of women must be heeded, not ignored. Even though Sharansky's plan faces tremendous obstacles, the fact that Netanyahu cared enough to send him to work and that he came up with any kind of reasonable plan was a huge moment of hope.

Then, remarkably, one judge changed everything. Truly and deeply changed everything. One female judge with a feminist voice, a sane voice, finally overturned the entire play and ruled that women cannot be arrested. "To arrest these women…is likened to blaming a rape victim for the clothing that she wears," she said.[39] But more importantly, when her ruling was naturally appealed by the police, the police *lost*. In that moment, the rules of the game completely changed. For the first time in twenty-five years, the police began protecting the Women of the Wall and arresting men who abuse them, both physically and psychologically. This is the change we have been waiting for.

That's not to say things are perfect. WOW board member Peggy Cidor had her house graffitied. And the Haredi community is not going down without a fight—at the WOW prayer services in May, they bused in thousands of seminary girls to counterprotest and abuse the women of WOW. And of course, a splinter group called OWOW, "Original Women of the Wall," has recently been created to protest Anat Hoffman's acceptance of the Sharansky proposal. That has undoubtedly cast a dark shadow on these developments. Still, there is no disputing that the protests and activism have changed the facts on the ground. The police and the government have paid heed and changed their views. That, in and of itself, is huge.

The story of WOW has become a positive example of change in action. Despite the fact that the story of WOW is in many ways similar to all the other issues described in this book—the police and local government took the side of Haredim out of perceptions of political expediency and votes; secular society for a long time didn't care and had all but abandoned the Western Wall to Haredim—despite all this, the women ultimately achieved some measures of change. Why? Because people spoke out. And it wasn't just "people"; it was a powerful alliance between Orthodox feminists and advocates for religious pluralism. It was also a powerful alliance between Israelis and Americans. These are the factors that led to the success of WOW. Women like Anat Hoffman simply did not give up and did not stop speaking out; Hoffman in particular is a wonderful model in this regard. She expresses tremendous respect for religious women, even though she is not Orthodox herself. That model of collaboration and cooperation toward a greater good is key for successfully advancing social change.

A question that emerges is why should the world outside of Israel care about this story? After all, this book is about Israel. Certainly, this is a compelling historical account. We are witnessing a very significant time in Israeli history. The country was founded on an earnest need to protect Jews and provide a safe refuge for them after the horrors of the Holocaust. But today, Israel is a nation among many and can no longer afford to have such a one-dimensional identity. It has a complex amalgamation of populations, each with individual rights and needs. It is no longer enough to say that Israel is the Jewish State. It is also a democracy, and it needs to figure out how to be both a democratic state and a Jewish state. The serious gender inequality issue can be a great opportunity for positive change in Israel, forcing leaders and policy makers to implement laws and practices that safeguard freedoms and ensure basic rights for all its residents and citizens. The activists pressing on lawmakers are doing the vital work of shaping democracy, but they need everyone's help. They need the support of citizens of Israel and of the world to speak out about what gender equality means to them.

This story is significant not only for Israelis, but for the rest of the world as well, because Israel is hardly the only country to face these kinds of challenges. Indeed, this book is not just about Israel. Countries around the world are facing similar threats of religious fundamentalism. The idea of women's bodies and sexuality as a "threat" to society—or to men—crosses cultural and religious divides, affecting places as free and democratic as America and as oppressive as Afghanistan and North Korea.

When you hear people—especially leaders and lawmakers—adopting language that has echoes of misogynistic religious radicalism, call them on it. Write, blog, tweet, comment, and share the stories and share your thoughts about them. The Internet is a great tool. Bloggers have had a tremendous impact on forcing change in Israel. As they say, sunlight is the best disinfectant—that is, bringing stories of injustice to the fore is the best way to advance change. Speak out and make sure that the world knows you care. The message will eventually get through. The world needs voices speaking out against religious radicalism. It is the only way to protect women and to protect freedom and human rights.

Afterword
AND THE BATTLE CONTINUES:
WHAT CAN WE DO?

I recently watched a video—one of those types that is so viral that several people send it to you at once—that shows a Muslim cleric speaking on a talk show about how and why it is okay for a man to beat his wife. He described it in language of compassion, about how a man should hit only the body and not the face (although he didn't say if this is out of respect for the woman or so that the whole world won't know). And then he started comparing her to a donkey: just as you have to use compassion toward the donkey when you hit it, not to beat with force but just enough for discipline, so too with the wife. Beat her, he said, with the force of a toothpick (and he took a rather large toothpick out of his pocket to demonstrate), like when you want her to pick up some garbage off the floor, because if you would afford the courtesy of a light beating to a donkey, you should certainly afford that same courtesy to a woman.[1]

What struck me about this clip was not only the bizarreness of this description, but also how certain this man was. He spoke as if he were Isaac Newton explaining the law of physics that he just discovered and was introducing to the world. He spoke as if he were personally delivering the most important message from

God himself. His face was not screwed up and angry but rather was joyful, eloquent, clear, almost prescient. If it weren't for the content of the words coming out of this person's mouth, I might have found myself saying, "Gee, I like this man. I want to learn from him."

There are some strange things happening in the world. Israel is just one case where religious extremism is threatening to take over women's bodies and minds. It's a mistake to think that this is simply a gender war, some kind of battle of power between men and women. There are plenty of men who decry religious extremism and plenty of women who don't. There are plenty of women who adopt opinions that are so self-damaging and so self-damning that it's difficult to understand how or why they speak that way. And it's a mistake to think that it's a battle between the religious and the secular. There are religious people backing openness and caring and there are secular people supporting backdoor politics and business that ultimately empower religious radicalism. And this radicalism is not limited to one religion. It's as ubiquitous as it is frightening.

Particularly difficult for me to observe is just how much force this misogynistic religious radicalism has in the minds of its leaders. Like the Muslim cleric—his posture of absolute certainty as he spewed forth ideas that to many of us can at best be described as rubbish was astonishing. He makes me think of lyrics from the Billy Joel song "Shades of Grey": "The only people I fear are those who never have doubts." That is indeed the problem: religious extremism is expressed through people who do not seem to have any doubts at all, who are so sure that their way is the right way and the only way that they don't hesitate when their practices hurt others. But for them, to think otherwise is unfathomable. Their worlds would shatter.

But it's more than that. The reason why religious people, especially women, get so upset by the idea that their lifestyles are based on sexism rather than the word of God is that it implies that they are nothing more than pawns who listen blindly in this system. Like any human being, more than anything, no religious woman in the world wants to think of herself as having no volition of her own. I hear this all the time, religious women who say things like, "Why do you act as if I'm oppressed? I'm not oppressed! I make my own choices! I choose this life!" Religious people for the most part *like* being religious, which I deeply understand as well. In many cases, religious women *choose* to abide by a set of rules, because at some point in their lives, they have made up their own minds that they want this package, that it's what works for them. They then take the whole thing, including all the rhetoric and rules that may oppress them, because with religion, it is often an all-or-nothing kind of deal. But what is important is that, for better or worse, they have *chosen* this path.

I want to be clear: I am not suggesting to anyone who is religious not to be religious. On the contrary: I believe religion can be a beautiful thing. Religious life can provide connection, meaning, purpose, community, structure, tradition, heritage, care, responsibility, and so much more. The religious life offers a certainty in which you know every waking moment what you are doing in this world and why. Even David Brooks wrote about this, giving homage to Orthodox Jews for having such a deeply meaningful and tradition-rooted existence. But more than that, I see religion as spirituality, as a search for life with some kind of mystical meaning, an awareness that we are more than a collection of atoms spinning in a random and anarchic universe, but part of some kind of unseen design. I love that worldview, and I live it, even if there might come a day when I may be proven wrong, after I die and discover that the truth bears no resemblance to these beliefs. Nevertheless, I think that holding on to a larger meaning of my own existence is just a better way of being. That is the true essence of religion. Above all, it should guide us to be better, kinder people and to deeply care about the state of humanity and work to improve it.

The problem is that so much of what is given to us under the guise of religiousness is just not actually religious at all. Whether it's a Muslim cleric comparing violence against women to training donkeys, a conservative American political candidate trying to control women's reproductive rights with an antiabortion platform, or a Haredi man spitting at a young woman on the bus, there are people in the world who claim to represent or do things in the name of religion but who simply aren't. This is fundamentally *not* what it means to be religious.

The most basic premise of religiousness is living compassionately. Karen Armstrong, a famous feminist author and scholar of religion, sums it up perfectly in her numerous books on religion: all religions of the world have at their core this truth—that to reach God, one must live a compassionate life, proactively, passionately, and profoundly. The key, Armstrong notes, is that compassion is not weakness, nor is it passive or ambivalent. Compassion is powerful, activist, and potentially world-changing.

In her 2008 "TED Prize Wish" marking her receipt of the TED Prize, this former nun who once swore off religion argues that religion can bring world peace.[2] She articulates more than any rabbi I have ever heard the most profound spiritual truths of the universe. "It is an arresting fact," she said, "that across the board in every one of the major faiths, compassion, the way to feel for the other, is not only the test of any true religiosity, it is also what will bring us into the presence of what Jews, Christians, and Muslims call God, or the Divine. It is compassion, says the Buddha, which is what brings you to Nirvana. We dethrone ourselves from the center of our world and we put another person there. Once we get rid of ego, then we're ready to see the Divine. Every single one of the major world religions has highlighted and put at the core of their tradition what has become known as the Golden Rule, first proposed by Confucius five centuries before Christ: do not do unto others what you would not like them to do unto you." She added, "People want to be religious, and religion should be made to be a force for harmony in the world, which it can and should be."

The forms of religious radicalism that I've explored in this book, the ones that so readily enact violence against women—emotional, spiritual, and even physical violence—are by definition not religious. If one's so-called religious doctrine forces one to act with violence against another human being, it is not representing the Divine spirit because it is not compassionate. It is just power and violence, a desire for control, or perhaps submission to others who have a desire for power and control. Armstrong sums it up well. "We are living in a world in which religion has been hijacked, in which terrorists cite verses of the Koran to justify their atrocities... We have Christians endlessly judging other people, using scriptures to put other people down. Throughout the ages, religion has been used to oppress others. This is because of human ego, human greed. We have a talent as a species for messing up wonderful things."[3]

To combat our habit of destroying beautiful things, it is essential to empower ourselves, especially women through whom men, societies, and cultures will also be empowered. Thus, to all the religious people who are sitting in on classes and lectures, watching videos, reading books, and studying the words of religious leaders, my message is this: talk back. Question the messages. Do not think that just because the person sitting in front of you has the poise and posture of a king that his words are indeed kingly. If someone tells you that they know the path to God and it involves looking down on or seeking to control another human being, do not believe him or her. Find your own voice, and let your ideas, beliefs, and actions be based first and foremost on care and compassion.

To everyone else reading this book, I would urge you to become aware of the language that surrounds you, because religious radicalism is creeping in everywhere in alarming and subtle ways. Do not fall into the trap of moral relativism, thinking that if other people are okay with their own suffering then it's none of our business, which is in many ways just another form of careless apathy. Not all ideologies are equal, and as cognizant, self-aware people, we have a responsibility to halt the spread of ideas that promote systematic harm of a particular group of people. As I have discussed in this book, when we listen to people spreading words that are used to hurt women, our job is to care about the women and help speak up for them, and through them, for humanity as a whole.

What You Can Do

So what can you do to help stop the spread of religious radicalism? Like I said, speak up! Use your networks—Facebook, Twitter, Tumblr, LinkedIn—to share information and let all your followers know that you care about this. Blog, share, and comment. The current changes that we are witnessing in Israel are a testament to the power of the Internet and social media for spreading the spirit of change.

If you want to do more, there are numerous amazing organizations that are dedicated to protecting women in Israel from the spread of radicalism. Here are a few worth supporting.

Organizations in Israel

Kolech–Religious Women's Forum

Kolech–Religious Women's Forum, the first Orthodox Jewish feminist organization in Israel, aims to increase public awareness and bring about change in Israeli religious society by: disseminating the values of gender equality and mutual respect between men and women; encouraging equal opportunities for women in the public arena; initiating equal opportunity legislation that benefits all Jewish women in Israel; advancing women's rights and women's leadership in religious and halachic (Jewish legal) spheres; encouraging greater equality for women in matters of personal status, such as marriage and divorce; and engaging in an uncompromising battle against all forms of gender violence.

Dr. Hannah Kehat, CEO
http://www.kolech.com/english/
8 Hat'asiya Street
P.O. Box 10502
Jerusalem, 91104
Israel
Phone: +972-2-672-0321
Fax: +972-2-673-0595
Email: kolech@kolech.com

Women of the Wall

Women of the Wall, or Nashot Hakotel, is a group of Jewish women from around the world who strive to achieve the right, as women, to wear prayer shawls, pray, and read from the Torah collectively and out loud at the Western Wall (Kotel) in Jerusalem, Israel. The Western Wall is Judaism's most sacred holy site and the principal symbol of Jewish peoplehood and sovereignty, and Women of the Wall works to make it a holy site where women can pray freely.

Anat Hoffman, Chair

http://womenofthewall.org.il/

P.O. Box 31936

Jerusalem, 91319

Israel

Tel: +972-2-620-3290

Fax: +972-2-625-6260

Email: media@womenofthewall.org.il

Center for Women's Justice

Established in 2004, the Center for Women's Justice (CWJ) is a recognized leader in the struggle to end injustices perpetrated against women in the name of religion. In Israel, where there are two government-funded court systems—civil and rabbinic— only rabbinic courts can decide matters concerning marriage and divorce. The pioneering legal solutions address the problems that occur when policies and rulings of Israel's rabbinic establishment violate the basic rights of women to equality and self-determination.

Susan Weiss, Founder and Executive Director

http://www.cwj.org.il/en

43 Emek Refaim St.

Jerusalem, 93141

Israel
Tel: +972-2-566-4390
Fax: +972-2-566-3317
Email: cwj@cwj.org.il

NCJW—National Council of Jewish Women

Shari Eshet is director of NCJW's Israel Office, based in Jerusalem. She oversees NCJW's funding and advocacy efforts in Israel and is active on NCJW's behalf in international coalitions on issues of concern to NCJW, including the International Coalition for Agunah Rights (ICAR) and the Forum of Foundations in Israel. She runs NCJW's Israel Granting Program; Yad B'Yad, NCJW's Initiative to Nurture Knowledge, which supports grassroots organizations serving at-risk children and their families in Israel; and Women to Women, NCJW's Empowerment Initiative, which supports efforts to empower women in Israel. Shari also represents NCJW at the NCJW Women Studies' Forum at Tel Aviv University and the NCJW Research Institute for Innovation in Education at Hebrew University (RIFIE).

Nancy Kaufman, CEO; Shari Eshet, Israel Director
www.ncjw.org

NCJW Headquarters

475 Riverside Drive, Suite 1901
New York, NY 10115
Tel: 212-645-4048
Fax: 212-645-7466
Email: action@ncjw.org

Israel Office

NCJW Research Institute for Innovation in Education, Room 267

Hebrew University, Mt. Scopus

Jerusalem, 91905

Israel

Tel: +972-2-588-2208

Fax: +972-2-581-3264

Email: ncjwisrael@gmail.com

ICAR—International Coalition for Agunah Rights

ICAR is a coalition of twenty-seven organizations working together to combat the issue of *agunot an mesoravot gett*, women denied divorce.

Robyn Shames, Executive Director

http://www.icar.org.il/

P.O. Box 68131

Jerusalem, 91680

Israel

Tel: +972-2-672-1401

Fax: +972-2-672-8901

Email: icar@icar.org.il

IRAC—Israel Religious Action Center

The public and legal advocacy arm of the Reform Movement in Israel, IRAC was founded in 1987 with the goals of advancing pluralism in Israeli society and defending the freedoms of conscience, faith, and religion. Today, IRAC is the preeminent civil and human rights organization in Israel, focusing on the issues of religion and state, and is the leading Jewish organization that advocates on behalf of a broadly inclusive Israeli democracy, infusing social justice advocacy with the spiritual energy and humane worldview of Progressive Judaism.

Anat Hoffman, Executive Director
http://www.irac.org/
13 King David Street, P.O. Box 31936
Jerusalem, 91319
Israel
Tel: +972-2-620-3323
Fax: +972-2-625-6260

Mavoi Satum

Mavoi Satum is a nonprofit organization founded in 1995 to provide legal and emotional support to women who have been refused a Jewish divorce (*gett*). They are also one of the leading organizations engaged in finding a solution to the problem of divorce refusal in the State of Israel.

Batya Kahana-Dror, Executive Director
http://www.mavoisatum.org
Hata'asiya 8, room 212B
P.O. Box 8712
Jerusalem, 91086
Israel
Tel: +972-2-671-2282
Fax: +972-2-671-1314
Email: mavoisatum@mavoisatum.org

Women Dance for Change

Women Dance for a Change is an international movement with a vision—to inspire women to become an active force in promoting full gender equality around the world by using dance as a key mode of social protest and transformation. The Israel organization, headed by Miri Shalem in Beit Shemesh, produces flash dances on demand in response to important women's rights issues. Custom-choreographed flash mobs vividly protest the disappearance of women from the public space simply by reappearing there with energy, impact, and joy.

Miri Shalem, Founding Director
Susan Reimer-Torn, Codirector
http://www.womendanceforachange.org
Email: mirigender@gmail.com

Isha L'Isha

Isha L'Isha, established in 1983, is the oldest grassroots feminist organization in Israel and one of the leading voices of women's rights in the country. Though based in Haifa and working primarily in the northern part of Israel, many of their projects focus on implementing system-wide solutions to issues pertaining to women's lives. As a result, Isha L'Isha has a national influence, reaching target audiences throughout the country. The mission is to advance the status and rights of women and girls, and to promote peace, security, and socioeconomic justice from a feminist perspective through: education, research, dissemination of knowledge, advancing legislation, and public events.

http://www.isha.org.il/eng/
118 Arlozorov St.
Haifa, 33276
Israel

Tel: +972-4-865-0977

Fax: +972-4-864-1072

Email: isha@isha.org.il

Ladaat (formerly SHILO—Jerusalem's Family Planning Educational and Counseling Center)

Ladaat–Choose Well, the organization for the promotion of sexual health, provides pregnancy and birth control counseling as well as sexual health education. The organization was established in 1976 under the name SHILO–Jerusalem's Family Planning Education and Counseling Center, the first service of its kind in Israel that integrated educational activities in the community, individual, and couple counseling as well as medical services, under one roof. Services are offered by a multidisciplinary staff comprised of social workers, gynecologists, guidance counselors, and health educators. The small staff is supplemented by a devoted team of volunteers. Ladaat's services are offered to the community—regardless of gender, age, family status, place of residence, religion, or nationality—and serve as a model for youth counseling services and educational programs throughout Israel.

http://www.ladaat.org.il

Even Yisrael 5

P.O. Box 2284

Jerusalem, 91022

Israel

Tel: +972-2-625-8841, +972-2-624-8412

Fax: +972-2-625-9741

Email: ladaat@ladaat.org.il

Hiddush

Hiddush works to implement the basic values guaranteed in Israel's Declaration of Independence, freedom of religion and equality, without which no enlightened democracy can exist.

Rabbi Uri Regev, President and CEO
http://hiddush.org/

U.S. Office

182 East 95th St., Suite 24G
New York, NY 10128

Israel Office

24 Ha'Uman Street
Jerusalem, 93420
Israel
Tel: +972-077-530-4131
Fax: +972-077-530-4130

Yisrael Hofshit—Be Free Israel

Be Free Israel is a Zionist nonpartisan movement which cleaves to the spirit of Israel's Declaration of Independence. At its core is the belief that all individuals have the right to live freely, as he or she chooses, and we extend that view toward all Israeli citizens regardless of their religion, gender, racial, or ethnic identity. The organization also demands Israeli recognition of the various streams of Judaism, beyond Orthodox, in Israel and around the world: Conservative, Reform, Reconstructionist, Liberal, Progressive, and Secular.

Micky Gitzin, Director

http://bfree.org.il/english/

Email: info@bfree.org.il

Kayan—Feminist Organization

Kayan is a group of feminists who aim to advance the status of Palestinian women in Israel. The women of Kayan envision a secure and just society in which Arab women in Israel enjoy full and equitable opportunities for self-expression and self-actualization. Kayan invests in the development of grassroots leadership to catalyze social change grounded in the elimination of gender disparity. Kayan values pragmatism in the democratization of the public sphere, fosters genuine agency among Arab women, and brings their influence directly to bear upon the realization of their rights.

http://www.kayan.org.il/en/

118 Arlozorov St.

Haifa, 33276

Israel

Tel: +972-4-864-1291, +972-4-866-1890

Fax: +972-4-862-9731

Email: kayan@netvision.net.il

Jerusalemites (Yerushalmim)

Yerushalmim is a not-for-profit civic organization working to build Jerusalem as a vibrant, pluralistic, and inclusive city, which will reflect the great human richness of all its people, help them live together with all their differences, provide a high quality of life for its citizens, and attract new and dynamic residents. Yerushalmim was founded in 2009 by a group of young Jerusalemite activists and professionals, religious and secular, who realized civil society must be mobilized to reverse negative directions in which the city is headed: high poverty levels, the steady exit of young professionals, and increasing religious extremism in its public sphere.

Rabbi Uri Ayalon, CEO

http://yerushalmim.info/eng/, http://yerushalmim.org.il

The Yerushalmim Movement

P.O. Box 10499

Jerusalem, 91104

Israel

Tel: +972-2-650-2306

Email: info@yerushalmim.org.il

New Israel Fund

The New Israel Fund (NIF) is the leading organization advancing democracy and equality for all Israelis. The NIF believes that Israel can live up to its founders' vision of a state that ensures complete equality of social and political rights to all its inhabitants, without regard to religion, race, gender, or national identity. Widely credited with building Israel's progressive civil society from scratch, the NIF has provided over $200 million to more than eight hundred cutting-edge organizations since its inception. Shatil, the New Israel Fund Initiative for Social Change, provides NIF grantees and other social change organizations with hands-on assistance, including training, resources, and workshops on various aspects of nonprofit management. Today, NIF/Shatil is a leading advocate for democratic values, builds coalitions, empowers activists, and often takes the initiative in setting the public agenda.

http://www.nif.org

New York Headquarters
New Israel Fund
330 Seventh Avenue, 11th Floor
New York, NY 10001-5010
Tel: +972-73-244-5000
Fax: +972-2-672-3099
Email: ny@nif.org

Israel Offices
New Israel Fund
P.O. Box 53410
Jerusalem, 91534
Israel
Tel: +972-73-244-5000
Fax: +972-2-672-3099
Email: nif@nif.org.il

SHATIL
P.O. Box 53395
Jerusalem, 91533
Israel
Tel: +972-2-672-3597
Fax: +972-2-673-5149
Email: shatil@shatil.nif.org.il

New Family Organization

Since 1998, New Family has distinguished itself as the leading
family rights advocates in Israel. New Family fills a crucial gap in

the theory and practice of law and human rights by working for equal rights for families in Israel, including the rights to marry, divorce, have children, register spouses and children, and conduct family life free of religious coercion regardless of religion, gender, nationality, sexual orientation, or status.

http://www.newfamily.org.il/en/about/
16 Tiomkin Street
Tel Aviv–Yafo, 65783
Israel
Tel: +972-3-566-0504
Fax: +972-3-560-0720
Email: newfamily@newfamily.org.il

Women and Their Bodies

Founded in 2005, Women and Their Bodies works to promote comprehensive social change in the health attitudes of Israeli women, Jewish and Arab. WTB is a member of the Our Bodies Ourselves (OBOS) international network of women's health organizations, focusing on all aspects of women's health, with particular focus on sexual and reproductive health rights. The organization provides accessible, pragmatic, research-based information about women's health and sexuality in order to raise awareness among women, regardless of age, socioeconomic status, and ethnicity, throughout Israel.

http://www.wtb.org.il/english/
Email: info@wtb.co.il

NOTES

Preface

1. Elana Sztokman, "My Daughter, the Soldier," *Lilith*, September 27, 2012, http://lilith.org/blog/2012/09/my-daughter-the-soldier/. Parts of this section are adapted from this post I originally wrote for the *Lilith* blog.

Introduction

1. Central Bureau of Statistics, *Israel in Statistics 1948–2007*, http://www1.cbs.gov.il/statistical/statistical60_eng.pdf.

2. Abigail Klein Leichman, "Israel's Top 45 Greatest Inventions of All Time," *Israel21c*, September 26, 2011, http://israel21c.org /technology /israels-top-45-greatest-inventions-of-all-time-2/; Nicky Blackburn, "The Top 65 Ways Israel Is Saving Our Planet," *Israel21c*, April 14, 2013, http://israel21c.org/social-action-2/the-top-65-ways-israel-is -saving-our-planet/; James K. Glassman, "Where Tech Keeps Booming," *Wall Street Journal*, November 23, 2009, http://online.wsj.com/news /articles/SB10001424052748704779704574553884271802474.

3. David Brooks, "The Tel Aviv Cluster," *New York Times*, January 10, 2010, http://www.nytimes.com/2010/01/12/opinion/12brooks .html?_r=1&.

4. Gal Beckerman, "Senor Decides against Running for Senate, Citing Family and Business," *Jewish Daily Forward*, March 24, 2010, http://forward.com/articles/126843/senor-decides-against-running-for-senate-citing-fa/.

5. Arabs, and Palestinians especially, are also excluded from these opportunities. However, my primary interest in this book is the plight of women. It's not that I'm not concerned about discrimination against Arabs or Palestinians; it's just that the Palestinian conflict is so widely researched, debated, and discussed, in both academic and journalistic settings about Israel, and gender is not. The topic of gender inequality in Israel is one whose time has come.

6. Tali Heruti-Sover, "In Israel, the Gender Wage Gap Is Worst at the Top," *Haaretz*, August 7, 2012, http://www.haaretz.com/business/in-israel-the-gender-wage-gap-is-worst-at-the-top-1.456471.

7. Ricardo Hausmann, Laura D. Tyson, and Saadia Zahidi, *The Global Gender Gap Report 2012*, World Economic Forum, October 16, 2012, http://www3.weforum.org/docs/WEF_GenderGap_Report_2012.pdf.

8. Ruth Eglash, "Israel Falls on Gender Gap Index," *Jerusalem Post*, November 4, 2011, http://www.jpost.com/National-News/Israel-falls-on-gender-gap-index.

9. Ruth Halperin-Kaddari, *Women in Israel: A State of Their Own* (Philadelphia: University of Pennsylvania Press, 2004), 35.

10. Lesley Hazleton, *Israeli Women: Reality behind the Myths* (New York: Simon & Schuster, 1977), 17.

11. Ibid., 21.

12. Letty Cottin Pogreben, "Golda Meir," Jewish Women's Archives, accessed March 1, 2014, http://jwa.org/encyclopedia/article/meir-golda.

13. Halperin-Kaddari, *Women in Israel*, 36.

14.   Hanna Herzog, "Feminism in Contemporary Israel," Jewish Women's Archives, accessed March 1, 2014, http://jwa.org/encyclopedia /article/feminism-in-contemporary-israel; Elana Maryles Sztokman, "Shulamit Aloni, One of Israel's First Feminist Leaders, Dies at 85," *Tablet*, January 24, 2014, http://www.tabletmag.com/scroll/160679 /shulamit-aloni-one-of-israels-first-feminist-leaders-dies-at-85.

15.   Linda Pressly, "Israel's Ultra-Orthodox Fight to be Exempt from Military Service," *BBC News Magazine*, September 11, 2012, http:// www.bbc.co.uk/news/magazine-19492627.

16.   Shahar Ilan, "Benefits Package for Avreichim: 17,000 NIS Gross" [in Hebrew], *Haaretz*, August 5, 2003, http://www.haaretz.co.il /misc/1.1538550.

17.   Telem Yahav, "Haredi Parties: Women Have Different Role," *Ynetnews*, December 18, 2012, http://www.ynetnews.com/articles /0,7340,L-4321510,00.html.

18.   Ido Kenan, "'I May Become Everyone's Enemy,'" *Haaretz*, February 14, 2014, http://www.haaretz.com/news/national/.premium-1.574108. In February 2014, the Jerusalem city council approved a woman as its representative.

19.   Elana Maryles Sztokman, "How Modern Orthodoxy Is Losing Touch with Modernity," *The Sisterhood* (blog), *Jewish Daily Forward*, May 27, 2010, http://blogs.forward.com/sisterhood-blog/128396 /how-modern-orthodoxy-is-losing-touch-with-modernit/.

20.   Shmulik Grossman, "Rabbi Bans Women from Public Office," *Ynetnews*, May 26, 2010, http://www.ynetnews.com/articles/0,7340,L -3893054,00.html.

21.   "Ladies Should Wear Overcoats," *Parshablog*, July 18, 2008, http:// parsha.blogspot.com/2008/07/ladies-should-wear-overcoats.html; "Tsnius and Cell Phones," *Truth, Praise, and Help* (blog), May 24, 2011, http://truthpraiseandhelp.wordpress.com/2011/05/24

/tsnius-and-cell-phones/; "Blogging Is Not Tznius," *Hadassah Sabo Milner* (blog), November 18, 2009, http://hadassahsabomilner.com /blogging-is-not-tznius/.

22.   Ari Galaher, "New Start-Up: Kosher Clothing Stores," *Ynet*, January 31, 2011, http://www.ynet.co.il/english/articles/0,7340,L -4007585,00.html.

23.   Ariel Finkelstein, "The Connection Between School Environment and Gender Segregation in Religious State-Primary School Education," *Neemanei Torah V'Avoda*, July 2013, http://toravoda .org.il/he/taxonomy/term/584.

24.   Tamar Rotem, "Israel's Religious Zionist Kids Growing Up in a World Where Females Are Taboo," *Haaretz*, May 27, 2013, http://www .haaretz.com/news/features/israel-s-religious-zionist-kids-growing -up-in-a-world-where-females-are-taboo.premium-1.526074.

25.   For more on the ways in which religious extremism threatens women around the world, see Lisa Fishbayne Joffe, "Introduction: Theorizing Conflicts between Women's Rights and Religious Laws," in *Gender, Religion, and Family Law: Theorizing Conflicts between Women's Rights and Cultural Traditions*, eds. Lisa Fishbayne Joffe and Sylvia Neil (Waltham, MA: Brandeis University Press, 2013), xiii-xxxvi.

26.   Tarek Amara, "Islamists Storm Tunisian School after It Bars Veiled Student," *Reuters*, April 10, 2013, http://www.reuters .com/article/2013/04/10/us-tunisia-school-salafists-idUSBRE9390 M620130410.

27.   "Turkey Sees Rise in Violence against Women," *United Press International,* March 14, 2012, http://www.upi.com/Top_News /World-News/2012/03/14/Turkey-sees-rise-in-violence -against-women/UPI-62861331730213/; see also Boris Kálnoky, "Majority of Turks Is for Violence against Women" [in German], *Die Welt*, April 19, 2013, http://www.welt.de/vermischtes

/article115427763/Mehrheit-der-Tuerken-ist-fuer-Gewalt-gegen -Frauen.html.

28. Gardiner Harris, "India's New Focus on Rape Shows Only the Surface of Women's Perils," *New York Times*, January 12, 2013, http://www .nytimes.com/2013/01/13/world/asia/in-rapes-aftermath-india -debates-violence-against-women.html.

29. Randa Abdel-Fattah, "Ending Oppression in the Middle East: A Muslim Feminist Call to Arms," *ABC.net*, April 29, 2013, http:// www.abc.net.au/religion/articles/2013/04/29/3747543.htm.

30. Allison Kaplan Sommer and Dahlia Lithwick, "The Feminists of Zion," *New Republic*, August 4, 2013, http://www.newrepublic .com/article/114124/israels-orthodox-women-new-face-feminism.

Chapter 1

1. Ron Friedman, "Transportation Minister OKs 'Mehadrin' Buses," *Jerusalem Post*, February 2, 2010, http://www.jpost.com/JewishWorld /JewishNews/Article.aspx?id=167516.

2. Ricky Shapira-Rosenberg, "Excluded, for God's Sake: Gender Segregation in Public Space in Israel," Israel Religious Action Center, Israel Movement for Progressive (Reform) Judaism, November 2010.

3. Shahar Ilan, "Haredim May Get Gender-Separated Bus Line," *Haaretz*, October 24, 2001, http://www.haaretz.com/print-edition /news/Haredim-may-get-gender-separated-bus-line-1.72777.

4. Betzalel Kahn, "Bus 402 from Bnei Brak to Jerusalem Launched," *Dei'ah VeDibur*, October 31, 2001, http://www.chareidi.org /archives5762/V62abus.htm.

5. Ibid.

6. Ibid.

7. Ilan, "Haredim."

8. Naomi Ragen, "Egged and the Taliban," NaomiRagen.com, August 1, 2004, http://www.naomiragen.com/israel/egged-and-the-taliban/.

9. Aaron Megid, "Egged Launches 11 'Mehadrin' Bus Lines," *Jerusalem Post*, December 1, 2006, http://www.jpost.com/Israel/Egged -launches-11-mehadrin-bus-lines.

10. Daphna Berman, "Woman Beaten on J'lem Bus for Refusing to Move to Rear Seat," *Haaretz*, December 15, 2006, http://www .haaretz.com/woman-beaten-on-j-lem-bus-for-refusing-to-move-to -rear-seat-1.207251.

11. Ibid.

12. Anat Tzruya, "Risking One's Life on the Bus," *Eretz Acheret*, August 7, 2010, http://acheret.co.il/en/?cmd=articles.398&act=read&id =2299. *Shiksa* literally means a cockroach but has come to be used as a slur meaning "non-Jewish woman." Some Haredim use this is an insult against Jewish women who are perceived as nonconforming, especially in their attire, as if to say being a gentile is akin to being evil, impure, dirty, or unworthy.

13. Sharon Shenhav, "Insult, Embarrass, Harass 'Uppity' Women," *Jerusalem Post*, July 13, 2011, http://www.jpost.com/Opinion /Editorials/Article.aspx?id=229255.

14. Ibid.

15. Tzruya, "Risking One's Life."

16. Ibid.

17. Ariela and Rachel, "A Mother and Daughter on Segregation in Beit Shemesh," *Women Talk about Segregation in Israel*, Israel Religious Action Center, January 2012.

18. Daphna Berman, "Canadian Woman Beaten on Egged Bus Joins High Court Petition," *Haaretz*, February 2, 2007, http://www .haaretz.com/weekend/anglo-file/canadian-woman-beaten-on -egged-bus-joins-high-court-petition-1.211790.

19. Shapira-Rosenberg, "Excluded, for God's Sake," 11.

20. Ron Friedman, "Segregate or Suffer," *Jerusalem Post*, February 12, 2010, http://www.jpost.com/Israel/Segregate-or-suffer; Friedman, "Transportation Minister."

21. Elana Maryles Sztokman, "Protesters of Extreme Gender Segregation Report Personal Threats," *The Sisterhood* (blog), *Jewish Daily Forward*, October 17, 2010, http://blogs.forward .com/sisterhood-blog/132203/protesters-of-extreme-gender -segregation-report-pe.

22. Ibid.

23. Ibid.

24. Ibid.

25. Interview with Dr. Hannah Kehat, March 20, 2012.

26. Anshel Pfeffer, "Charedi Women Refuse Bus Gender [Segregation]," *Jewish Chronicle*, September 18, 2009, http://www.thejc.com/news /israel-news/charedi-women-refuse-bus-gender-segragation.

27. Sztokman, "Protesters."

28. Shapira-Rosenberg, "Excluded, for God's Sake," 11.

29. Elana Maryles Sztokman, "On Segregated Buses, a Choice That Isn't," *The Sisterhood* (blog), *Jewish Daily Forward*, March 21, 2012, http:// blogs.forward.com/sisterhood-blog/153395/on-segregated-buses -a-choice-that-isnt/.

30. Marcy Oster, "Gender Segregation Still OK on Israeli Buses, with Caveats," *JTA*, January 6, 2011, http://www.jta.org/2011/01/06 /news-opinion/israel-middle-east/gender-segregation-still-ok-on -israeli-buses-with-caveats; High Court of Israel, "Naomi Ragen versus the Ministry of Transport," file 746/07, decision January 5, 2011, signed by Justice Elyakim Rubinstein. Original transcript available at www.court.gov.il.

31. Ron Friedman, "Egged Faces Contempt Charges over Haredi

Newspaper Ads," *Jerusalem Post*, February 10, 2011, http://www
.jpost.com/NationalNews/Article.aspx?id=207575.

32.   Daphna Berman, "Woman Beaten on J'lem Bus for Refusing to
Move to Rear Seat," *Haaretz*, Dec. 15, 2006, http://www.haaretz
.com/woman-beaten-on-j-lem-bus-for-refusing-to-move-to-rear
-seat-1.207251.

33.   Diana Bletter, "Israel's Freedom Riders," *Tablet*, June 25, 2012,
http://www.tabletmag.com/jewish-news-and-politics/103038
/israels-freedom-riders.

34.   Interview with Shari Eshet, December 2012.

35.   Dan Klein, "Israeli Bus Company Ordered to Pay Woman Forced
to Sit in Back," *Jewish Telegraph Agency*, December 8, 2011,
http://www.jta.org/2011/12/08/news-opinion/israel-middle-east
/israeli-bus-company-ordered-to-pay-woman-forced-to-sit-in-back.

36.   Izzy Lemberg and Kevin Flower, "Israel's 'Rosa Parks' Refuses to
Take Back Seat," *CNN*, December 19, 2011, http://www.cnn
.com/2011/12/19/world/meast/israel-rosa-parks/.

37.   Noam (Dabul) Dvir, "Superbus to Compensate Passenger over
Women's Exclusion," *Ynetnews*, July 11, 2012, http://www.ynetnews
.com/articles/0,7340,L-4254181,00.html.

38.   Oz Rosenberg, "Israeli Female Soldier Accosted for Rebuffing
Haredi Bus Segregation," *Haaretz*, December 28, 2011, http://www
.haaretz.com/news/national/israeli-female-soldier-accosted-for
-rebuffing-Haredi-bus-segregation-1.404158.

39.   Dawn Hzlkoren, "We Will Punish All Those Involved in Assaulting
a Student," *Ynet*, February 18, 2013, http://www.ynet.co.il/articles
/0,7340,L-4346218,00.html.

40.   "Ultra-Orthodox Men Order Woman to Rear of Bus," *Times of Israel*,
February 15, 2013, http://www.timesofisrael.com/ultra-orthodox
-men-order-woman-to-rear-of-bus/.

41. Neri Brenner, "Young Woman Harassed on Bus by Haredim," *Ynetnews*, February 17, 2013, http://www.ynetnews.com/articles /0,7340,L-4346017,00.html.

42. Danny Adeno Abebe, "Woman Verbally Abused by Haredi Bus Passengers," *Ynetnews*, January 9, 2013, http://www.ynetnews.com /articles/0,7340,L-4330287,00.html.

43. Maayan Lubell, "Religious Zealots Attack 'Immodest' Jerusalem Shops," *Reuters*, October 18, 2011, http://www.reuters.com/article/2011/10/18 /cnews-us-israel-ultraorthodox-idCATRE79H1HT20111018.

44. Naomi Ragen, "Moving Backward: A Look at 'Mehadrin' Bus Lines," *Jewish Ideas*, November 3, 2009, http://www.jewishideas .org/articles/moving-backward-look-mehadrin-bus-lines.

45. Magid, "Egged Launches."

46. Ibid.

47. Sasha Chavkin and Josh Nathan-Kazis, "Outside New York City, Sexes Separated on State-Funded Bus," *New York World*, November 4, 2011, http://www.thenewyorkworld.com/2011/11/04/outside-new -york-city-sexes-separated-on-state-funded-bus/.

48. Naomi Zeveloff, "Sex-Segregation Spreads among Orthodox: Buses, Public Sidewalks, and Streets Split Between Men and Women," *Jewish Daily Forward*, October 28, 2011, http://forward .com/articles/144987/sex-segregation-spreads-among-orthodox/; Shmarya Rosenberg, "Hasidic Bus Company Still Illegally Gender Segregating Public Buses," *Failed Messiah* (blog), October 13, 2013, http://failedmessiah.typepad.com/failed_messiahcom/2013/10 /hasidic-bus-company-still-illegally-gender-segregating-public -buses-123.html

49. Ibid.

50. Joseph Berger, "Out of Enclaves, a Pressure to Accommodate Traditions," *New York Times*, August 21, 2013, http://www.nytimes

.com/2013/08/22/nyregion/hasidic-jews-turn-up-pressure-on-city
-to-accommodate-their-traditions.html?pagewanted=all&_r=0.

51.   Dina Kraft, "Growing Gender Segregation among Israeli Haredim Seen
        as Repressing Women," *Jewish Telegraph Agency*, November 13, 2011,
        http://www.jta.org/2011/11/13/news-opinion/israel-middle-east
        /growing-gender-segregation-among-israeli-haredim-seen-as
        -repressing-women.

Chapter 2

1.   J. J. Goldberg, "Women Honorees Barred from Science Award
      Stage," *Forward Thinking* (blog), *Jewish Daily Forward*, December 20,
      2011, http://blogs.forward.com/forward-thinking/148220/women
      -honorees-barred-from-science-award-stage/; "Exclusion of Women
      in the Health Care System: Female Researchers Who Won a Prize
      Were Banned from Going on Stage to Accept the Prize and Were
      Asked to Sit in the Balcony," *Doctors Only*, December 19, 2011,
      http://doctorsonly.co.il/2011/12/27443/.

2.   Ricky Shapira-Rosenberg, "Excluded, for God's Sake." A good portion
      of the items on this list come from the Knesset report on the issue filed
      by Ricky Shapira-Rosenberg on behalf of IRAC and presented by
      IRAC and Kolech at a special session on gender segregation in Israel in
      November 2010. I've added a few items to the list as well.

3.   Dafna Liel and Rina Matzliach, "In the Middle of Beit Shemesh, a
      Sign Reads 'Women—Cross Over to the Other Side of the Road'"
      [in Hebrew], Channel 2 News, December 21, 2011, http://reshet.tv
      /%D7%97%D7%93%D7%A9%D7%95%D7%AA/News/Domestic
      /internal/Article,85957.aspx.

4.   Shapira-Rosenberg, "Excluded, for God's Sake," 22.

5.   Idan Roth and Anna Bord, "Watch: Passengers Ask a Woman to
      Leave the Train Car so That They Can Pray" [in Hebrew], Channel

10 News, December 12, 2011, http://news.nana10.co.il/Article/?ArticleID=854585&sid=126.

6. Yossi Mizrachi, "Because of Two Religious Men, All the Female Students Were Removed from the Gym at the Technion" [in Hebrew], Channel 2 News, December 13, 2011, http://www.mako.co.il/news-israel/education/Article-bc608f50ac83431017.htm&sCh=31750a2610f26110&pId=786102762.

7. Omri Maniv, "When Men Swim on Campus, Women Wait Outside" [in Hebrew], *NRG*, December 13, 2011, http://www.nrg.co.il/online/54/ART2/315/724.html?hp=54&cat=869&loc=4.

8. Omri Efraim, "Women Banned from Economic Conference," *Ynetnews*, July 12, 2011, http://www.ynetnews.com/articles/0,7340,L-4094000,00.html; Shapira-Rosenberg, "Excluded, for God's Sake," 11–29.

9. Orly Erez-Likhovski, "Discrimination in the Cemetery," *Women Talk about Segregation in Israel*, Israel Religious Action Center, January 2012, http://www.irac.org/userfiles/women-talk-about-segregation-in-israel.pdf.

10. Ibid.

11. Elana Maryles Sztokman, "Women Barred from Funerals in Israel," *The Sisterhood* (blog), *Jewish Daily Forward*, December 5, 2011, http://blogs.forward.com/sisterhood-blog/147243/women-barred-from-funerals-in-israel/.

12. Judy Siegel-Itzkovich, "Exclusion of Women Makes Waves for Conference," *Jerusalem Post*, January 9, 2012, http://www.jpost.com/Health-and-Science/Exclusion-of-women-makes-waves-for-conference; see also "Puah Conference—Kolech Response," Kolech–Religious Women's Forum, accessed March 1, 2014, http://www.kolech.com/english/show.asp?id=48888.

13. Erin Gloria Ryan, "Hillary Clinton Photoshopped Out of Situation

Room Photo," *Jezebel* (blog), May 8, 2011, http://jezebel.com /5799724/hillary-clinton-photoshopped-out-of-situation-room-photo.

14.   "Israel: Women Photoshopped from Cabinet Picture to Cater to the Ultra-Orthodox," *Huffington Post*, April 3, 2009, http:// www.huffingtonpost.com/2009/04/03/israel-women-photoshopped _n_182822.html.

15.   Nir Hasson, "Gila Almagor Was Removed from Billboards of IsraCard in Jerusalem" [in Hebrew], *Haaretz*, January 1, 2012, http:// www.haaretz.co.il/news/education/1.1609383.

16.   *Haaretz* staff, "Pictures of Women Were Removed from Edi Ads," *Haaretz*, November 8, 2011, http://www.haaretz.co.il/news /education/1.1560721.

17.   "Photos of Women Removed from Adi Card Banners," *Haaretz*, November 8, 2011, http://www.haaretz.co.il/news /education/1.1560721.

18.   Nir Hasson, "Jerusalem Women Challenge Ultra-Orthodox Ban on 'Immodest' Posters," *Haaretz*, November 2, 2011, http:// www.haaretz.com/jewish-world/jerusalem-women-challenge-ultra -orthodox-ban-on-immodest-posters-1.393227.

19.   Noam (Dabul) Dvir, "Shaare Zedek: Women's Pictures Covered by Stickers," *Ynetnews*, July 12, 2012, http://www.ynetnews.com /articles/0,7340,L-4254903,00.html.

20.   "Haredi Kiruv Organization Censors Women's Pictures," *Failed Messiah* (blog), May 11, 2009, http://failedmessiah.typepad.com /failed_messiahcom/2009/05/Haredi-kiruv-organization-censors -womens-pictures.html.

21.   Peggy Cidor, "Jerusalem 2012—The State of Things," *Jerusalem Post*, May 17, 2012, http://www.jpost.com/In-Jerusalem/City-Front /Jerusalem-2012-the-state-of-things.

22.   Reuven Weiss, "Bnei Brak vs. Female Teachers, Haredi,"

Ynetnews, September 12, 2011, http://www.ynetnews.com/articles
/0,7340,L-4118073,00.html.

23. Hasson, "Jerusalem Women."

24. Rabbi Jason Miller, "Hasidic Newspaper Photoshops Hillary
Clinton from Iconic Photo," *Jewish Techs* (blog), *Jewish Week*,
May 8, 2011, http://www.thejewishweek.com/blogs/jewish_techs
/hasidic_newspaper_photoshops_hillary_clinton_iconic_photo.

25. Aviad Glickman, "Petition: Stop Exclusion of Women in Ads,"
Ynetnews, January 2, 2012, http://www.ynetnews.com/articles
/0,7340,L-4170199,00.html.

26. Aviel Magnezi, "State to Ban Women's Exclusion from Bus
Ads," *Ynetnews*, July 19, 2012, http://www.ynetnews.com/articles
/0,7340,L-4254428,00.html.

27. Interview with Rabbi Uri Ayalon, March 2013.

28. Ibid.

29. "A New Scandal in Rechovot" [in Hebrew], *BE106*, April 24, 2013,
http://www.be106.net/news_inner.php?city=233&id=3382.

30. Yitzhak Tessler, "Haredi Weekly Censors Female Holocaust
Victims," *Ynetnews*, March 28, 2013, http://www.ynetnews.com
/articles/0,7340,L-4361353,00.html.

31. Interview with Robyn Shames, May 2012.

32. Debra Nussbaum Cohen, "Silent and Invisible on Purim," *The Sisterhood*
(blog), *Jewish Daily Forward*, February 25, 2013, http://blogs.forward
.com/sisterhood-blog/171850/silent-and-invisible-on-purim/.

33. Renee Ghert-Zand, "Controversial Suspension for Contestant on
Israel's 'The Voice,'" *The Sisterhood* (blog), *Jewish Daily Forward*,
January 27, 2013, http://blogs.forward.com/sisterhood-blog/170011
/controversial-suspension-for-contestant-on-israels/.

34. Ibid.

35. Shira Hecht-Koller, "Silencing Women's Voices: Time to Speak Up,"

Jewish Week, February 15, 2013, http://www.thejewishweek.com
/editorial-opinion/opinion/silencing-womens-voices-time-speak-up.

36. Kobi Nahshoni, "Rabbi Bigman: Women Can Sing 'in Innocence,'" *Ynetnews*, July 14, 2008, http://www.ynetnews.com /articles/0,7340,L-3567666,00.html.

37. Kobi Nahshoni, "Givat Shmuel Singing Contest Causes Division in Bnei Akiva," *Ynetnews*, July 10, 2008, http://www.ynetnews.com /articles/0,7340,L-3565972,00.html.

38. Gili Cohen and Ilan Lior, "Segregation of the Sexes Reaches Israeli Youth Club," *Haaretz*, November 1, 2011, http://www .haaretz.com/jewish-world/segregation-of-the-sexes-reaches-israeli -youth-club-1.393140.

39. Arik Bender, "Because of the Opposition of the Haredim, Rivlin Stops the Knesset Choir" [in Hebrew], *NRG News*, January 15, 2012, http://www.nrg.co.il/online/1/ART2/326/874.html.

40. Eric Bander, "Because of Haredi Opposition: The End of the Knesset Choir" [in Hebrew], *NRG*, January 15, 2012, http://www.nrg.co.il /online/1/ART2/326/874.html?hp=1&cat=404&loc=12.

41. Akiva Novick, "Cadets Walk Out as Female Soldier Sings," *Ynetnews*, September 7, 2011, http://www.ynetnews.com/articles /0,7340,L-4119085,00.html.

42. See, for example: Yaakov Katz, "IDF: Religious Soldiers Cannot Leave Ceremonies," *Jerusalem Post*, January 2, 2012, http://www.jpost.com /Defense/IDF-Religious-soldiers-cannot-leave-ceremonies; Susan Hattis Rolef, "'Exclusion of Women Is Form of Violence,'" *Jerusalem Post*, November 27, 2011, http://www.jpost.com/National-News /Exclusion-of-women-is-form-of-violence; Lahav Harkov, "'IDF Religious Won't Hear Women Sing? Use Earplugs,'" *Jerusalem Post*, December 14, 2011, http://www.jpost.com/Diplomacy-and-Politics /IDF-religious-wont-hear-women-sing-Use-earplugs.

43.   Kobi Nahshoni, "Metzger: Let Troops Avoid Women's Singing," *Ynetnews*, September 27, 2011, http://www.ynetnews.com/articles /0,7340,L-4128078,00.html.

44.   Kobi Nahshoni, "Haredi Soldier Warns: We'll Leave IDF Over Women's Singing," *Ynetnews*, January 4, 2012, http://www .ynetnews.com/articles/0,7340,L-4171199,00.html.

45.   Harkov, "'IDF Religious.'"

46.   Orly Erez-Likhovski, "All the Truth about the Exclusion of Women on Kol Berama Radio" [in Hebrew], Kolech–Religious Women's Forum, accessed March 1, 2014, http://www.kolech.com/show .asp?id=51305.

47.   Jeremy Sharon and Lahav Harkov, "Parliamentarians Slam No-Women Policy at Ration Station," *Jerusalem Post*, November 8, 2011, http://www.jpost.com/National-News/Parliamentarians -slam-no-women-policy-at-radio-station.

48.   "Dati Leumi MKs Target Kol Berama Radio for Not Interviewing Females on Air," *Yeshiva World News*, November 7, 2011, http:// www.theyeshivaworld.com/article.php?p=108187.

49.   Sharon and Harkov, "Parliamentarians."

50.   "Dati Leumi MKs."

51.   Nati Toker, "Organizations to Chair of the Second Authority: Do Not Allow Women's Exclusion on Kol Berama" [in Hebrew], *Marker*, April 22, 2012, http://www.themarker.com/advertising/1.1691278.

52.   Sharon and Harkov, "Parliamentarians."

53.   Jeremy Sharon, "Women's Group Sues Haredi Radio for Discrimination," *Jerusalem Post*, August 29, 2012, http://www.jpost.com/National-News /Womens-group-sues-Haredi-radio-for-discrimination.

54.   Edna Adato, "Petition Filed against Haredi Radio Station over Gender Discrimination," *Israel Hayom*, August 29, 2012, http:// www.israelhayom.com/site/newsletter_article.php?id=5590.

55.   Sharon, "Women's Group Sues."

56.   Alexander Katz, "Because of the Exclusion of Women: The Transmission License for Kol Berama Was Extended by One Year Only" [in Hebrew], *ICE*, March 19, 2013, http://www.ice.co.il /article/view/355129; "Will Exclusion of Women Cost Radio 'Kol Barama' Its Franchise?," *Behadrey Haradim*, March 11, 2013, http:// www.bhol.co.il/Article_EN.aspx?id=52033.

57.   New Israel Fund, "Victory in the Fight against Women's Exclusion," January 30, 2014, http://www.nif.org/our-issues/social-and-economic -justice/1598-victory-in-the-fight-against-women-s-exclusion.

58.   Religious law only applies to post-bar-mitzvah-age boys.

59.   Almog Boker, "The Basketball Game Exploded: 'We Can't Touch Girls'" [in Hebrew], *Nana 10*, December 27, 2012, http://news .nana10.co.il/Article/?ArticleID=947156; Allison Kaplan Sommer, "When Exclusion of Women Hits the Basketball Court," *Routine Emergencies* (blog), *Haaretz*, December 31, 2012, http://www.haaretz .com/blogs/routine-emergencies/when-exclusion-of-women-hits -the-basketball-court.premium-1.491075.

60.   Monia Ghanmi, "Religious Extremism Worries Tunisians," *Magharebia*, April 12, 2013, http://magharebia.com/en_GB/articles /awi/features/2013/04/12/feature-01.

61.   Annie-Rose Strasser and Tara Culp-Ressler, "How 'Slut Shaming' Has Been Written into School Dress Codes across the Country," *ThinkProgress*, May 6, 2013, http://thinkprogress.org/health/2013 /05/06/1969001/slut-shaming-dress-codes/.

62.   Elana Koriel, "A Girl Worked in a Restaurant with Boys—and Was Expelled from School," *Ynet*, May 3, 2012, http://www.ynet .co.il/articles/0,7340,L-4198712,00.html.

63.   Allison Kaplan Sommer, "Exclusion of Women."

Chapter 3

1. "Ladies Should Wear Overcoats," *Parshablog*; "Tsnius and Cell Phones," *Truth, Praise, and Help* (blog); "Blogging Is Not Tznius," *Hadassah Sabo Milner* (blog).

2. Debra Nussbaum Cohen, "How 'Modesty' Turns Women into Sex Objects," *The Sisterhood* (blog), *Jewish Daily Forward*, January 11, 2012, http://blogs.forward.com/sisterhood-blog/149447/how -modesty-turns-women-into-sex-objects/.

3. Galaher, "Kosher Clothing Stores."

4. Jeremy Sharon, "Court Denies Appeal by Haredi Extremist over J'lem Attack," *Jerusalem Post*, November 22, 2011, http://www .jpost.com/Jewish-World/Jewish-News/Court-denies-appeal-by -Haredi-extremist-over-Jlem-attack.

5. Lubell, "Religious Zealots."

6. Shmarya Rosenberg, "Following Ultra-Orthodox Money Trail," *Jewish Daily Forward*, February 01, 2012, http://forward.com /articles/150571/following-ultra-orthodox-money-trail/.

7. Tzipi Malkov, "Haredim to Set Up 'Modest' Market," *Ynetnews*, August 25, 2011, http://www.ynetnews.com/articles/0,7340,L -4113767,00.html.

8. Eli Senyor, "Beitar Illit Mayor Suspected in 'Modesty Squad' Affair," *Ynetnews*, February 18, 2013, http://www.ynetnews.com /articles/0,7340,L-4346546,00.html.

9. Oz Rosenberg, "Woman in Beit Shemesh Attacked by Ultra-Orthodox Extremists," *Haaretz*, January 25, 2012, http://www.haaretz.com /print-edition/news/woman-in-beit-shemesh-attacked-by-ultra -orthodox-extremists-1.409065.

10. Nir Cohen and Noam Dvir, "Beit Shemesh: Woman Attacked for Dressing 'Immodestly,'" *Ynetnews*, June 20, 2012, http://www .ynetnews.com/articles/0,7340,L-4245127,00.html.

11.   Aviad Glickman, "Man Accused of Spitting at 'Immodest' Women," *Ynetnews*, June 4, 2012, http://www.ynetnews.com /articles/0,7340,L-4238192,00.html.

12.   Interview with Nili Phillip, March 31, 2013.

13.   Glickman, "Man Accused of Spitting."

14.   Moshe Heller, "Exclusion of Female Cashiers: Haredim Boycott Supermarket Where Women Are Employed" [in Hebrew], *NRG*, December 23, 2011, http://www.nrg.co.il/online/54/ART2/319 /261.html?hp=54&cat=869&loc=60.

15.   Neta Sela, "'Modesty Police' Patrols Bridge Ceremony," *Ynetnews*, June 26, 2008, http://www.ynetnews.com/articles/0,7340,L-356 0615,00.html.

16.   Noam (Dabul) Dvir, "Women Excluded from Performing in Jerusalem Festival," *Ynetnews*, March 24, 2013, http://www.ynetnews.com /articles/0,7340,L-4360264,00.html.

17.   Zeveloff, "Sex-Segregation Spreads."

18.   Tristin Hopper, "York University Professor Who Refused Student's Request to be Separated from Female Classmates Broke 'Obligation to Accommodate': Officials," *National Post*, January 8, 2014, http:// news.nationalpost.com/2014/01/08/york-university-professor-who -refused-students-request-to-be-separated-from-female-classmates -broke-obligation-to-accommodate-officials/.

19.   Jillian Scheinfeld, "The Circus, Kosher for Passover," *Tablet*, March 29, 2013, http://www.tabletmag.com/jewish-news-and -politics/128186/the-circus-kosher-for-passover.

20.   Joseph Berger, "Modesty in Ultra-Orthodox Brooklyn Is Enforced by Secret Squads," *New York Times*, January 29, 2013, http:// www.nytimes.com/2013/01/30/nyregion/shadowy-squads-enforce -modesty-in-hasidic-brooklyn.html.

21.   Debra Nussbaum Cohen, "New York City Suing Ultra-Orthodox for

Posting Modesty Guidelines in Stores," *Haaretz*, February 15, 2013, http://www.haaretz.com/jewish-world/jewish-world-news/new-york-city-suing-ultra-orthodox-for-posting-modesty-guidelines-in-stores.premium-1.503804.

22. Noam (Dabul) Dvir, "Beit Shemesh 'Helpless' Fighting Women's Exclusion," *Ynetnews*, July 4, 2012, http://www.ynetnews.com/articles/0,7340,L-4251544,00.html.

23. Sztokman, "On Segregated Buses."

24. Ibid.

25. Tova Hartman Halbertal, *Appropriately Subversive: Modern Mothers in Traditional Religions* (Cambridge: Harvard University Press, 2002), 26–27.

26. Matthew Wagner, "Beit Shemesh 'Burka' Cult Unveiled," *Jerusalem Post*, March 27, 2008, http://www.jpost.com/Israel/Beit-Shemesh-Burka-cult-unveiled.

27. Allison Kaplan Sommer, "Jewish Women, Behind the Veil," *The Sisterhood* (blog), *Jewish Daily Forward*, July 29, 2010, http://blogs.forward.com/sisterhood-blog/129728/jewish-women-behind-the-veil/.

28. Elana Maryles Sztokman, "Why Jewish Women Are Wearing Burqas," *The Sisterhood* (blog), *Jewish Daily Forward*, April 7, 2010, http://blogs.forward.com/sisterhood-blog/127114/why-jewish-women-are-wearing-burqas/.

29. Sommer, "Jewish Women."

30. Wagner, "Beit Shemesh 'Burka' Cult Unveiled."

31. Adrian Blomfield, "Israeli Rabbis Clamp Down on Burka," *Telegraph*, July 30, 2010, http://www.telegraph.co.uk/news/worldnews/middleeast/israel/7919501/Israeli-rabbis-clamp-down-on-burka.html; "Rejecting the Burka," *Jerusalem Post*, April 27, 2010, http://www.jpost.com/Opinion/Editorials/Rejecting-the-burka.

32. Lisa Fishbayne Joffe, "Introduction: Theorizing Conflicts between Women's Rights and Religious Laws."

33. "Modest Is Hottest? The Revealing Truth," *Beauty Redefined* (blog), September 27, 2012, http://www.beautyredefined.net /modest-is-hottest-the-revealing-truth/.

34. Strasser and Culp-Ressler, "'Slut Shaming.'"

35. "The Ugly Side of Modesty," *Friendly Atheist* (blog), *Patheos*, June 27, 2012, http://www.patheos.com/blogs/friendlyatheist/2012/06/27 /the-ugly-side-of-modesty/.

36. Matthew Paul Turner, "Is Modest Really Hottest?," *Relevant*, August 19, 2011, http://www.relevantmagazine.com/life/current-events /op-ed-blog/26523-is-modest-really-hottest.

37. Marinda Valenti, "What Do Dress Codes Say about Girls' Bodies?," *Ms.*, May 24, 2013, http://msmagazine.com/blog/2013/05/24 /what-do-dress-codes-say-about-girls-bodies/.

Chapter 4

1. Phyllis Chesler and Rivka Haut, "Introduction," *Women of the Wall: Claiming Sacred Ground at Judaism's Holy Site*, ed. Phyllis Chesler and Rivka Haut (Woodstock: Jewish Lights Publishing, 2003), xix.

2. Bat Sheva Marcus and Ronnie Becher, "Women's Tefillah Movement," Jewish Women's Archives, http://jwa.org/encyclopedia /article/womens-tefillah-movement.

3. Chesler and Haut, "Introduction," xx.

4. Bonna Devora Haberman, "Drama in Jerusalem," *Women of the Wall: Claiming Sacred Ground at Judaism's Holy Site*, 5-6.

5. Ibid., 7.

6. Ibid., 8.

7. Ibid., 11.

8. Ibid., 13–14.

9. Ibid., 19.

10. Pnina Lahav, "The Woes of WoW: The Women of the Wall as a

Religious Social Movement and as a Metaphor" (Boston University School of Law Working Paper No. 13-2, January 23, 2013), 4, http://www.bu.edu/law/faculty/scholarship/workingpapers/TheWoes ofWoW.html.

11. Ibid., 11.

12. Ibid., 15.

13. Ibid., 14.

14. Chesler and Haut, *Women of the Wall*, 365-367.

15. Ibid., 365–367.

16. "Israeli Legislators Propose Prison for Women Worshipers," *JTA*, June 1, 2000, http://www.jta.org/2000/06/01/archive /israeli-legislators-propose-prison-for-women-worshipers#ixzz351 pKggJX.

17. Chesler and Haut, *Women of the Wall*, 118.

18. Ibid., 10.

19. Interview with Frances Raday, May 2013.

20. Lahav, "The Woes of WoW," 34.

21. Nofrat Frenkel, "The 'Crime' of Praying with a *Tallit*, and a Plea for Tolerance," *Jewish Daily Forward*, November 24, 2009, http://forward .com/articles/119509/the-crime-of-praying-with-a-tallit-and-a-ple.

22. Ibid.

23. Efrat Weiss, "Police Arrest Woman Praying at Western Wall," *Ynetnews*, November 18, 2009, http://www.ynetnews.com/articles/0,7340,L -3807090,00.html.

24. Elana Maryles Sztokman, "Anger over Arrest at Kotel of Woman Carrying Torah," *Jewish Daily Forward*, July 23, 2010, http://forward .com/articles/129362/anger-over-arrest-at-kotel-of-woman-carrying -torah/.

25. Ibid.

26. Ibid.

27.   Jodi Rudoren, "Arrests of 10 Women Praying at Western Wall Add to Tensions Over Holy Site," *New York Times*, February 11, 2013, http://www.nytimes.com/2013/02/12/world/middleeast/Women -Praying-at-Western-Wall-Detained.html?_r=0.

28.   Ibid.

29.   Elana Maryles Sztokman, "Woman Arrested for Carrying Torah Speaks with The Sisterhood," *The Sisterhood* (blog), *Jewish Daily Forward*, July 12, 2010, http://blogs.forward.com/sisterhood-blog/129300 /woman-arrested-for-carrying-torah-speaks-with-the/.

30.   Daphna Berman, "Anat Hoffman Dares to Take on Israel's Orthodox Establishment. Can She Win?," *Moment*, February 26, 2013, http:// www.momentmag.com/anat-hoffman-dares-to-take-on-israels -orthodox-establishment-can-she-win/.

31.   Dahlia Lithwick, "Wall Flowers: Women Fight to Pray at the Western Wall," *Slate*, February 12, 2013, http://www.slate.com /articles/double_x/doublex/2013/02/women_at_the_western_wall _they_should_be_allowed_to_pray_the_way_they_want.single.html.

32.   Avi Shafran, "The 'War of the Wall' Secret Weapon," *Jewish Journal*, January 2, 2013, http://www.jewishjournal.com/opinion/article /the_war_of_the_wall_secret_weapon.

33.   Anat Hoffman, "What the Women of the Wall Want," *Jewish Daily Forward*, January 13, 2010, http://forward.com/articles/123353 /what-the-women-of-the-wall-want/.

34.   Arianna Melamed, "The High Court Ruled? It's Time to Break the Law" [in Hebrew], *Ynet*, April 4, 2013, http://www.ynet.co.il /articles/0,7340,L-4364117,00.html.

35.   Aaron Kalman, "Women Can't Say Mourner's Prayer at Western Wall, Police Announce," *Times of Israel*, April 4, 2013, http://www .timesofisrael.com/women-cant-say-mourners-prayer-at-western -wall-police-announce/; Debra Nussbaum Cohen, "Anger over Kotel

Kaddish Ban Leads to Reversal," *The Sisterhood* (blog), *Jewish Daily Forward*, April 4, 2013, http://blogs.forward.com/sisterhood-blog /174300/anger-over-kotel-Kaddish-ban-leads-to-reversal/.

36. "Women Challenge Western Wall Rules," Odyssey Networks video, 3:57, March 21, 2013, http://www.odysseynetworks.org/video /women-challenge-western-wall-rules.

37. Jodi Rudoren, "At a Sacred Site, a Fight over Women and Prayer," *New York Times*, December 22, 2012, http://www.nytimes .com/2012/12/23/world/middleeast/at-western-wall-a-divide -over-prayer-deepens.html?_r=0.

38. Judy Maltz, "URJ President Jacobs Throws Support behind Sharansky's Western Wall Proposal," *Haaretz*, May 3, 2013, http:// www.haaretz.com/jewish-world/jewish-world-news/urj-president -jacobs-throws-support-behind-sharansky-s-western-wall-proposal .premium-1.519111.

39. Judy Maltz, "The New Orthodox Face of Women of the Wall," *Haaretz*, April 19, 2013, http://www.haaretz.com/jewish-world /jewish-world-features/the-new-orthodox-face-of-women-of-the -wall.premium-1.516416.

40. Ronit Irshai, "Whose Kotel Is This?," *Ma'ariv*, May 26, 2013, http:// www.kolech.com/show.asp?id=59917.

41. Ron Friedman and Gavriel Fiske, "Court Frees Female Activists, Calls Western Wall Arrests Groundless," *Times of Israel*, April 11, 2013, http:// www.timesofisrael.com/female-worshipers-released-from-custody/.

42. Yair Ettinger, "On 1st of Sivan, 5773, Women of the Wall Became a Legitimate Stream of Judaism," *Haaretz*, May 10, 2013, http://www .haaretz.com/jewish-world/jewish-world-news/on-1st-of-sivan -5773-women-of-the-wall-became-a-legitimate-stream-of-judaism .premium-1.523417.

43. Michal Shmulovich and Yoel Goldman, "Ultra-Orthodox Teens

Clash with Women of the Wall at Holy Site," *Times of Israel*, May 10, 2013, http://www.timesofisrael.com/Haredi-women-mass-at -kotel-for-standoff-with-feminist-group/.

44. Judy Maltz, "Women of the Wall Splinter Group Takes Uncompromising Stance," *Haaretz*, January 12, 2014, http://www .haaretz.com/jewish-world/.premium-1.568166.

45. Susan Aranoff, "Original Women of the Wall (OWOW)—A Cord of Three Strands Is Not Easily Broken," (blog), *Times of Israel*, December 11, 2013, http://blogs.timesofisrael.com/original-women-of-the -wallowow-a-cord-of-three-strands-is-not-easily-broken/.

Chapter 5

1. Elana Maryles Sztokman, "No Touching: As Israel's Military Becomes More Religious, Women Are Having a Really Hard Time Showing Men How to Hold a Rifle," *Slate*, October 11, 2012, http://www .slate.com/articles/double_x/doublex/2012/10/women_in_israel _as_the_idf_becomes_more_religious_the_rights_of_female_soldiers .html. Sections of chapter 5 originally appeared in this article.

2. Shani Boianjiu, "What Happens When the Two Israels Meet," *New York Times*, September 7, 2012, http://www.nytimes .com/2012/09/09/opinion/sunday/what-happens-when-the-two -israels-meet.html?pagewanted=all&_r=0.

3. "More Female Soldiers in More Positions in the IDF," Israel Defense Forces, November 30, 2011, http://www.idf.il/1086 -14000-EN/Dover.aspx; "60 Years of Women's Service in the IDF," Israel Defense Forces, http://www.idfblog.com/reports/60-years -of-women's-service-in-the-idf/; Amos Harel and Anshel Pfeffer, "IDF Appoints First-Ever Female Major General," *Haaretz*, May 26, 2011, http://www.haaretz.com/news/national/idf-appoints -first-ever-female-major-general-1.364280.

4. "More Female Officers in More Positions in the IDF," Israel Defense Forces, November 30, 2011, http://www.idf.il/1086-14000-EN /Dover.aspx.

5. Gili Cohen, "Cash Incentives Could Kills the IDF Ideal of Being a People's Army," *Haaretz*, January 16, 2012, http://www.haaretz .com/print-edition/features/cash-incentives-could-kills-the-idf -ideal-of-being-a-people-s-army-1.407522.

6. Hadass Ben-Eliyahu and Zeev Lehrer, "Gender Aspects of the Cancellation of the Tal Law" [in Hebrew], Open University symposium YouTube video, 15:30, posted September 10, 2012, http://www.youtube.com/watch?v=RLqnOPu6E3A.

7. Yoav Zeitun, "Bamachane IDF Newspaper: Army Version That's Kosher for Passover" [in Hebrew], *Ynet*, March 29, 2013, http:// www.ynet.co.il/articles/0,7340,L-4362062,00.html.

8. Asher Zeiger, "Tens of Thousands of Ultra-Orthodox Men Rally against Army Service," *Times of Israel*, May 16, 2013, http://www .timesofisrael.com/ultra-orthodox-turn-out-en-masse-to-protest -draft/.

9. Mitch Ginsburg, "On a Wing and a Prayer," *Times of Israel*, January 2, 2013, http://www.timesofisrael.com/on-a-wing-and-a-prayer/.

10. Interview with Rabbi Avraham Shapira, in *Hatsofe*, April 13, 1987 [in Hebrew].

11. Marissa Newman, "Education Minister Backs Rabbis' Ban on Orthodox Women in IDF," *Times of Israel*, January 13, 2014, http://www.timesofisrael.com/education-minister-backs-rabbis -ban-on-female-enlistment/.

12. Haim Lev, "Rabbinic Council Forbids Religious Girls' IDF Service," *Arutz* 7, January 9, 2014, http://www.inn.co.il/News/News .aspx/268578.

13. Ginsburg, "On a Wing and a Prayer."

14. Naomi Darom, "Safed Chief Rabbi Launches Campaign against Women Serving in the Military," *Haaretz*, January 12, 2014, http://www.haaretz.com/news/national/.premium-1.568179.

15. Ibid.

16. Newman, "Education Minister Backs Rabbis' Ban."

17. Yehoshua Breiner, "IDF Recruits Religious Women" [in Hebrew], *Walla*, March 20, 2008, http://news.walla.co.il/?w=/9/1252758.

18. Jeremy Sharon, "Rabbinical Association Says Permissible in Jewish Law for Women to Serve in IDF," *Jerusalem Post*, May 28, 2014, http://www.jpost.com/Defense/Rabbinical-association-says -permissible-in-Jewish-law-for-women-to-enlist-to-IDF-354648

19. Sigal Arbitman, "We Stayed Religious in the Army Too" [in Hebrew], *Walla*, January 20, 2012, http://news.walla.co.il/?w=//2501945.

20. Ibid.

21. Asher Zeiger, "Shas Spiritual Leader Calls on Haredim to Emigrate Rather Than Join Army," *Times of Israel*, January 7, 2013, http://www.timesofisrael.com/shas-spiritual-leader-calls-on-Haredim-to -emigrate-rather-than-join-army/.

22. Haggai Matar, "Tens of Thousands Protest Plan to Draft Ultra-Orthodox into Israeli Army," *+972 Magazine*, May 17, 2013, http://972mag.com/tens-of-thousands-protest-plan-to-draft-ultra -orthodox-into-israeli-army/71636/.

23. Boianjiu, "What Happens When."

24. Amos Harel, "The IDF Struggles with the Domination of the Skullcap" [in Hebrew], *Haaretz*, July 22, 2011, http://www.haaretz .co.il/misc/1.1181332.

25. Batsheva Sobelman, "Balancing Needs of Women, Ultra-Orthodox Men in Israel's Military," *Los Angeles Times*, March 29, 2013, http://articles.latimes.com/2013/mar/29/world/la-fg-israel-soldiers-qa -20130330.

26.   Harel, "The IDF Struggles."

27.   Ben-Eliyahu and Lehrer, "Gender Aspects."

28.   Ibid.

29.   Ibid.

30.   Nir Cohen and Moran Azoulay, "The Law to Recruit Haredi Soldiers: It's Just a Game and a Ploy" [in Hebrew], *Ynet*, May 23, 2013, http://www.ynet.co.il/articles/0,7340,L-4383451,00 .html.

31.   Aviel Magnezi, "State: Universal Draft Not Best for IDF," *Ynetnews*, January 8, 2013, http://www.ynetnews.com/articles /0,7340,L-4330071,00.html.

32.   Pressly, "Israel's Ultra-Orthodox Fight."

33.   Ibid

34.   Zeiger, "Tens of Thousands."

35.   "IDF Says It Might Allow Haredim to Get Induction Physical from Private Doctors to Avoid Testicles Issue," *Failed Messiah* (blog), December 25, 2012, http://failedmessiah.typepad.com/failed_messiah com/2012/12/idf-says-it-might-allow-Haredim-to-get-induction -physical-from-private-doctors-to-avoid-testicles-is-345.html.

36.   Ginsburg, "On a Wing and a Prayer."

37.   Anshel Pfeffer, "One Hundred Female Soldiers Abandoned an Event on Simchat Torah Because They Were Forced to Celebrate Separately" [in Hebrew], *Haaretz*, October 23, 2011, http://www.haaretz .co.il/news/education/1.1528402.

Chapter 6

1.   Keren Nathanson, "Noa Tishby: Only in Israel Do People Get into My Womb" [in Hebrew], *Ynet*, November 19, 2011, http://www .ynet.co.il/articles/0,7340,L-4150094,00.html.

2.   "Israel: Reproduction and Abortion: Law and Policy," Law Library

of Congress, February 2012, http://www.loc.gov/law/help/reports /pdf/2012-007460_IL_FINAL.pdf.

3. Carmel Shalev and Sigal Gooldin, "The Uses and Misuses of In Vitro Fertilization in Israel: Some Sociological and Ethical Considerations," *Nashim: A Journal of Jewish Women's Studies & Gender Issues* 12, Fall 5767/2006, 151–176.

4. "Birth Grant," National Insurance Institute of Israel, http://www .btl.gov.il/English%20Homepage/Benefits/Maternity%20Insurance /Birthgrant/Pages/default.aspx; "Children–Child Allowance Rates," National Insurance Institute of Israel, http://www.btl.gov.il /English%20Homepage/Benefits/Children/Pages/Rates%20of%20 child%20allowance.aspx. Figures as of May 1, 2013.

5. Carol Ungar, "Hey Marissa, Ever Consider Aliya? The Israeli Government, the Yahoo CEO, and the Work Life Balance," (blog), *Times of Israel*, July 22, 2012, http://blogs.timesofisrael.com/hey -marissa-ever-consider-aliya-the-israeli-government-the-yahoo-ceo -and-the-work-life-balance/.

6. Hannah Katsman, "The Good, the Bad, and the Fantastic: 65 Surprising Things about Parenting in Israel," (blog), *Times of Israel*, April 14, 2013, http://blogs.timesofisrael.com/65-surprising-things -about-israeli-parenting/.

7. Susan Sered, *What Makes Women Sick? Maternity, Modesty, and Militarism in Israeli Society* (Hanover: Brandeis University Press, 2000), 25.

8. Yael Hashiloni Dolev, "Between Mothers, Fetuses, and Society: Reproductive Genetics in the Israeli Jewish Context," *Nashim: A Journal of Jewish Women's Studies & Gender Issues* 12, Fall 5767/2006: 130.

9. Ibid.

10. Yali Hashash, "Medicine and the State: The Medicalization of Reproduction in Israel," in *Kin, Gene, Community: Reproductive*

Technologies among Jewish Israelis, ed. Daphna Birenbaum-Carmeli and Yoram S. Carmeli (New York: Berghahn Books, 2010).

11.   Nitza Berkovitch, "Motherhood as a National Mission: The Construction of Womanhood in the Legal Discourse of Israel," *Women's Studies International Forum* 20, no. 5 (September 1997): 605–619.

12.   Halperin-Kaddari, *Women in Israel*, 35.

13.   David Regev, "Within Five Years, Double the Number of Men Are Taking Parental Leave" [in Hebrew], *Ynet*, September 8, 2011, http://www.ynet.co.il/articles/0,7340,L-4119563,00.html.

14.   E. Teman, T. Ivry, and B. A. Bernhardt, "Pregnancy as a Proclamation of Faith: Ultra-Orthodox Jewish Women Navigating the Uncertainty of Pregnancy and Prenatal Diagnosis," *American Journal of Medical Genetics* Part A, no. 155 (2011): 69; see also R. Haimov-Kochman and Hochner-Celinkier, "Contraceptive Counseling for Orthodox Jewish Women," *European Journal of Contraceptive and Reproductive Health Care* 12, no. 1 (March 2007): 13–18.

15.   Judy Brown (Eshes Chayil), "I'm a Mother, Not a Baby Machine," *The Sisterhood* (blog), *Jewish Daily Forward*, March 14, 2013, http://blogs.forward.com/sisterhood-blog/172918/im-a-mother -not-a-baby-machine/.

16.   Tsipy Ivry, "Kosher Medicine and Medicalized Halacha: An Exploration of Triadic Relations among Israeli Rabbis, Doctors, and Infertility Patients," *American Ethnologist* 37, no. 4 (November 2010): 662–680.

17.   D. Birenbaum-Carmeli, "Your Faith or Mine: A Pregnancy Spacing Intervention in an Ultra-Orthodox Jewish Community in Israel," *Reproductive Health Matters* 16, no. 32 (November 2008): 185–91.

18.   Uri P. Dior et al., "Association between Number of Children and Mortality of Mothers: Results of a 37-Year Follow-Up Study," *Annals of Epidemiology* 23, no. 1 (January 2013): 8–13.

19.   Sarit Rosenblum, "Children Bring Long Life?," *Ynetnews*, January 10, 2011, http://www.ynetnews.com/articles/0,7340,L-4001699,00 .html.

20.   Itai Gal, "Study: Please Wait Two Years between This Birth and the Next Pregnancy" [in Hebrew], *Ynet*, December 17, 2009, http:// www.ynet.co.il/articles/0,7340,L-3821393,00.html.

21.   Dr. Hannah Kehat, Survey of Women's Health: Summary Document (January 2011), presented to MK Gila Gamliel, Deputy Minister for the Advancement of Women, Youth, and Students in the Prime Minister's Office and the Authority for the Advancement of Women. Data gathered between December 28, 2010, and January 3, 2011, with a sample representation of 928 women ages 25 to 50 from three sectors: Arab, Haredi, and non-Haredi Jewish. The full presentation can be viewed at http://www.slideshare.net/nachshon/ss-8303601 [in Hebrew] and a review of the survey can be found at http://www .kan-naim.co.il/artical.asp?id=16868 [in Hebrew]. I received the reports and correspondence directly via Kolech.

22.   Interview with Dr. Hannah Kehat, May 2013.

23.   Claire Bates, "IVF 'May Increase Breast Cancer Risk in Younger Women,'" *Daily Mail*, June 25, 2012, http://www.dailymail.co.uk /health/article-2164261/IVF-increase-breast-cancer-risk-younger -women.html.

24.   Shalev and Gooldin, "Uses and Misuses," 165.

25.   Ibid.

26.   R. Haimov-Kochman, D. Rosenak, R. Orvieto, and A. Hurwitz, "Infertility Counseling for Orthodox Jewish Couples," *Fertility and Sterility* 93, no. 6 (April 2010): 1816–9.

27.   Daniel Rosenak, *To Restore the Splendor: The Real Meaning of Severity in Applying Jewish Marital Tradition* (Tel Aviv: Yediot Books, 2011).

28.   Karni Eldad, "Rabbis! Get Out of Our Wombs!" [in Hebrew], *Ynet*, November 30, 2011, http://www.ynet.co.il/articles/0,7340,L -4155091,00.html.

29.   "Why Blog," *Nice Jewish Girl* (blog), February 22, 2005, http:// shomernegiah.blogspot.com/2005/02/why-blog.html.

30.   Ma'ayan Alexander, "Directive from Israeli Supreme Court to State-Funded Rabbinate: Explain Why Women Can't Use Mikvah without Being Questioned as to Purpose," CWJ Blog, Center for Women's Justice, September 6, 2012, https://sites.google.com/site /centerforwomensjustice/cwj-blog/directivefromisraelisupremecourt tostate-fundedrabbinateexplainwhywomencan%E2%80%99tusethe mikvahwithoutbeingquestionedastopurpose.

31.   Ibid.

32.   Haviva Ner-David, "Mikveh and the Single Girl," *Times of Israel*, May 12, 2013, http://blogs.timesofisrael.com/mikveh-and-the-single -woman/.

33.   Seth Farber, "The Court and the 'Mikve,'" *Jerusalem Post*, September 09, 2012, http://www.jpost.com/Opinion/Op-Ed-Contributors /The-court-and-the-mikve.

34.   Yair Ettinger, "Bennett Deputy Permits Use of Ritual Baths for Non-Orthodox Jews, Then Recants," *Haaretz*, May 22, 2013, http://www .haaretz.com/news/national/bennett-deputy-permits-use-of-ritual -baths-for-non-orthodox-jews-then-recants.premium-1.525455.

35.   Rabbi Yuval Cherlow, "My Opinion on the Petition by Women's Organizations to Allow Single Women to Immerse" [in Hebrew], Yeshivat Orot Shaul Kfar Batya, http://www.ypt.co.il/show.asp?id =48717.

36.   Ner-David, "Mikveh and the Single Girl."

37.   Ronit Irshai, *Fertility and Jewish Law: Feminist Perspectives on Orthodox Responsa Literature*, Brandeis Series on Gender, Culture, Religion, and

Law, HBI Series on Jewish Women (Hanover: Brandeis University Press, 2012).

38. Tamar Traubman, "Education as Contraception," *Haaretz*, September 15, 2004, http://www.haaretz.com/education-as -contraception-1.134883.

39. Katie Mcdonough, "Israel Admits Ethiopian Jewish Immigrants Were Given Birth Control Shots," *Salon*, January 28, 2013, http:// www.salon.com/2013/01/28/israel_admits_ethiopian_jewish _immigrants_were_given_birth_control_shots/; see also Brendan O'Neill, "How True Is It That Israel Deceitfully Gave Ethiopian Jews Birth Control Injections?.," *Telegraph*, January 31, 2013, http://blogs.telegraph.co.uk/news/brendanoneill2/100200874 /how-true-is-it-that-israel-deceitfully-gave-ethiopian-jews-birth -control-injections/.

40. Elana Maryles Sztokman and L. Ariella Zeller, "Abortion in Israel: When the Nation Enters the Womb," *Lilith*, Winter 2011–2012, http://lilith.org/articles/abortion-in-israel/. The following section was written with Dr. L. Ariella Zeller and originally published in *Lilith* magazine. It's reproduced here with permission.

41. Birth and Fertility Statistics, Central Bureau of Statistics, 2011, http:// www.cbs.gov.il/reader/?MIval=cw_usr_view_SHTML&ID=638; see also Yaron Druckman, "CBS: Jewish Births Up, Muslim Births Down," *Ynetnews*, January 14, 2013, http://www.ynetnews.com /articles/0,7340,L-4332386,00.html.

42. Penal Law 5737–1977, Laws of the State of Israel, 1977.

43. E. F. Sabatello, "The Impact of Voluntary Induced Abortions on Fertility in Israel," *Entre Nous Cph Den* 24 (October 1993): 15, 17.

44. Sztokman and Zeller, "Abortion in Israel."

45. Orli Lotan, "Limitations in Abortion Legislation—A Comparative Study" [in Hebrew], Knesset Center for Research and Information,

Jerusalem, 2007, http://www.knesset.gov.il/mmm/doc.asp?doc
=m01861&type=pdf.

46. Sztokman and Zeller, "Abortion in Israel."

47. Interview with Irit Rosemblum, November 2011.

48. Sztokman and Zeller, "Abortion in Israel."

49. Interview with "Ruti," November 2011.

50. Rebecca Steinfeld, "Abortions in Israel: Is the Law as Liberal as They Claim?," *Haaretz*, February 13, 2014, http://www.haaretz.com/jewish-world/the-jewish-thinker/.premium-1.574039.

51. Interview with Dana Weinberg, November 2011.

52. Interview with Irit Rosemblum, November 2011.

53. United Nations Population Fund, "Empowering Women," accessed March 1, 2014, http://www.unfpa.org/gender/empowerment.htm.

54. Ryan Jones, "Abortion Numbers Still Falling in Israel," *Israel Today*, December 12, 2011, http://www.israeltoday.co.il/NewsItem/tabid/178/nid/23042/Default.aspx.

55. "How Efrat Began," Efrat website, accessed March 1, 2014, http://www.efrat.org.il/english/about/?id=64.

56. Interview with Ruth Tidhar by L. Ariella Zeller, November 2011.

57. Interview with Hedva Eyal by L. Ariella Zeller, November 2011.

58. Oz Rosenberg, "Following the Death of Raz Atias: The Organization Efrat Is the Focus of Criticism" [in Hebrew], *Haaretz*, October 21, 2012, http://www.haaretz.co.il/news/education/1.1847178.

59. Yair Ettinger, "Israel's Chief Rabbis Back Anti-Abortion Group: 'Killing Fetuses Is Murder,'" *Haaretz*, January 2, 2013, http://www.haaretz.com/news/national/israel-s-chief-rabbis-back-anti-abortion-group-killing-fetuses-is-murder.premium-1.491531.

60. Melanie Lidman, "Feminists to Protest Anti-Abortion Group's Prize," *Jerusalem Post*, December 30, 2012, http://www.jpost.com/NationalNews/Article.aspx?id=297858.

61. "Efrat—Society for the Encouragement of the Birth of the Jewish People" [in Hebrew], Guidestar Israel, http://www.guidestar.org.il /organization/580009363.

62. Interview with Zahava Gal-On, November 2011.

63. Interview with Joanne Zack-Pakes by L. Ariella Zeller, November 2011.

64. Amnon Miranda and Meital Yisur, "Proposal: To Illegalize Abortions after 22nd Week of Pregnancy," *Ynet*, December 3, 2007, http://www.ynet.co.il/articles/0,7340,L-3478510,00.html [in Hebrew]; Shari Eshet, "Don't Set Back Reproductive Rights for Israeli Women," *JTA*, July 9, 2012, http://www.jta.org/2012/07/09 /news-opinion/opinion/op-ed-dont-set-back-reproductive-rights -for-israeli-women.

65. Steinfeld, "Abortions in Israel."

66. Interview with Dr. Jordana Hyman, November 2011.

67. Interview with Orly Hasson Tsitsuashvili by L. Ariella Zeller, November 2011.

68. Debra Kamin, "Israel's Abortion Law Now among World's Most Liberal," *Times of Israel*, January 6, 2014, http://www.timesofisrael .com/israels-abortion-law-now-among-worlds-most-liberal/

69. Steinfeld, "Abortions in Israel."

70. Ari Yashar, "NGO: 'C'tee Robs From the Sick to Fund Abortions,'" *Arutz Sheva*, January 1, 2014, http://www.israelnationalnews.com /News/News.aspx/175792#.U4xv_HZ2SMk.

Chapter 7

1. David Robson, "There Really Are 50 Eskimo Words for 'Snow,'" *Washington Post*, January 14, 2013, http://articles.washingtonpost .com/2013-01-14/national/36344037_1_eskimo-words-snow-inuit.

2. "21 Untranslatable Words Worth Spreading," *TED Blog*, June

25, 2012, http://blog.ted.com/2012/06/25/21-untranslatable-words
-worth-spreading/.

3.   Emily Taitz, Sondra Henry, and Cheryn Tallan, *The JPS Guide to
Jewish Women: 600 BCE-1900 CE* (Philadelphia: Jewish Publication
Society, 2003). A Jewish legal document found dated from the second
century CE shows that a woman named "Shlomtzion, daughter of
Joseph Qebshan" gave her husband a *gett* in order to get divorced.
And according to Josephus, King Herod's wife Salome sent her
husband a *gett*.

4.   Babylonian Talmud Yevamot 14:1.

5.   Polygamy is technically against the law in Israel, although unregistered
marriages are not uncommon. Actually, the community with the
biggest polygamy problem is the Bedouin, but that's a whole different
discussion.

6.   Gail Lichtman, "Jerusalem Organizations Are Working to Ease the
Plight of 'Agunot,' Women Denied Divorce," *In Jerusalem Magazine*,
January 7, 2000, http://www.come-and-hear.com/editor/agunot
/legalaid/index.html

7.   Susan M. Weiss and Netty C. Gross-Horowitz, *Marriage and Divorce
in the Jewish State: Israel's Civil War* (Hanover: Brandeis University
Press, 2012), 7.

8.   "Agunot: 462 Too Many," *Jewish Week*, October 25, 2011, http://
www.thejewishweek.com/editorial_opinion/editorial/agunot_462
_too_many.

9.   Weiss and Gross-Horowitz, *Marriage and Divorce*, 8.

10.   Interview with Robyn Shames, May 2012.

11.   Lichtman, "Jerusalem Organizations."

12.   Neta Sela, "Poll: More Women Refuse Divorce than Men," *Ynetnews*,
June 29, 2007, http://www.ynetnews.com/articles/0,7340,L
-3418502,00.html.

13. Rivkah Lubitch, "Who's Counting Agunot?," *Ynetnews*, March 16, 2010, http://www.ynetnews.com/articles/0,7340,L-3861525,00.html.

14. Orli Lotan, "Background Document on the Subject of: Women Denied Divorce in Israel," presented to the Committee for the Advancement of Women, the Knesset, November 28, 2005.

15. Ruth Halperin-Kaddari and Inbal Karo, *Women and Family in Israel: Statistical Bi-Annual Report* [in Hebrew] (Ramat Gan: Bar-Ilan University, Rackman Center, 2009), 73–80.

16. Lichtman, "Jerusalem Organizations."

17. Anat Silverstone, "I Was an Agunah: I Was Like Air" [in Hebrew], Ne'emanei Torah Va'Avodah, http://toravoda.org.il/node/110.

18. Tali Farkash, "Poll: 1 in 3 Women Extorted by Ex-Husband," *Ynetnews*, July 7, 2013, http://www.ynetnews.com/articles/0,7340,L-4400770,00.html.

19. Leslie Morgan Steiner, "Why Domestic Violence Victims Don't Leave," TED Talks video, 15:59, filmed November 2012, http://www.ted.com/talks/leslie_morgan_steiner_why_domestic_violence_victims_don_t_leave.html.

20. Susan Moller Okin, "When Cultural Values Clash with Universal Rights: Is Multiculturalism Bad for Women?," presentation on October 29, 2001, as part of the Markkula Ethics Center Lecture Series. See also Susan Moller Okin, *Justice, Gender, and the Family* (New York: Basic Books, 1989); *Women in Western Political Thought* (Princeton: Princeton University Press, 1979); *Is Multiculturalism Bad for Women?* (Princeton: Princeton University Press, 1999).

21. Farkash, "Poll."

22. Silverstone, "I Was an Agunah."

23. Weiss and Gross-Horowitz, *Marriage and Divorce*, 40.

24. Jeremy Sharon, "Bill Passed on Sanctions for 'Recalcitrant Husbands,'"

Jerusalem Post, November 2, 2011, http://www.jpost.com/National
-News/Bill-passed-on-sanctions-for-recalcitrant-husbands;   Yair
Ettinger, "Israeli Rabbinical Couts Now Must Track Men Who
Won't Grant Gets," *Haaretz*, March 21, 2012, http://www.haaretz
.com/print-edition/news/israeli-rabbinical-courts-now-must-track
-men-who-won-t-grant-gets-1.419847.

25.   Supreme Court ruling, Avraham Yihye 164/67. For an explanation
of the ruling in context, see Diana Hareven, "Agunot" [in
Hebrew], Hareven website, http://www.hareven-law.co.il/?page
=piskay&id=35.

26.   "Jerusalem: Recalcitrant Husband Flees Police via Courthouse
Bathroom Window," *Yeshiva World News*, March 7, 2013, http://
www.theyeshivaworld.com/article.php?p=159802.

27.   "Husband Who Kept Wife Agunah Loses Burial Rights in Israel,"
Yeshiva World News, May 23, 2013, http://www.theyeshivaworld
.com/article.php?p=169092.

28.   Weiss and Gross-Horowitz, *Marriage and Divorce*, 80.

29.   Neta Sela, "Knesset Committee: Division of Property before
Divorce," *Ynetnews*, January 10, 2008, http://www.ynetnews.com
/articles/0,7340,L-3492690,00.html.

30.   Susan Weiss, Rivkah Lubitch, and Elana Maryles Sztokman,
"The Interrogation of the Convert 'X' by the Rabbinical
Courts in Israel," November 2010, http://www.cwj.org.il/sites
/default/files/interrogation%20of%20converts%20-%202013%20
07%2007.pdf.

31.   Lahav Harkov, "Bills to Let Women Choose Rabbinical Judges
Passes Hurdle," *Jerusalem Post*, May 1, 2013, http://www.jpost.com
/Diplomacy-and-Politics/Bills-to-let-women-choose-rabbinical
-judges-passes-hurdle-311711; Yonah Jeremy Bob, "Knesset C'tee
Adds Women to Panel Picking Rabbinic Judges," *Jerusalem Post*,

May 13, 2013, http://www.jpost.com/National-News/Knesset
-Ctee-adds-women-to-panel-picking-rabbinic-judges-313051.

32. Michele Chabin, "Israel's Divorce Ruling Leaves Matter Unsettled," *WeNews*, November 30, 2010, http://womensenews.org/story /religion/101126/israels-divorce-ruling-leaves-matter-unsettled.

33. Susan Weiss, "From Religious 'Right' to Civil 'Wrong': Using Israeli Tort Law to Unravel the Knots of Gender Equality," in *Gender, Religion, and Family Law: Theorizing Conflicts Between Women's Rights and Cultural Traditions*, eds. Lisa Fishbayne Joffe and Sylvia Neil (Waltham, MA: Brandeis University Press), 119–135.

34. Ibid.

35. Rivkah Lubitch, "Recalcitrant Husband to Pay NIS 680,000," *Ynetnews*, October 10, 2011, http://www.ynetnews.com/articles /0,7340,L-4132961,00.html.

36. Weiss, "From Religious 'Right' to Civil 'Wrong.'"

37. Weiss and Gross-Horowitz, *Marriage and Divorce*, xviii.

38. Ibid, 113.

39. Jeremy Sharon, "Rabbinic Body Touts Prenups to Avoid 'Get' Refusal," *Jerusalem Post*, May 27, 2013, http://www.jpost.com/National-National -News/Rabbinic-body-touts-prenups-to-prevent-get-refusal-314490.

40. Weiss and Gross-Horowitz, *Marriage and Divorce,*198.

41. Ibid., 164–188.

Chapter 8

1. Susan Weiss, Rivkah Lubitch, and Elana Maryles Sztokman, "The Interrogation of Convert 'X' by the Rabbinical Courts in Israel," Center for Women's Justice, November 2010, http://www.cwj .org.il/sites/default/files/interrogation%20of%20converts%20-%20 2013%2007%2007.pdf.

2. Rabbinic Courts Jurisdiction (Marriage and Divorce) Law, 5713

-1953, http://www.knesset.gov.il/review/data/eng/law/kns2
_rabbiniccourts_eng.pdf.

3. "Differing View of Dealing with Agunah & Conversion Issues within
   Orthodoxy," American Friends of Bar-Ilan University video, 6:40,
   http://www.afbiu.org/learn/agunot-chained-women.

4. Yechiel Spira, "Supreme Rabbinical Court Disqualifies Rav
   Druckman's Conversions," *Yeshiva World News*, May 4, 2008, http://
   www.theyeshivaworld.com/article.php?p=17569.

5. "RCA Affirms Its Support for Israel's Conversion Authority,"
   Rabbinical Council of America, May 6, 2008, http://www.rabbis
   .org/news/article.cfm?id=105297.

6. Sara Aeder, "The Public Role of the Chief Rabbinate as Factor in
   Israel-Diaspora Relations," Colloquium Report, ACJ Global Jewish
   Activism, November 27, 2012.

7. Seth Farber, "Druckman's Legacy," *Jerusalem Post*, February 15, 2012, http://
   www.jpost.com/Opinion/Op-Ed-Contributors/Druckmans-legacy.

8. Rivkah Lubitch, "Rabbinic Court Defeats Public 2-0," *Ynetnews*, June 19,
   2011, http://www.ynetnews.com/articles/0,7340,L-4083037,00.html.

9. Yair Ettinger, "IDF Rabbi: Soldiers Who Converted during Army
   Service Are Real Jews," *Haaretz*, September 6, 2010, http://
   www.haaretz.com/news/national/idf-rabbi-soldiers-who-converted
   -during-army-service-are-real-jews-1.312583.

10. Marcy Oster, "Orthodox Conversions in Israel Down Dramatically,
    Study Shows," *JTA*, May 21, 2012, http://www.jta.org/2012/05/21
    /news-opinion/israel-middle-east/orthodox-conversions-in
    -israel-down-dramatically-study-shows.

11. Nathan Jeffay, "David Stav Aims to Oust Haredim from Israeli
    Ashkenazi Chief Rabbi Post," *Jewish Daily Forward*, April 9,
    2013, http://forward.com/articles/174267/david-stav-aims-to-oust
    -Haredim-from-israeli-ashke/.

12.   Idit Hila Nachman and Naama Sari-Levi, "Report Conversion in Advance of the Holiday of Shavuot 2012" [in Hebrew], Itim Resources and Advocacy for Jewish Life, http://www.knesset.gov .il/protocols/data/rtf/maamad/2013-05-13.rtf.

13.   Yair Ettinger, "Holy Wars in Store for Bennett over Reform of Israel's Rabbinate," *Haaretz*, May 20, 2013, http://www.haaretz .com/news/national/holy-wars-in-store-for-bennett-over-reform-of -israel-s-rabbinate.premium-1.524912.

14.   Daniel Estrin, "Getting Married in Israel: Why It So Often Means Hiring a Detective," *The Atlantic*, February 13, 2013, http:// www.theatlantic.com/international/archive/2013/02/why-getting -married-in-israel-sometimes-means-hiring-a-detective/273127/.

15.   "Mamzerim: Real People, Real Problems," *Mamzerim Hakodesh* (blog), September 21, 2010, http://mamzerhakodesh.blogspot .co.il/2010/09/mamzerim-real-people-real-problems.html.

16.   Rivkah Lubitch, "So What if the Rabbi Said You Can Marry?," *Ynetnews*, May 17, 2009, http://www.ynetnews.com/articles /0,7340,L-3715305,00.html.

17.   Rivkah Lubitch, "Solution to Illegitimacy Problem," *Ynetnews*, September 19, 2010, http://www.ynetnews.com/articles/0,7340,L -3952988,00.html.

18.   Pinhas Shifman, *Safa Ahat Udvarim Ahadim: Iyyunim Bemishpat Vehevra* (*One Language and One Set of Words—Studies in Law, Halacha, and Society*) (Jerusalem: Shalom Hartman Institute, Bar-Ilan University and Keter Publishing House, 2013).

19.   Weiss and Gross-Horowitz, *Marriage and Divorce*, 28.

20.   Irit Rosenblum, "Where Is the Protest?," *Haaretz*, December 28, 2012, http://www.haaretz.com/opinion/where-is-the-protest .premium-1.490472.

21.   Samuel C. Heilman, *Sliding to the Right: The Contest for the Future of*

American Jewish Orthodoxy (Oakland, CA: University of California Press, 2006), 1–10.

22.   David Breakstone, "Identity Theft: An National Epidemic," *Jerusalem Post*, July 8, 2011, http://www.jpost.com/Opinion/Columnists /Identity-theft-An-national-epidemic.

23.   Rosenblum, "Where Is the Protest?"

24.   Weiss and Gross-Horowitz, *Marriage and Divorce*, 22.

25.   Yair Ettinger, "The Conversion Bill Demystified," *Haaretz*, July 13, 2010, http://www.haaretz.com/print-edition/news/the-conversion -bill-demystified-1.301565.

26.   "RCA Statement Regarding the Rotem Knesset Legislation Pertaining to Conversions," Rabbinical Council of America, July 19, 2010, http://www.rabbis.org/news/article.cfm?id=105576.

27.   Rabbi Andrew Sacks, "Rabbi Riskin, Conversion and the Real Facts," *Masorti Matters* (blog), *Jerusalem Post*, August 28, 2011, http:// blogs.jpost.com/content/rabbi-riskin-conversion-and-real-facts.

28.   Jonah Mandel, "Rotem Revises Conversion Bill," *Jerusalem Post*, July 12, 2010, http://www.jpost.com/Israel/Rotem-revises -conversion-bill.

29.   Rosenblum, "Where Is the Protest?"

30.   "Israeli Lawmaker David Rotem under Fire for Saying Reform 'Is Not Jewish,'" *JTA*, February 5, 2014, http://www.jta.org/2014/02/05 /news-opinion/israel-middle-east/israeli-lawmaker-david-rotem -under-fire-for-saying-reform-isnt-jewish.

31.   "New Agreement on Conversion in Israel Reached," Jewish Federations of North America, January 10, 2011, http://www .jewishfederations.org/page.aspx?id=236254.

32.   Jeremy Sharon, "Politicians Slam Shas Election Ad as Racist," *Jerusalem Post*, January 9, 2013, http://www.jpost.com/Diplomacy -and-Politics/Politicians-slam-Shas-election-ad-as-racist; Gabe Fisher,

"Shas vs. Shiksa?," *Times of Israel*, January 8, 2013, http://www. timesofisrael.com/shas-vs-shiksa/.

33. Rosenblum, "Where Is the Protest?"

34. "On Hiddush's Freedom of Marriage World Map, Israel Receives '0' for Religious Monopoly and Severe Restrictions on Marriage," Hiddush, April 29, 2013, http://hiddush.org/article-2450-0-In _Hiddushs_Freedom_of_Marriage_World_Map_Israel_receives_0 _for_religious_monopoly_and_severe_restrictions_on_marriage.aspx.

35. Nancy K. Kaufman, "End Orthodox Monopoly on Jewish Marriage in Israel," *Jewish Daily Forward*, May 22, 2013, http://forward .com/articles/176953/end-orthodox-monopoly-on-jewish-marriage -in-israel/.

36. Asher Zeiger, "Religious Affairs Ministry to Promote Wedding Reform," *Times of Israel*, May 19, 2013, http://www.timesofisrael .com/religious-affairs-ministry-to-promote-wedding-reform/.

37. Ettinger, "Holy Wars."

38. Kobi Nachshoni, "Reform in Religious Services Slammed," *Ynetnews*, May 20, 2013, http://www.ynetnews.com/articles/0,7340,L -4381798,00.html.

39. Tomer Nir, "Tzipi Livni's Revenge: Veto on the Religious Services Revolution" [in Hebrew], *Srugim*, May 30, 2013, http://www .srugim.co.il/46539-%D7%94%D7%A0%D7%A7%D7%9E%D7%94 -%D7%A9%D7%9C-%D7%A6%D7%99%D7%A4%D7%99 -%D7%9C%D7%91%D7%A0%D7%99-%D7%95%D7%98%D7 %95-%D7%A2%D7%9C-%D7%94%D7%9E%D7%94%D7 %A4%D7%9B%D7%94-%D7%91%D7%A9%D7%99%D7%A8%D7 %95%D7%AA?di=1.

40. Yair Ettinger, "The Bennet Plan for Strengthening Jewish Identity: Former IDF Rabbi Rontzki to Head the 'Jewish Identity Authority,'" *Haaretz*, May 21, 2013, http://www.haaretz.co.il/news

/education/.premium-1.2025365; Yehoshua Breiner, "Bennet Plans: Strengthening 'Jewish Identity' in Schools," *Walla News*, May 7, 2013, http://news.walla.co.il/?w=/9/2639769; Gershom Gorenberg, "Ronski Heads New Jewish identity Administration," *Daily Beast*, May 28, 2013, http://www.thedailybeast.com/articles/2013/05/28 /ronski-heads-new-jewish-identity-administration.html.

41.   Rabbi David Stav, "The Future of the Chief Rabbinate: A National Rabbinate or a Sectoral Rabbinate?" (public lecture, Jerusalem, February 2013).

42.   Nachman and Sari-Levi, "Report Conversion in Advance of the Holiday of Shavuot 2012" [in Hebrew].

43.   Ibid.

44.   Aeder, "Public Role."

45.   "Israelis Chafe under Orthodox Grip on Marriage, Divorce, and Conversion," *Jewish Daily Forward*, April 28, 2013, http://forward .com/articles/175614/israelis-chafe-under-orthodox-grip-on -marriage-div.

46.   Nachman and Sari-Levi, "Report Conversion in Advance of the Holiday of Shavuot 2012" [in Hebrew].

47.   Dov S. Zakheim and Steven M. Bayme, "Whither the Chief Rabbinate?," *Jerusalem Post*, December 25, 2012, http://www.jpost .com/Opinion/Op-EdContributors/Article.aspx?id=297304.

48.   Liora Minka, "Women Should Be Seen and Heard," *Israel Hayom*, May 26, 2013, http://www.israelhayom.com/site/newsletter _opinion.php?id=4445.

49.   Yair Ettinger, "Israeli Women's Groups Petition AG for Say in Picking Chief Rabbis," *Haaretz*, January 2, 2013, http://www .haaretz.com/news/national/israeli-women-s-groups-petition-ag -for-say-in-picking-chief-rabbis.premium-1.491457.

50.   "10 Women Appointed to Chief Rabbinate Voting Body," *Yeshiva*

World News, June 30, 2013, http://www.theyeshivaworld.com/news/General+News/175350/10-Women-Appointed-to-Chief-Rabbinate-Voting-Body.html.

51.   Lubitch, "Solution to Illegitimacy Problem."

52.   Mazal Mualem, "Israeli Author Yoram Kaniuk Asks Court to Cancel His 'Jewish' Status," *Haaretz*, May 15, 2011, http://www.haaretz.com/print-edition/news/israeli-author-yoram-kaniuk-asks-court-to-cancel-his-jewish-status-1.361720.

53.   Rosenblum, "Where Is the Protest?"

54.   Center for Women's Justice Facebook page, posted May 30, 2013, https://www.facebook.com/Centerforwomensjustice/posts/615038275175147.

Chapter 9

1.   Allison Kaplan Sommer, "Stink Bomb Welcomes Girls Back to School," *The Sisterhood* (blog), *Jewish Daily Forward*, October 25, 2011, http://blogs.forward.com/sisterhood-blog/144826/stink-bomb-welcomes-girls-back-to-school/; Allison Kaplan Sommer, "Throwing Eggs and Jeers at Little Girls," *The Sisterhood* (blog), *Jewish Daily Forward*, September 19, 2011, http://blogs.forward.com/sisterhood-blog/143027/throwing-eggs-and-jeers-at-little-girls/.

2.   Allison Kaplan Sommer, "Tense Return to School for Beit Shemesh Girls," *The Sisterhood* (blog), *Jewish Daily Forward*, September 1, 2011, http://blogs.forward.com/sisterhood-blog/142186/tense-return-to-school-for-beit-shemesh-girls/.

3.   Ibid.

4.   Elizabeth Flock, "Naama Margolese, Israeli Schoolgirl, Says She Was Bullied and Spit On by Jewish Extremists," *WorldViews* (blog), *Washington Post*, December 27, 2011, http://www.washingtonpost.com/blogs/blogpost/post/naama-margolese-israeli-schoolgirl-says

-she-was-bullied-and-spit-on-by-jewish-extremists/2011/12/27 /gIQATNgRKP_blog.html; Katy Waldman, "Why Did Ultra-Orthodox Jews Bully an Israeli Second Grader?," *The XX Factor* (blog), *Slate*, December 30, 2011, http://www.slate.com/blogs/xx _factor/2011/12/30/naama_margolese_why_did_the_Haredim _call_her_a_whore_.html; Yair Altman, "Haredim Riot in Beit Shemesh after Segregation Signs Removed," *Ynetnews*, December 26, 2011, http://www.ynetnews.com/articles/0,7340,L-4166659,00 .html.

5. Aron Heller, "Thousands in Israel Protest Against Jewish Extremists," *NBC News*, December 27, 2011, http://www.nbcnews .com/id/45794260/.

6. Elana Maryles Sztokman, "Was Yesterday's Rally Really About Gender?," *The Sisterhood* (blog), *Jewish Daily Forward*, December 28, 2011, http://blogs.forward.com/sisterhood-blog/148728/was -yesterdays-rally-really-about-gender/. The next few paragraphs were originally published in this blog.

7. Ibid.

8. Ibid.

9. Ibid.

10. Ibid.

11. Ibid.

12. Martha C. Nussbaum, *Women and Human Development: The Capabilities Approach* (Cambridge: Cambridge University Press, 2000).

13. "Beit Shemesh, Israel's Town of Ultra-Orthodox Hate, Steps Back from Brink," *Jewish Daily Forward*, February 15, 2013, http://forward.com/articles/171264/beit-shemesh-israels-town -of-ultra-orthodox-hate-s/.

14. Interview with Hadassa Margolese, July 2013.

15. Ariella Zeller and Elana Maryles Sztokman, "Noa: We're Headed

Toward a 'Taliban State,'" *The Sisterhood* (blog), *Jewish Daily Forward*, December 20, 2011, http://blogs.forward.com/sisterhood -blog/147970/noa-were-headed-toward-a-taliban-state/. A version of this section originally appeared as this blog.

16.   Interview with Hadas Bandel by L. Ariella Zeller, December 2011.

17.   Ibid.

18.   Ibid.

19.   L. Ariella Zeller and Elana Sztokman, "Noa: We're Headed Toward a 'Taliban State,'" *The Forward*, December 20, 2011, http:// blogs.forward.com/sisterhood-blog/147970/noa-were-headed -toward-a-taliban-state/#ixzz3546KVhzd.

20.   Ibid.

21.   Interview with Miri Shalem, June 2013.

22.   Ibid.

23.   Ibid.

24.   Ibid.

25.   Ibid.

26.   "Official Bet Shemesh Women Flashmob," YouTube video, 2:26, January 6, 2012, https://www.youtube.com/watch?v=pZd0kL WP01c.

27.   Interview with Miri Shalem, June 2013.

28.   Ibid.

29.   Liron Nagler-Cohen, "Beit Shemesh women dance for change," *Ynetnews,* January 10, 2012, http://www.ynetnews.com/articles /0,7340,L-4173737,00.html.

30.   "If We Can't Be Elected, We're Not Voting," *Lo Nivharot, Lo Boharot* Facebook page [in Hebrew], accessed March 1, 2014, https://www .facebook.com/lo.bocharot?fref=ts.

31.   Esty Shushan, "If We Can't Be Elected, We're Not Voting," *Ynet*, December 31, 2012, http://www.ynet.co.il/articles/0,7340,L

-4326016,00.html; Nathan Jeffay, "Israeli Elections: Charedi Women Refuse to Vote," *Jewish Chronicle Online*, January 10, 2013, http://www.thejc.com/news/israel-news/97420/israeli-elections -charedi-women-refuse-vote.

32. Ibid.

33. "If We Can't Be Elected, We're Not Voting."

34. Yair Ettinger, "United Torah Judaism Wins the Israeli Election—In Demographics: For the First Time Ever, the Ultra-Orthodox Community's Growth Has Been Translated into Votes; the Party Has Won Seven Knesset Seats," *Haaretz*, January 24, 2013, http://www .haaretz.com/news/national/united-torah-judaism-wins-the-israeli -election-on-demographics.premium-1.496009.

35. Anat Yatach, "Shas Rabbi against Shira: Women's Place Is at Home" [in Hebrew], *MyNet*, May 26, 2013, http://www.mynet.co.il /articles/0,7340,L-4382952,00.html.

36. "Rachel Ibenboim Forced to Step Away from Politics," *Life in Israel* (blog), September 3, 2013, http://lifeinisrael.blogspot.co.il/2013/09 /rachel-ibenboim-forced-to-step-away.html.

37. Meital Menashe, "Exclusion of Women? Haredi Women Try Their Luck at Local Elections" [in Hebrew], *Mako*, June 5, 2013, http:// www.mako.co.il/special-mako-news/Article-44d5b33147a0f31006 .htm.

38. Hannah Katsman, "Bnei Baruch Kabbalah Laam: Politics and Money," *A Mother in Israel* (blog), October 4, 2013, http://www.amotherinisrael .com/bnei-baruch-kabbalah-cult-politics-elections-money/.

39. Ron Friedman and Gavriel Fiske, "Court Frees Female Activists, Calls Western Wall Arrests Groundless," *Times of Israel*, April 11, 2013, http://www.timesofisrael.com/female-worshipers-released -from-custody/#ixzz34AayKi8m.

Afterword

1. "Imam Explains the Proper Etiquette on Beating Your Wife," *Sharia Unveiled* (blog), video, 3:04, October 6, 2013, http://www.boreme.com/posting.php?id=15927#.U4yoKHKSxPs.

2. Karen Armstrong, "2008 TED Prize Wish: Charter for Compassion," YouTube video, 21:27, posted March 19, 2008, http://www.youtube.com/watch?v=SJMm4RAwVLo.

3. Ibid.

INDEX

ACKNOWLEDGMENTS

I have been intensely writing about the issues described in this book since at least 2009, when I started writing for the *Jewish Daily Forward*'s *The Sisterhood* blog, and even before, when I was blogging on my own. I have also been active in many of the on-the-ground initiatives since the 1990s, from when I was involved with Mavoi Satum and ICAR as a volunteer and much later when I worked for the CWJ, and then with JOFA, the Jewish Orthodox Feminist Alliance, based in New York. My deepest admiration, gratitude, and awe go to all the people of these important organizations who are on the front lines of the battle to protect women and Judaism from radical takeover. I am personally indebted to the people at all these organizations who have provided me with homes over the years from which to work on building a better world.

There are so many people who I encountered over the years whose ideas shaped what I wrote here, so many inspiring women—and men—who have dedicated their lives and their bodies to fighting injustice. You all deserve the eternal thanks of anyone who would like to see Israel and Judaism thrive.

To those who agreed to be interviewed for this book and

whose lifework is the subject of the book: Dr. Hannah Kehat; Anat Hoffman; Dr. Susan Weiss; Ricky Shapira-Rosenberg; Ayelet Wieder-Cohen; Shari Eshet; Robyn Shames; Brig. Gen. Hadass Ben-Eliyahu; Rabbi Uri Ayalon; Rabbi Uri Regev; Joel Katz; MK Zahava Gal-On; Hadassa Braun Margolese; Nili Phillip; Cheryl Birkner Mack; Dr. Aliza Berger Cooper; Nancy Kaufman; Rachel Azaria; Micky Gitzin; Shira Ben-Sasson Furstenberg; Tami Katsabian; Miri Shalem; Dr. Bonna Devora Haberman; Prof. Frances Raday; Peggy Cidor; Irit Rosenblum; Sharon Orshalimy; Dr. Jordana Hyman; Joanne Zack-Pakes; Ruth Tidhar; Hedva Eyal; Susan Silverman; and Hallel Silverman. I sincerely hope that I haven't forgotten anyone, and if I did, please accept my apologies—and my deepest thanks.

To those who supported this work in various ways: Fern Reiss, agent par excellence, who saw the vision way before I did and has an incredible ability to get things done; Stephanie Bowen, my editor at Sourcebooks, for her enthusiastic and unwavering support from the beginning, for her dedication to the topic, and for her truly exceptional editing skills; Nicole Villeneuve at Sourcebooks, for phenomenal publicity and marketing; Susan Weidman Schneider— editor, mentor, cheerleader, and friend—at the always remarkable *Lilith* magazine, as well as the wonderful Sonia Isard and Naomi Danis; Jane Eisner, Gabrielle Birkner, Abigail Jones, and Naomi Zeveloff at the *Forward*; and Blu Greenberg, Zelda Stern, Carolyn Hochstadter Dicker, Sylvia Barack Fishman, Professor Tamar Ross, and Phyllis Shapiro of JOFA.

To the many friends who nurtured me along the way: Rabbi Dr. Haviva Ner-David; Mona Farkas Berdugo; Tammy Braverman; Dr. Malka (Melanie) Landau; Ilana Teitelbaum Reichert; Dr. Chaya Gorsetman; Fred Gorsetman; Dr. L. Ariella Zeller (who cowrote two important sections of this book); Chaim Kram; Robin Alexander; Helen Maryles Shankman; Susan Goodman Jackson; Vivian Lazar; Ariella Rand; Annie Eisen; Jay Engelmeyer; Elise Rynhold; Jonny Rynhold; Hillary Gordon; Rachel Karlin; Ken Quinn; Elli Sacks; Adina Sacks; Jessica Kaz; Jackie Bitensky; Shirley Glance; and Di Hirsch. And to all my virtual friends on Facebook, Twitter, and the blogosphere who constantly engage. This book was crafted in all those conversations.

To my wonderful writer colleagues who have remained steadfast on this beat: Debra Nussbaum Cohen (who also brought me to the *Forward*—very special thank you!); Allison Kaplan Sommer; Renee Ghert Zand; Michele Chabin; Amanda Borschel-Dan; Rivkah Lubitch; Susan Reimer-Torn; Naomi Zeveloff; Sara Selzer; Batya Ungar-Sargon; Shmarya Rosenberg (*Failed Messiah*); Dan Brown (E-Jewish Philanthropy); Yerachmiel Lopin (Frum Follies); Dorron Katzin; Ruth Marks Eglash; Hannah Katsman (*A Mother in Israel*); Nehama Zibitt Blumenreich; Eetta Gibson Prince; Sara Tuttle-Singer; Frimet Goldberger; Ruchama Weiss; and the rest of you out there doing this kind of writing. Keep up the great work! The telling is such a vital component of the process of social change. As they say, sunlight is the best disinfectant. So grateful to be part of this fabulous posse!

To some of my teachers and guides: Professor Alice Shalvi, Karen Abrams, Inbal Gal, Wendy Murphy, Ori Arbell, Eva Har-Even, and Zita Frederic.

To my mother-in-law, Claire Sztokman, and to Alex Haber, for always being such wonderful supporters.

To Ilona Fischer, for invaluable friendship and loving care.

To my father, Matthew Maryles, for lots of lunches in New York.

To my wonderful children, Avigayil, Effie, Yonina, and Meital, for always being awesome and full of wisdom and fun. I pray that this book makes your Israel a better Israel and works to improve life for you, your friends, and generations to come.

To my extraordinary spouse, Jacob, after more than two decades together, for always being a willing and joyful partner on the journey and surprising me each time with new wellsprings of support and new dimensions of loving-kindness.

Finally, to my Creator, for enabling these words to come through my lips and through my fingers in a way that is kind, caring, and reflective of divine compassion, and for supporting me in my ongoing quest to be a vehicle for *tikkun olam* and the empowerment of women in this world.

ABOUT THE AUTHOR

Photo credit: Ingrid Muller

Dr. Elana Maryles Sztokman, former executive director of JOFA, the Jewish Orthodox Feminist Alliance, is a leading author and activist on the issue of religious feminism in Jewish life. Her first book, *The Men's Section: Orthodox Jewish Men in an Egalitarian World*, won the 2012 National Jewish Book Council Award for Women's Studies. Her second book, *Educating in the Divine Image: Gender Issues in Orthodox Jewish Day Schools* (with Chaya Gorsetman), won the National Jewish Book Council Award for Education and Identity 2013. She lives in Modi'in, Israel, and blogs at *A Jewish Feminist*, www.jewfem.com.